HUNGRY FOR PROFIT

HUNGRY FOR PROFIT

THE AGRIBUSINESS THREAT TO FARMERS, FOOD, AND THE ENVIRONMENT

edited by **FRED MAGDOFF, JOHN BELLAMY FOSTER,**
and **FREDERICK H. BUTTEL**

MONTHLY REVIEW PRESS
New York

Library of Congress Cataloging-in-Publication Data

Hungry for profit: the agribusiness threat to farmers, food and the environment /
edited by Fred Magdoff, John Bellamy Foster, and Frederick H. Buttel.
p. cm.
ISBN: 1-58367-016-5 (pbk.) — ISBN: 1-58357-015-7 (cloth)
1. Agricultural industries. 2. Agriculture—Economic aspects. 3. Sustainable agriculture.
I. Magdoff, Fred, 1942- II. Foster, John Bellamy. III. Buttel, Frederick H.

HD9000.5 .H86 2000
338.1—dc21

00-056000

Monthly Review Press
122 West 27th Street
New York, NY 10001

Printed in Canada

10 9 8 7 6 5 4 3 2

CONTENTS

AN OVERVIEW

FRED MAGDOFF, JOHN BELLAMY FOSTER
AND FREDERICK H. BUTTEL

The conventional view that agriculture was displaced by industry in two stages—by the industrial revolution in the late nineteenth century and, as a result of the rise of the agribusiness system in the mid-twentieth century—has left many observers of the contemporary issues with the impression that to deal with agriculture is essentially to focus on political-economic history rather than contemporary political economy. Nothing could be further from the truth. The purpose of this book is to help compensate for the neglect that agriculture has often suffered in political-economic literature of the late twentieth century, and to assist what is fast becoming a powerful resistance movement in the agricultural realm.

Historically, the significance of agriculture to the origin and development of capitalism cannot be overemphasized. The development of capitalism in England depended on the increasing surpluses resulting from an agriculture in the throes of major technical and social transformations. And England's distinctive patterns of land holding created a new kind of market dependency in agricultural production that was critical to the initiation of dynamic capitalist relations geared to constant productivity growth (see Wood, chapter 1). In subsequent development, the rise of industry in no way left agriculture behind but was mirrored (indeed in some cases prefigured) at each stage by changes in the latter.

7

Agriculture, which has been dominated for decades in the United States and, more recently in the rest of the world, by large agribusiness corporations, is now once again undergoing rapid, even unprecedented change. To be sure, much of this story—concentration and centralization of capital and exodus of peasants and farmers from the land—is not new. But the trends witnessed in agriculture in the late twentieth century are distinctive in several important respects. Concentration and centralization and rural dispossession within this sector are being reinforced by new technological innovations, particularly in the area of biotechnology, leading to such developments as the proletarianization of the farmer, and to the appropriation of ownership and control of indigenous plants and animals in third world countries. The global commodification of agriculture has its counterpart in the destruction of peasant and small-scale agriculture throughout the world. Subsistence farming is in decline in the third world while the production of luxury crops for export to the rich countries is being expanded as never before. The result is a rise in world food supplies, together with an increase in world hunger. So sharp are these contradictions that hunger is expanding in the United States itself, at the very heart of the system, where it is no longer surprising to see food lines and soup kitchens even during economic expansions. The growth of agribusiness has also generated more and more ecological problems through the subdivision of traditional diversified farming into specialized production, the break in the soil nutrient cycle, the pollution of land and water (and food itself) with chemicals, soil erosion and other forms of destruction of agricultural ecosystems, and so on. These developments in world agriculture, however, have not gone unanswered. Movements dedicated to promoting sustainable agriculture, fighting hunger, supporting family- and small-scale farming, and staving off ecological destruction have sprouted from the rural and urban grassroots everywhere: locally, nationally, and globally. Our purpose in compiling the essays for this book is to provide the basis for a coherent analysis of these developments.

The essays in *Hungry for Profit* are focused on the political economy of agriculture, food, and ecology. Each article adopts a historical approach while at the same time focusing on issues of current concern and of importance for the future. Further, each of the essays is a critique in the classical sense of striving to penetrate a contradictory reality in order to develop the means for transcending it. Capitalism presents us with the paradoxical reality of a rapid growth of food production and perpetuation of overproduction (relative to markets and income distribution) on one hand, accompanied by the reinforcement of social exclusion and thus the growth of hunger on the other. The latter is not, as is sometimes thought, mainly a result of population growth (which has generally been surpassed by the growth of productivity in agriculture), but instead a consequence of the fact that the immediate object of food production is not human sustenance and well-being but the growth of profits. The coincidence of hungry mouths with overflowing grain silos may seem to be a paradox, but it is a paradox not of our analysis, but of capitalist agribusiness itself.

HISTORICAL TURNING POINT

There can no longer be any doubt today, at the turn of the twenty-first century, that we are in the midst of an unusually rapid change in all aspects of the world's agriculture-food system. This system consists of the farmers who produce the food, but also the huge industry that supplies farmers with inputs, from seeds to fertilizers to tractors to fuel, and the even larger industry that processes, packages, and distributes the food. And, although international trade in agricultural products has occurred for centuries, the pace at which the world is being bound together by trade and the penetration of third world agriculture by the largest of corporations is also quickening (see McMichael, chapter 7).

Traditionally, the various activities of different parts of the agriculture-food system have involved many players—numerous suppliers of inputs, millions of farmers, many purchasers of agricultural commodities, and processors and distributors of food—and have often been portrayed as the textbook example of free-market competition. In *Monopoly Capital* (1966), Paul Baran and Paul Sweezy discussed the process of the increasing concentration and centralization of production under a mature capitalism, which results in a few "corespective" firms dominating most industrial sectors. Under these conditions, a handful of giant corporations control the bulk of a particular market, and the struggle over market share is more by advertising, product differentiation, and brand identification than price competition.

The process of concentration and centralization of the agriculture and food sectors of the economy is occurring later than in the nonfarm industrial sectors. But recent decades have witnessed a startling pace of concentration of suppliers of agricultural inputs that farmers must purchase (such as seeds, fertilizers, pesticides, and machinery) as well as concentration in the food processing, distribution, and retail sectors, where a relatively small number of food conglomerates now play a dominant role (see Heffernan, chapter 3).

How food is produced and how it gets from farm fields to people's tables (the entire food system) is something that obviously concerns everyone. Today there is growing popular fear over possible pesticide contamination of food as well as with the microbiological safety of the food supply. Recent outbreaks of illness have been associated with a variety of contaminated products—meat, juice, fruits, and vegetables. Concern also is growing in the United States and abroad over the safety of food made from genetically modified crops. But the food safety question so much on people's minds is only one small part of the picture. Other important issues include concentration of ownership and control in the production, processing, and marketing of food; safety of farmers and farmworkers when using pesticides; the heavy dependence on nonrenewable resources; environmental consequences of widespread use of genetically modified plants, animals, and microorganisms; contamination of surface- and groundwaters with pesticides and nutrients; low returns for most farmers; low wages and poor working and living conditions for farmworkers; cruel treatment of livestock; and inadequate access to food by poor people. The negative influences of current agricultural practices on ecological systems at the local, regional, and global levels affect the lives of all of us as well as many other species (see Foster and Magdoff, chapter 2, and Altieri, chapter 4). The environmental, social, and economic problems are intertwined, and all are related to the structure of agriculture as it has developed in the late twentieth century.

There are now few buyers for most raw agricultural products. This has left farmers without truly free markets to sell their commodities. Although supply and demand forces, when at their extremes, certainly influence the prices of agricultural commodities, prices for most agricultural commodities have generally remained low and the farmer's share of the food dollar (after paying for input costs) has steadily declined from about 40 percent in 1910 to less than 10 percent in 1990. The enormous power exerted by the largest agribusiness/food corporations allows them essentially to control the cost of their raw materials purchased from farmers while at the same time keeping prices of food to the general public at high enough levels to ensure large profits. It is no accident that the food industry is the second most profitable one in the United States, following pharmaceuticals!

While Baran and Sweezy wrote persuasively and perceptively about how concentration and centralization of capital was occurring and would decisively affect national economies and societies, several of the essays in this collection point to how these concentration and centralization processes are being shaped by the globalization of capital in agriculture and agro-food systems. Heffernan's essay portrays the breakneck pace of concentration and centralization of agribusiness capital at a global scale. McMichael notes that the emergence of new global trade rules over the past twenty-five years—culminating in the World Trade Organization, the North American Free Trade Agreement, other regional trade agreements, and the proposed Multilateral Agreement on Investment (MAI)—has contributed to the expansion of global sourcing of foodstuffs and to the growth of export-oriented production in the third world.

Just as remarkable as the globalization of the agro-industrial chain of production and distribution are the trends in the United States and most other nations toward the industrialization of agriculture and contractual integration. Recognizing that farming tends not to be very profitable and that cheapening the cost of obtaining raw food products is a key to corporate profitability, agribusiness firms have begun to develop "industrial"—or factory-style—production systems and contractual integration arrangements in which the decisions about how to produce crops and animals are increasingly being taken over by the large agribusinesses (see Lewontin, chapter 5). In the extreme situation, such as poultry growers under contract to Tyson or Perdue, or hog producers under contract to Murphy Family Farms, independent farmers are reduced to the position of laborers, but without the rights of workers to collectively bargain.

Contractual integration in the white and red meat sectors (especially broilers and hogs) is closely associated with industrialized or "factory" farming. Meat packers and processors prefer factory farming because it provides them with large, predictable quantities of uniform commodities. Though factory farming and contractual integration are often justified in terms of the need to respond to "consumer preferences," consumers more often than not oppose factory farming, and there appear to be few benefits for consumers from these types of production systems. The development of factory farms, which produce animals under the most cruel conditions as part of a vertically integrated production system, has also resulted in the separation of the animals from the land that produces their feed (see Foster and Magdoff, chapter 2). This phenomenon is in addition to the separation of the mass of the population from the land that occurred when industrialization caused the migrations to urban centers (a process that continues to this day in Third World countries, with or without commensurate industrialization). The ecological consequences of that earlier process were outlined by Marx in *Capital*.

TECHNOLOGY AND EVER-INCREASING SCALE

As is generally the case for relatively small-scale producers of commodities under capitalism, farmers are on a treadmill in which the downward pressure on prices they receive—and/or the upward pressure on inputs needed for production—force them to adopt new technologies and to increase the scale of production in an attempt to stay in business. (It has been said that farming is one of the few businesses that pays retail prices for inputs and sells its products at wholesale prices.) As the financial returns of farmers decline per unit of output, in order to reap the same returns as before the farmers are told that they must get larger or get out. The treadmill that this creates is indicated by an old New England saying: "we grow more corn, to feed more cows, to make more milk, to buy more land, to grow more corn." However, a recent study of dairy farmers in New York State showed that their profit per cow decreased as production per cow and herd size increased. More production is needed just to stand still!

The physical advantages that accrue to increasing production scale (mainly more efficient use of labor and machinery) reach their limits fairly quickly in agriculture. For most commodities medium-sized family farms are as or more efficient than larger, more industrial ones. But that doesn't mean that there aren't real pecuniary advantages to very large farms in a capitalist economy—they typically receive a premium for the commodities they sell because of their large volumes, pay less for purchased inputs and for interest on borrowed money, and have more opportunity for making profits through the use of hired labor.

In the most industrialized and "integrated" sectors such as broilers, "open markets" disappear, and only those producers who have production contracts with processors and other agribusiness "integrators" are able to find a market for their products. A number of publicly funded agricultural experiment stations have also tended to give more attention to factory producers—who account for a very small share of their clientele—than to the far more numerous, but less influential family-scale farmers.

Those who can't keep up with the treadmill of producing on an ever-increasing scale tend to be forced out of farming, and their children are discouraged from entering farming. This is what has been responsible for the drastic decline in the numbers of farms in many countries; in the United States from close to 7 million in the 1930s to about 1.8 million by the mid-1990s. And as farmers left the land, the effects on minorities were devastating. From a high of 14 percent of all U.S. farms being owned by blacks in the 1930s, today less than 1 percent are black-owned. The bulk of decline in farms occurred from the end of the Second World War through the early 1970s, when farm numbers stabilized at approximately 2.0 million and declined by only 0.2 percent a year through the early 1980s. (Although there has recently been an increase in the number of minority-owned farms, mainly among Mexicans and Asians, they still represent a very small percent of total farms.) During the severe "farm crisis" of the 1980s, U.S. farm numbers again declined at a rapid pace (of approximately 17 percent per decade), but are now declining at a slower rate. The rates of decline in farms have been particularly startling in the livestock sectors that are undergoing the most rapid industrialization and movement toward factory farming. Since the early 1980s the numbers of broiler, hog, and dairy farmers have declined at about 4.0 to 4.5 percent per year.

Philip McMichael (chapter 7) stresses that one of the key provisions of the Uruguay General Agreement on Tariffs and Trade (GATT) Round which culminated in the establishment of the World Trade Organization (WTO) was the dismantling of agricultural commodity programs, which since the Second World War have served, albeit very imperfectly, to put a floor under domestic commodity prices. The U.S. government wasted little time in complying with the Uruguay Round Agreement, having done so, in the form of the Federal Agricultural Improvement and Reform Act (FAIR) of 1996. As this book goes to press we are in the midst of another era of hardship and bankruptcies caused by the phasing out of the farm commodity program safety net, and by continuing low prices received by farmers for the basic agricultural commodities such as wheat, corn, and soybeans. This year, as last, an "emergency" farm-aid bill was passed by the U.S. Congress in response to the low prices of farm products.

As farm numbers declined during the last half century, the average farm size increased and the largest of farms have come to account for a sizable proportion of production. At present, the 122,000 largest farms in the United States, representing only 6 percent of the total number, receive close to 60 percent of total farm receipts. These large farms have also been able to reap a disproportionate amount of government support payments, receiving over 30 percent of the payments for the commodity programs.

In the Third World, displacement of farmers under internal pressures, as well as external pressures arising from growing imports from the first world, has led to a loss of huge numbers of people from the land, and has resulted in the swelling of cities (see Araghi, chapter 8). One of the consequences has been increased hunger because of less non-market access to sources of food, particularly by way of peasant self-provisioning from household plots of land. The unfair advantages of the more powerful transnational corporations in shaping world trade in food only accelerates these trends toward "depeasantization."

As U.S. farmers have been squeezed by the trends mentioned above and as Third World farmers have left their fields in increasing numbers, the conditions of U.S. farmworkers have remained dismal (see Majka and Majka, chapter 9). Many of the gains made by the successful unionization drives of the 1970s and early 1980s have been reversed. The increased immigration of farmworkers from Mexico and Central America, and the high rate of worker turnover has made it exceedingly difficult to maintain the organizing momentum.

TECHNOLOGY TO THE RESCUE?

A number of technological fixes have been proposed for the environmental problems of agriculture and food. For example, instead of solving food safety problems by shortening the distance between the point of production and the point of consumption, and producing animals in a small-scale, stress-free, pleasant and clean environment, industry has been promoting irradiation of meat as a cure to bacterial contamination.

A good example of misplaced priorities is that of "precision farming." Over the past few years chemical and farm-machinery companies have been pushing precision (or "Prescription") farming, whereby through the use of global positioning technology (developed by military contractors as part of Reagan's "Star Wars" initiative), yield monitors, extensive field sampling and mapping, and variable application rate machinery, it is possible to apply agrichemicals according to the supposed needs of different parts of a field. It is clearly the case that for decades many fertilizers and pesticides have been applied at higher rates than are economically justifiable. Proponents of precision farming believe that this technology can tailor doses of chemicals to the specific characteristics of small parts of a field, and thereby avoid overusing chemicals on plots of land where the chemicals result in little additional yield. There is little evidence, however, that the precision technology brings any better environmental results than could be obtained with common sense reductions in the use of agrichemicals based on previously available methods. And in many cases it has been found that farmers employing precision farming techniques use a greater overall level of chemicals than they did before.

The push toward biotechnology is being driven by corporations looking for ways to expand their profit-making potential (see Lewontin and Middendorf et al., chapters 5 and 6). While the quest for profits is hardly unique to biotechnology firms, the way that the biotechnology industry developed historically has made this quest a particularly frantic one. The agricultural biotechnology industry dates from the early 1980s. With a very few exceptions, the billions of dollars invested in crop and livestock biotechnology research since the early 1980s yielded virtually no commercial products by the mid-1990s. Thus, with staggering investments but no significant revenues, agricultural biotechnology firms have been particularly intent in the 1990s on the need to speed up the introduction of products into the market. The tendency has been for these corporations to release as many products as possible, many of which have some significant shortcomings, and then convince farmers that they need the particular products that have been developed. Bovine growth hormone, for example, can increase milk production by 10 percent or more per cow. This is a dubious advantage, however, when the price of milk received by farmers has declined in real terms (corrected for inflation) by over half since the early 1980s, and when the number of dairy farmers is already declining by about 40 percent each decade. As noted by Lewontin, other first-generation biotechnology products, such as Bt-engineered and herbicide-tolerant crop varieties, have significant liabilities as well. Even the more environmentally benign "identity-preserved" biotechnology products, which can potentially increase the quality of food products, are likely to serve as the newest frontier for capital to extract profits from agriculture, and through "integration" will serve to convert more farmers into essentially being a proletariat that nominally "owns," but has lost control over, its own land (see Lewontin, chapter 5).

RESPONSES TO THE ONSLAUGHT

There have been many responses around the world to the negative effects of the developing monopoly capital control of the agriculture-food system. In Third World countries there have been efforts against the patenting of plant genetic information (which really constitutes the common heritage of the world's people, and is to a large extent the cultural product of indigenous peoples over many generations), as well as struggles against the trade treaties, such as the World Trade Organization and NAFTA, that tie countries closer together by exposing all to the full force of the market in which the more powerful gain and the less powerful lose out. Farmers and the general public in Europe are trying to resist the importation of genetically modified grains (like "Roundup Ready" soybeans) and beef produced using hormone stimulants.

In the United States, literally hundreds of organizations have been formed to struggle against one or another of the many problems (see Henderson, chapter 10). These organizations and groups have fought for changes in state and national laws, have promoted research aimed at developing practices that are appropriate for environmentally sound farming on a small to medium scale, have specifically promoted organic agriculture, and have provided direct assistance for farmers to help them survive in a very hostile climate.

Critical developments during 1999 have put the purveyors of genetically modified seeds on the defensive. There was an immense reaction in the Third World and Europe to the possible introduction of technology that would produce sterile crop seeds, so that farmers would be forced to buy new seeds annually (see Lewontin and Middendorf et al., chapters 5 and 6, for discussion of the "terminator" gene.) This backlash has forced Monsanto first to put the introduction of the technology on hold and then to back out of the acquisition that would have given them access to the terminator technology. In response to concerns both at home and abroad about environmental and food safety effects, it is projected that lower prices will be paid to farmers growing genetically modified crops. This, combined with the meager returns even before there was a price differential, has made many farmers question the economics of continuing to grow these crops. For the first time since their introduction, a major decrease in acreage planted to genetically modified crops is projected for 2000 (*Wall Street Journal*, Nov. 19, 1999). Activists are convincingly and loudly arguing for mandatory labeling of foods made from genetically modified crops. For years biotechnology firms, along with U.S. government officials, have tirelessly made the case that "the market" should control the introduction of new technologies. Now, however, these firms and government agencies are fighting against labeling of biotechnology food—the only way that the public can actually have a choice. The biotech industry, including Monsanto, DuPont, and Novartis, has launched a counter-offensive to take on the critics of genetically modified crops (*New York Times*, Nov. 12, 1999). The fight against genetically modified foods is currently the leading edge of a struggle by farmers and the general public against complete corporate control of the food system.

It has often been suggested that most farmers can't survive by selling undifferentiated commodities such as wheat, corn, apples, milk, and meat to wholesale processors because of the unequal power relations between direct producers and agribusinesses. Thus, it is believed that to thrive in an era dominated by giant agribusiness corporations farmers must either find a niche crop that few others are growing, start their own processing business (to capture some of the added value to their agricultural product), or sell directly to the public through farmers markets or Community Supported Agriculture (CSA) farms, where people buy shares in the production of the farm before the season starts. Some of these groups concede the loss of the mass of agricultural production to corporate agribusiness and the largest farms. Each of the proposed solutions may help those individual farmers with entrepreneurial skills, or boost those who enjoy working with the public. But while there certainly are some niches available, once they are developed and other farmers start to get into the same enterprise, the niche becomes less lucrative. It cannot offer relief for the mass of farmers. Moreover, once a particular niche grows into a large-scale operation (as in the case of today's organic food industry) it will inevitably face new pressures from agribusiness determined to monopolize all large-scale, lucrative markets.

A parallel social movement has developed in response to the persistence of hunger in the midst of plenty and the decrease in support of food distribution through governmental programs. Many efforts have taken place all over the United States to remedy this problem, including soup kitchens, the opening up and expanding of food shelf pantries that distribute food to the poor, and many corporate or organizational food drives that collect food for later distribution. Nevertheless, the focus has all too often been simply on hunger and what can be done to alleviate it, without going deeper to underlying causes (see Poppendieck, chapter 11).

In the noncapitalist world (i.e., Cuba) and the formerly noncapitalist world (i.e., China), two countries are attempting very different pathways in a sea of change. Cuba is facing severe dislocations caused by the breakup of the Soviet Union. It is under severe pressure because of the lack of fuel and access to other inputs needed to run the high-input, large-scale production system they copied from the Russians. The Cuban state and farmers have turned to small-scale production, in many cases using animal power and organic agricultural techniques (see Rosset, chapter 12). They are also encouraging urban gardening to help provide food during this crisis.

China, in contrast, is moving in a very different direction. The government, as part of its program to achieve and maintain very high rates of income growth through reintroducing capitalist relations, has largely disbanded the agricultural cooperatives. Agricultural plots have been sliced up into narrow strips (see Hinton, chapter 13). Because there is little animal power available and the individual strips are too small to justify use of tractors (which are now mainly used for transportation), most farmers are not able to do a good job of managing their fields. Farmers routinely burn crop residues, just to get rid of them, instead of incorporating them into the soil to make it more fertile, improve its structure, and make it more healthy. Instead of supporting small-scale, resource-efficient agriculture as in Cuba, the infrastructure being developed under government direction (fertilizer and other agrichemical factories) is aimed at high-input systems. Better soil and crop management under these conditions would seem to call for consolidating small strips into larger units of production. Ironically, the effects of the extensive land reform of 1947, a critical part of the success to date of the country's agriculture, has provided an important buffer to the Chinese peoples' food supply as the government heads in the direction of privatization.

WHAT CAN BE DONE?

It is clear that the current food system in all its ramifications is not beneficial for the mass of farmers or the environment, nor does it ensure a plentiful supply of food for all people. However, it does meet the needs of a limited group of large farmers and, of course, the sellers of agricultural inputs as well as the processors, distributors, and sellers of food. Can tinkering with the existing capitalist system realistically be expected to make the changes needed toward a more environmentally sound and humane food system? Such a sound and humane system would, minimally, be one in which:

(1) People would live in greater proximity to agricultural land and animals would be raised more humanely and reunited with the cropland that produces their feed (so nutrients can be recycled more easily with fewer environmental problems).

(2) The power of a few corporations to control so much of food production, processing, and sales would be broken (to make a better deal for farmers growing the food and encourage more environmentally sound farming practices).

(3)   There would be a plentiful and healthy food supply for all people.

Clearly, the changes needed are huge and go to the very foundation of capitalism. The job of creating a just and environmentally sound food system cannot be separated from the creation of a just and environmentally sound society. As pointed out by Poppendieck (chapter 11), hunger is only a symptom of a larger problem—inequality and poverty. And it is critical to emphasize the problem and not to dwell on the symptom. Can the grassroots efforts for food security, growing healthy food, and direct selling of food from farms to consumers be mobilized to help in the efforts to completely transform the food system? Certainly, many sustainable agriculture and food security activists—from a diversity of perspectives—are dedicated to making substantial changes in the food system.

Yet the range of groups with a stake in the transformation of agriculture is both a strength and weakness of this movement. Family farmers, sustainable agriculture proponents, migrant farmworkers, environmentalists, health- and environmentally-conscious consumers, and third world peasants all share an interest in changing the system. This will be a difficult alliance to cement on more than an intermittent basis. Family farmers, for example, are petty property owners whose political leanings are seldom consistent with reducing the prerogatives of property. Family farmers tend to be more comfortable with "right to farm" laws (which insulate producers from "nuisance" lawsuits and from many local land use or environmental regulations) and "food disparagement" laws (like the Texas law that was the basis of the Texas Cattlemen's Association suit against Oprah Winfrey) than they are with environmental regulations or public programs to feed the hungry. Farmworkers continue to strive for improved working conditions as well as higher wages. Environmental groups tend to find wilderness issues and global environmental concerns most important, and do not usually give much emphasis to agriculture. Consumer movements can wield great power over the short term–for example, the boycott of grapes during the California farmworker unionization drive three decades ago was critical to its success, and consumer resistance to biotechnology products such as bovine growth hormone and herbicide-tolerant crop varieties has recently been significant. But consumer movements tend not to focus on any one issue for very long—a particularly dramatic example being the decline of anti-BGH (bovine growth hormone) activities in the United States over the past three years. There continue to be major barriers to cooperation between farmers, farmworkers, environmental groups, sustainable agriculture groups, and consumer organizations.

These groups' struggles offer many opportunities for left activity by those who believe that a complete transformation of society is needed to meet the goals of a truly just and environmentally sound food system. Their differing interests, however, raise the difficult question of how to unite the many groups that focus on individual but interrelated issues, all best approached with a unified focus.

THE MORAL OF THE TALE

Those who wish to radically transform the present agricultural-food system often focus on issues such as the proper scale of agriculture, the question of whether food should be organized in local or global systems, and the appropriate technology to be adopted. Although all of these questions are significant—and we should emphasize the importance of relatively small-scale (by today's standards), local production in agriculture, using technology appropriate to a given set of social/historical/ecological conditions—it is well to remember that such issues are essentially secondary under present circumstances to the question of the commodification of agriculture (and indeed of nature itself) promoted by the capitalist economy with only one end in mind: the production of profits. "The moral of the tale," Marx wrote in *Capital* (vol. III, chapter 6, section 2),

> is that the capitalist system runs counter to a rational agriculture, or that a rational agriculture is incompatible with the capitalist system (even if the latter promotes technical development in agriculture) and needs either small farmers working for themselves or the control of the associated producers.

Chapter One

THE AGRARIAN ORIGINS OF CAPITALISM

ELLEN MEIKSINS WOOD

One of the most well established conventions of Western culture is the association of capitalism with cities. Capitalism is supposed to have been born and bred in the city. But more than that, the implication is that *any* city—with its characteristic practices of trade and commerce—is by its very nature potentially capitalist from the start, and only extraneous obstacles have stood in the way of any urban civilization giving rise to capitalism. Only the wrong religion, the wrong kind of state, or any kind of ideological, political, or cultural fetters tying the hands of urban classes, have prevented capitalism from springing up anywhere and everywhere, since time immemorial—or at least since technology has permitted the production of adequate surpluses.

What accounts for the development of capitalism in the West, according to this view, is the unique autonomy of its cities and of their quintessential class, the burghers or bourgeois. In other words, capitalism emerged in the West less because of what was *present* than because of what was *absent*: constraints on urban economic practices. In those conditions, it took only a more or less natural expansion of trade to trigger the development of capitalism to its full maturity. All that was needed was a quantitative growth, which occurred almost inevitably with the passage of time (in some versions, of course, helped along but *not* originally caused, by the Protestant Ethic).

There are many things to be said against these assumptions about the natural connection between cities and capitalism. Among the objections is the fact that these assumptions tend to *naturalize* capitalism, to disguise its distinctiveness as a historically specific social form, with a beginning and (no doubt) an end. The tendency to identify capitalism with cities and urban commerce has generally been accompanied by an inclination to make capitalism appear as a more or less automatic consequence of practices as old as human history, or even the automatic consequence of human nature, the "natural" inclination, in Adam Smith's words, to "truck, barter, and exchange."

Perhaps the most salutary corrective to these assumptions—and their ideological implications—is the recognition that capitalism, with all its very specific drives of accumulation and profit-maximization, was born not in the city but in the countryside, in a very specific place, and very late in human history. It required not a simple extension or expansion of barter and exchange but a complete transformation in the most basic human relations and practices, a rupture in age-old patterns of human interaction with nature in the production of life's most basic necessities. If the tendency to identify capitalism with cities is associated with a tendency to obscure the *specificity* of capitalism, one of the best ways of understanding that specificity is to consider the agrarian origins of capitalism.

WHAT WAS "AGRARIAN CAPITALISM"?

For millennia, human beings have provided for their material needs by working the land. And probably for nearly as long as they have engaged in agriculture they have been divided into classes, between those who worked the land and those who appropriated the labor of others. That division between appropriators and producers has taken many forms in different times and places, but one general characteristic they have had in common is that the direct producers have typically been peasants. These peasant producers have remained in possession of the means of production, specifically land. As in all precapitalist societies, these producers have had direct access to the means of their own reproduction. This has meant that when their surplus labor has been appropriated by exploiters, it has been done by what Marx called "extra-economic" means—that is, by means of direct coercion, exercised by landlords and/or states employing their superior force, their privileged access to military, judicial, and political power.

Here, then, is the most basic difference between all precapitalist societies and capitalism. It has nothing to do with whether production is urban or rural and everything to do with the particular property relations between producers and appropriators, whether in industry or agriculture. Only in capitalism is the dominant mode of surplus appropriation based on the dispossession of the direct producers, whose surplus labor is appropriated by purely "economic" means. Because direct producers in a fully developed capitalism are propertyless, and because their only access to the means of production, to the requirements of their own reproduction, even to the means of their own labor, is the sale of their labor-power in exchange for a wage, capitalists can appropriate the workers' surplus labor without direct coercion.

This unique relation between producers and appropriators is, of course, mediated by the "market." Markets of various kinds have existed throughout recorded history and no doubt before, as people have exchanged and sold their surpluses in many different ways and for many different purposes. But the market in capitalism has a distinctive and unprecedented function. Virtually everything in capitalist society is a commodity produced for the market. And even more fundamentally, both capital and labor are utterly dependent on the market for the most basic conditions of their own reproduction. Just as workers depend on the market to sell their labor-power as a commodity, capitalists depend on it to buy labor-power, as well as the means of production, and to realize their profits by selling the goods or services produced by the workers. This market-dependence gives the market an unprecedented role in capitalist societies, as not only a simple mechanism of exchange or distribution but as the principal determinant and regulator of social reproduction. The emergence of the market as a determinant of social reproduction presupposed its penetration into the production of life's most basic necessity, food.

This unique system of market-dependence entails some very distinctive "laws of motion," specific systemic requirements and compulsions shared by no other mode of production: the imperatives of competition, accumulation, and profit-maximization. And these imperatives, in turn, mean that capitalism can, and must, constantly expand in ways and degrees unlike any other social form—constantly accumulating, constantly searching out new markets, constantly imposing its imperatives on new territories and new spheres of life, on human beings and the natural environment.

Once we recognize just how distinctive these social relations and processes are, how different from other social forms which have dominated most of human history, it becomes clear that more is required to explain the emergence of this distinctive social form than the question-begging assumption that it has always existed in embryo, just needing to be liberated from unnatural constraints. The question of its origins, then, can be formulated this way: given that producers were exploited by appropriators in noncapitalist ways for millennia before the advent of capitalism, and given that markets have also existed "time out of mind" and almost everywhere, how did it happen that producers and appropriators, and the relations between them, came to be so market dependent?

Now obviously the long and complex historical processes that ultimately led to this condition of market dependence could be traced back indefinitely. But we can make the question more manageable by identifying the first time and place that a new social dynamic is clearly discernible, a dynamic that derives from the market dependence of the main economic actors. And we can then explore the specific conditions surrounding that unique situation.

As late as the seventeenth century, and even much later, most of the world, including Europe, was free of the market-driven imperatives outlined here. A vast system of trade certainly existed, by now extending across the globe. But nowhere, neither in the great trading centers of Europe nor in the vast commercial networks of the Islamic world or Asia, was economic activity, and production in particular, driven by the imperatives of competition and accumulation. The dominant principle of trade everywhere was "profit on alienation," or "buying cheap and selling dear"—typically, buying cheap in one market and selling dear in another.

International trade was essentially "carrying" trade, with merchants buying goods in one location to be sold for a profit in another. But even within a single, powerful, and relatively unified European kingdom like France, basically the same principles of noncapitalist commerce prevailed. There was no single and unified market, a market in which people made profit not by buying cheap and selling dear, not by carrying goods from one market to another, but by producing more cost-effectively in direct competition with others in the same market.

Trade still tended to be in luxury goods, or at least goods destined for more prosperous households or answering to the needs and consumption patterns of dominant classes. There was no mass market for cheap everyday consumer products. Peasant producers would typically produce not only their own food requirements but other everyday goods like clothing. They might take their surpluses to local markets, where the proceeds could be exchanged for other commodities not produced at home. And farm produce might even be sold in markets further afield. But here again, the principles of trade were basically the same as in manufactured goods.

These noncapitalist principles of trade existed side-by-side with noncapitalist modes of exploitation. For instance, in Western Europe, even where feudal serfdom had effectively disappeared, other forms of "extra-economic" exploitation still prevailed. In France, for example, where peasants still constituted the vast majority of the population and still remained in possession of most land, office in the central state served as an economic resource for many members of the dominant classes, a means of extracting surplus labor in the form of taxes from peasant producers. And even rent-appropriating landlords typically depended on various extra-economic powers and privileges to enhance their wealth.

So peasants had access to the means of production, the land, without having to offer their labor-power as a market commodity. Landlords and office-holders, with the help of various "extra-economic" powers and privileges, extracted surplus labor from peasants directly in the form of rent or tax. In other words, while all kinds of people might buy and sell all kinds of things in the market, neither the peasant-proprietors who produced, nor the landlords and office-holders who appropriated what others produced, depended directly on the market for the conditions of their self-reproduction, and the relations between them were not mediated by the market.

But there was one major exception to this general rule. England, by the sixteenth century, was developing in wholly new directions. Although there were other relatively strong monarchical states, more or less unified under the monarchy (such as Spain and France), none was as effectively unified as

England (and the emphasis here is on England, not other parts of the "British Isles"). In the sixteenth century, England—already more unified than most in the eleventh century, when the Norman ruling class established itself on the island as a fairly cohesive military and political entity—went a long way toward eliminating the fragmentation of the state, the "parcellized sovereignty," inherited from feudalism. The autonomous powers held by lords, municipal bodies, and other corporate entities in other European states were, in England, increasingly being concentrated in the central state. This was in contrast to other European states where even powerful monarchies continued for a long time to live uneasily alongside other post-feudal military powers, fragmented legal systems, and corporate privileges whose possessors insisted on their autonomy against the centralizing power of the state.

The distinctive political centralization of the English state had material foundations and corollaries. Already in the sixteenth century, England had an impressive network of roads and water transport that unified the nation to a degree unusual for the period. London, becoming disproportionately large in relation to other English towns and to the total population of England (and eventually the largest city in Europe), was also becoming the hub of a developing national market.

The material foundation on which this emerging national economy rested was English agriculture, which was unique in several ways. The English ruling class was distinctive in two major and related respects.[1] On the one hand, as part of an increasingly centralized state, in alliance with a centralizing monarchy, they did not possess to the same degree as their Continental counterparts the more or less autonomous "extra-economic" powers on which other ruling classes could rely to extract surplus labor from direct producers. On the other hand, land in England had for a long time been unusually concentrated, with big landlords holding an unusually large proportion of land. This concentrated landownership meant that English landlords were able to use their property in new and distinctive ways. What they lacked in "extra-economic" powers of surplus extraction they more than made up for by their increasing "economic" powers.

This distinctive combination had significant consequences. On the one hand, the concentration of English landholding meant that an unusually large proportion of land was worked not by peasant-proprietors but by tenants (the word "farmer," incidentally, literally means "tenant"—a usage suggested by phrases familiar today, such as "farming out"). This was true even before the waves of dispossession, especially in the sixteenth and eighteenth centuries, conventionally associated with "enclosure," in contrast, for example, to France, where a larger proportion of land remained, and long continued to remain, in the hands of peasants.

On the other hand, the relatively weak "extra-economic" powers of landlords meant that they depended less on their ability to squeeze more rents out of their tenants by direct, coercive means than on their tenants' productivity. Landlords had a strong incentive, then, to encourage—and, wherever possible, to compel—their tenants to find ways of increasing their output. In this respect, they were fundamentally different from rentier aristocrats who throughout history have depended for their wealth on squeezing surpluses out of peasants by means of simple coercion, enhancing their powers of surplus extraction not by increasing the productivity of the direct producers but rather by improving their own coercive powers—military, judicial, and political.

As for the tenants themselves, they were increasingly subject not only to direct pressures from landlords but to market imperatives that compelled them to enhance their productivity. English tenancies took various forms, and their were many regional variations, but a growing number were subject to economic rents, that is, rents not fixed by some legal or customary standard but responsive to market conditions. By the early modern period, even many customary leases had effectively become economic leases of this kind.

The effect of the system of property relations was that many agricultural producers (including prosperous "yeomen") were market-dependent, not just in the sense that they were obliged to sell produce on the market but in the more fundamental sense that their access to land itself, to the means of production, was mediated by the market. There was, in effect, a market in leases, in which prospective tenants had to compete. Where security of tenure depended on the ability to pay the going rent, uncompetitive production could mean outright loss of land. To meet economic rents in a situation where other potential tenants were competing for the same leases, tenants were compelled to produce cost-effectively, on penalty of dispossession.

But even those tenants who enjoyed some kind of customary tenure which gave them more security, but who might still be obliged to sell their produce in the same markets, could go under in conditions where competitive standards of productivity were being set by farmers responding more directly and urgently to the pressures of the market. The same would increasingly be true even of landowners working their own land. In this competitive environment, productive farmers prospered and their holdings were likely to grow, while less competitive producers went to the wall and joined the propertyless classes.

In all cases, the effect of market imperatives was to intensify exploitation in order to increase productivity—whether exploitation of the labor of others or self-exploitation by the farmer and his family. This pattern would be reproduced in the colonies, and indeed in post-Independence America, where independent small farmers, who were supposed to be the backbone of a free republic, from the beginning faced the stark choice of agrarian capitalism: at best, intense self-exploitation, and at worst, dispossession and displacement by larger, more productive enterprises.

THE RISE OF CAPITALIST PROPERTY

So English agriculture, already in the sixteenth century, was marked by a unique combination of conditions, at least in certain regions, which would gradually set the economic direction of the whole economy. The result was an agrarian sector more productive than any other in history. Landlords and tenants alike became preoccupied with what they called "improvement," the enhancement of the land's productivity for profit.

It is worth dwelling for a moment on this concept of "improvement," because it tells us a great deal about English agriculture and the development of capitalism. The word "improve" itself, in its original meaning, did not mean just "making better" in a general sense but literally (based on the old French for "into," *en*, and "profit," *pros*—or its oblique case, *preu*) doing something for monetary profit, and especially cultivating land for profit. By the seventeenth century, the word "improver" was firmly fixed in the language to refer to someone who rendered land productive and profitable, especially by enclosing or reclaiming waste. Agricultural "improvement" was by then a well-established practice, and in the eighteenth century, in the golden age of agrarian capitalism, "improvement," in word and deed, came truly into its own.

The word was, at the same time, gradually acquiring a more general meaning, in the sense that we know it today (we might like to think about the implications of a culture in which the word for "making better" is rooted in the word for monetary profit); and even in its association with agriculture, it eventually lost some of its old specificity—so that, for example, some radical thinkers in the nineteenth century might embrace "improvement" in the sense of scientific farming, without its connotation of commercial profit. But in the early modern period, productivity and profit were inextricably connected in the concept of "improvement," and it nicely sums up the ideology of a rising agrarian capitalism.

In the seventeenth century, then, a whole new body of literature emerged, a literature spelling out in unprecedented detail the techniques and benefits of improvement. Improvement was also a major preoccupation of the Royal Society, which brought together some of England's most prominent scientists (Isaac Newton and Robert Boyle were both members of the Society), with some of the more forward-looking members of England's ruling classes—like the philosopher John Locke's mentor, the first Earl of Shaftesbury, and Locke himself, both of whom were keenly interested in agricultural improvement.

Improvement did not, in the first instance, depend on significant technological innovations—although new equipment was used, like the wheelplow. In general, it was more a matter of developments in farming techniques: for example, "convertible" or "up and down" husbandry—alternating cultivation with fallow periods; crop rotation; drainage of marsh and plowlands; and so on.

But improvement meant something more than new methods and techniques of farming. It meant, even more fundamentally, new forms and conceptions of property. "Improved" farming, for the enterprising landlord and his prosperous capitalist tenant, ideally required enlarged and concentrated landholdings. It also—and perhaps even more—demanded the elimination of old customs and practices that interfered with the most productive use of land.

Peasant communities have, since time immemorial, employed various means of regulating land use in the interests of the village community. They have restricted certain practices and granted certain rights, not in order to enhance the wealth of landlords or states but in order to preserve the peasant community itself, perhaps to conserve the land or to distribute its fruits more equitably, and often to provide for the community's less fortunate members. Even "private" ownership of property has been typically conditioned by such customary practices, giving non-owners certain use-rights to property "owned" by someone else. In England, there were many such practices and customs. There existed common lands, on which members of the community might have grazing rights or the right to collect firewood, and there were also various kinds of use-rights on private land—such as the right to collect the leavings of the harvest during specified periods of the year.

From the standpoint of improving landlords and capitalist farmers, land had to be liberated from any such obstruction to their productive and profitable use of property. Between the sixteenth and eighteenth centuries, there was growing pressure to extinguish customary rights that interfered with capitalist accumulation. This could mean various things: it might mean disputing communal rights to common lands and claiming exclusive private ownership; it might mean eliminating various use-rights on private land; or it might mean challenging the customary tenures which gave many small-holders rights of possession without unambiguous legal title. In all these cases, traditional conceptions of property had to be replaced by new, capitalist conceptions of property—property as not only "private" but also exclusive, literally excluding other individuals and the community, by eliminating village regulation and restrictions on land use, by extinguishing customary use-rights, and so on.[2]

These pressures to transform the nature of property manifested themselves in various ways, in theory and in practice. They surfaced in court cases, in conflicts over specific property rights, over some piece of common land or some private land to which different people had overlapping use-rights. In such cases, customary practices and claims often directly confronted the principles of "improvement"—and judges often recognized reasons of improvement as legitimate claims against customary rights that had been in place as long as anyone could remember.[3]

New conceptions of property were also being theorized more systematically, most famously in John Locke's *Second Treatise of Government.*[4] Chapter 5 of that work is the classic statement of a theory of property based on the principles of improvement. Here, property as a "natural" right is based on what Locke regards as the divine injunction to make the earth productive and profitable, to *improve* it. The conventional interpretation of Locke's theory of property suggests that *labor* establishes the right to property, but a careful reading of Locke's chapter on property makes it clear that what really is at issue is not labor as such but the productive and profitable utilization of property, its improvement. An enterprising, improving landlord establishes his right to property not by his own direct labor but by the productive exploitation of his land and other people's labor on it. Unimproved land, land not rendered productive and profitable (such as the lands of indigenous peoples in the Americas), is "waste," and it is the right, even the duty, of improvers to appropriate it.

The same ethic of improvement could be used to justify certain kinds of dispossession not only in the colonies but at home, in England. This brings us to the most famous redefinition of property rights: *enclosure*. Enclosure is often thought of as simply the privatization and fencing in of formerly common land, or of the "open fields" that characterized certain parts of the English countryside. But enclosure meant, more particularly, the extinction (with or without a physical fencing of land) of common and customary use-rights on which many people depended for their livelihood.

The first major wave of enclosure occurred in the sixteenth century, when larger landowners sought to drive commoners off lands that could be profitably put to use as pasture for increasingly lucrative sheep farming. Contemporary commentators held enclosure, more than any other single factor, responsible for the growing plague of vagabonds, those dispossessed "masterless men" who wandered the countryside and threatened social order.[5] The most famous of these commentators, Thomas More, though himself an encloser, described the practice as "sheep devouring men." These social critics, like many historians after them, may have overestimated the effects of enclosure alone, at the expense of other factors leading to the transformation of English property relations. But it remains the most vivid expression of the relentless process that was changing not only the English countryside but the world: the birth of capitalism.

Enclosure continued to be a major source of conflict in early modern England, whether for sheep or increasingly profitable arable farming. Enclosure riots punctuated the sixteenth and seventeenth centuries, and enclosure surfaced as a major grievance in the English Civil War. In its earlier phases, the practice was to some degree resisted by the monarchical state, if only because of the threat to public order. But once the landed classes had succeeded in shaping the state to their own changing requirements—a success more or less finally consolidated in 1688, in the so-called "Glorious Revolution"—there was no further state interference, and a new kind of enclosure movement emerged in the eighteenth century, the so-called Parliamentary enclosures. In this kind of enclosure, the extinction of troublesome property rights that interfered with some landlord's powers of accumulation took place by acts of Parliament. Nothing more neatly testifies to the triumph of agrarian capitalism.

So in England, in a society where wealth still derived predominantly from agricultural production, the self-reproduction of *both* major economic actors in the agrarian sector—both direct producers and the appropriators of their surpluses—were, at least from the sixteenth century, increasingly dependent on what amounted to capitalist practices: the maximization of exchange value by means of cost-cutting and improving productivity, by specialization, accumulation, and innovation.

This mode of providing for the basic material needs of English society brought with it a whole new dynamic of self-sustaining growth, a process of accumulation and expansion very different from the age-old cyclical patterns that dominated material life in other societies. It was also accompanied by the typical capitalist processes of expropriation and the creation of a propertyless mass. It is in this sense that we can speak of "agrarian capitalism" in early modern England.

WAS AGRARIAN CAPITALISM REALLY CAPITALIST?

We should pause here to emphasize two major points. First, it was not merchants or manufacturers who were driving this process. The transformation of social property relations was firmly rooted in the countryside, and the transformation of English trade and industry was result more than cause of

England's transition to capitalism. Merchants could function perfectly well within noncapitalist systems. They prospered, for example, in the context of European feudalism, where they profited not only from the autonomy of cities but also from the fragmentation of markets and the opportunity to conduct transactions between one market and another.

Secondly, and even more fundamentally, readers will have noticed that the term "agrarian capitalism" has so far been used without reference to wage labor, which we have all learned to think of as the essence of capitalism. This requires some explanation.

It should be said, first, that many tenants did employ wage labor, so much so that the "triad" identified by Marx and others—the triad of landlords living on capitalist ground rent, capitalist tenants living on profit, and laborers living on wages—has been regarded by many as the defining characteristic of agrarian relations in England. And so it was—at least in those parts of the country, particularly the east and southeast, most noted for their agricultural productivity. In fact, the new economic pressures, the competitive pressures that drove unproductive farmers to the wall, were a major factor in polarizing the agrarian population into larger landholders and propertyless wage laborers and promoting the agrarian triad. And, of course, the pressures to increase productivity made themselves felt in the intensified exploitation of wage labor.

It would not, then, be unreasonable to define English agrarian capitalism in terms of the triad. But it is important to keep in mind that competitive pressures, and the new "laws of motion" that went with them, depended in the first instance not on the existence of a mass proletariat but on the existence of market-dependent tenant-producers. Wage laborers, and especially those who lived entirely on wage labor, depending on it for their livelihood and not just for seasonal supplements (the kind of seasonal and supplementary wage labor that has existed since ancient times in peasant societies) remained very much a minority in seventeenth century England.

Besides, these competitive pressures operated not just on tenants who did employ wage laborers but also on farmers who—typically with their families—were themselves direct producers working without hired labor. People could be market-dependent—dependent on the market for the basic conditions of their self-reproduction—without being completely dispossessed. To be market-dependent required only the loss of direct non-market access to the means of production. In fact, once market imperatives were well established, even outright ownership was no protection against them. And market-dependence was a cause, not a result, of mass proletarianization.

This is important for various reasons—and I'll have more to say later about its broader implications. For the moment, the important point is that the specific dynamics of capitalism were already in place, in English agriculture, before the proletarianization of the work force. In fact, those dynamics were a major factor in bringing about the proletarianization of labor in England. The critical factor was the market-dependence of producers, as well as appropriators, and the new social imperatives created by that market-dependence.

Some people may be reluctant to describe this social formation as "capitalist," precisely on the grounds that capitalism is, by definition, based on the exploitation of wage labor. That reluctance is fair enough—as long as we recognize that, whatever we call it, the English economy in the early modern period, driven by the logic of its basic productive sector, agriculture, was already operating according to principles and "laws of motion" different from those prevailing in any other society since the dawn of history. Those laws of motion were the *preconditions*—which existed nowhere else—for the development of a mature capitalism that would indeed be based on the mass exploitation of wage labor.

What, then, was the outcome of all this? First, English agriculture was uniquely productive. By the end of the seventeenth century, for instance, grain and cereal production had risen so dramatically that England became a leading exporter of those commodities. The important point here is that these advances in production were achieved with a relatively small agricultural labor force. This is what it means to speak of the unique *productivity* of English agriculture.

Some historians have tried to challenge the very idea of agrarian capitalism by suggesting that the "productivity" of French agriculture in the eighteenth century was more or less equal to that of England. But what they really mean is that *total agricultural production* in the two countries was more or less equal. What they fail to point out is that in one country, that level of production was achieved by a population the vast majority of which still consisted of peasant producers, while in the other country, the same total production was achieved by a much smaller work force, in a declining rural population. In other words, the issue here is not total output but productivity in the sense of output per unit of work.

The demographic facts alone speak volumes. Between 1500 and 1700, England experienced a substantial growth in population—as did other European countries. But English population growth was distinctive in one major respect: the percentage of the urban population more than doubled in that period (some historians put the figure at just under a quarter of the population already by the late seventeenth century). The contrast with France is telling: here, the rural population remained fairly stable, still about 85 to 90 percent at the time of the French Revolution in 1789 and beyond. By 1850, when the urban population of England and Wales was about 40.8 percent, France's was still only 14.4 percent (and Germany's 10.8 percent).

So agriculture in England, already in the early modern period, was productive enough to sustain an unusually large number of people no longer engaged in agricultural production. This fact, of course, testifies to more than just particularly efficient farming techniques. It also bespeaks a revolution in social property relations. While France remained a country of peasant proprietors, land in England was concentrated in far fewer hands, and the propertyless mass was growing rapidly. While agricultural production in France still followed traditional peasant practices (nothing like the English body of improvement literature existed in France, and the village community still imposed its regulations and restrictions on production, affecting even larger landholders), English farming was responding to the imperatives of competition and improvement.

It is worth adding one other point about England's distinctive demographic pattern. The unusual growth of the urban population was not evenly distributed among English towns. Elsewhere in Europe, the typical pattern was an urban population scattered among several important towns—so that, for example, Lyons was not dwarfed by Paris. In England, London became disproportionately huge, growing from about 60,000 inhabitants in the 1520s to 575,000 in 1700 and becoming the largest city in Europe, while other English towns were much smaller.

This pattern signifies more than is apparent at first glance. It testifies, among other things, to the transformation of social property relations in the heartland of agrarian capitalism, the south and southeast, and the dispossession of small producers, a displaced and migrant population whose destination would typically be London. The growth of London also represents the growing unification not only of the English state but of a national market. That huge city was the hub of English commerce—not only as a major transit point for national and international trade but as a huge consumer of English products, not least its agricultural produce. The growth of London, in other words, in all kinds of ways stands for England's emerging capitalism: its increasingly single, unified, integrated, and competitive market; its productive agriculture; and its dispossessed population.

The long-term consequences of these distinctive patterns should be fairly obvious. Although this is not the place to explore the connections between agrarian capitalism and England's subsequent development into the first "industrialized" economy, some points are self-evident. Without a productive agricultural sector that could sustain a large non-agricultural workforce, the world's first industrial capitalism would have been unlikely to emerge. Without England's agarian capitalism, there would have been no dispossessed mass obliged to sell its labor-power for a wage. Without that dispossessed non-agrarian work force, there would have been no mass consumer market for the cheap everyday goods—such as food and textiles—that drove the process of industrialization in England. And without its growing wealth, together with wholly new motivations for colonial expansion—motivations different from the old forms of territorial acquisition—British imperialism would have been a very different thing than the engine of industrial capitalism it was to become. And (this is no doubt a more contentious point) without English capitalism there would probably have been no capitalist system of any kind: it was competitive pressures emanating from England, especially an industrialized England, that compelled other countries to promote their own economic development in capitalist directions.

THE LESSONS OF AGRARIAN CAPITALISM

What, then, does all this tell us about the nature of capitalism?

First, it reminds us that capitalism is not a "natural" and inevitable consequence of human nature, or even of age-old social practices like "truck, barter, and exchange." It is a late and localized product of very specific historical conditions. The expansionary drive of capitalism, to the point of virtual universality today, is not the consequence of its conformity to human nature or to some transhistorical natural laws but the product of its own historically specific internal laws of motion. And those laws of motion required vast social transformations and upheavals to set them in train. It required, again, a transformation in the human metabolism with nature, in the provision of life's basic necessities.

The second point is that capitalism has from the beginning been a deeply contradictory force. We need only consider the most obvious effects of English agrarian capitalism: on the one hand, the conditions for material prosperity existed in early modern England as nowhere else; yet on the other hand, those conditions were achieved at the cost of widespread dispossession and intense exploitation. It hardly needs to be added that these new conditions also established the foundation for new and more effective forms of colonial expansion and imperialism, as well as new needs for such expansion, in search of new markets and resources.

And then there are the corollaries of "improvement": on the one hand, productivity and the ability to feed a vast population; on the other hand, the subordination of all other considerations to the imperatives of profit. This means, among other things, that people who could be fed are often left to starve. In fact, it means that there is in general a great disparity between the productive capacities of capitalism and the quality of life it delivers. The ethic of "improvement" in its original sense, in which production is inseparable from profit, is also the ethic of exploitation, poverty, and homelessness.

The ethic of "improvement," of productivity for profit, is also, of course, the ethic of irresponsible land use, environmental destruction, and mad cow disease. Capitalism was born at the very core of human life, in the interaction with nature on which life itself depends, and the transformation of that interaction by agrarian capitalism revealed the inherently destructive impulses of a system in which the very fundamentals of existence are subjected to the requirements of profit. In other words, it revealed the essential secret of capitalism.

The expansion of capitalist imperatives throughout the world has constantly reproduced some of the effects that it had at the beginning within its country of origin. The process of dispossession, extinction of customary property rights, the imposition of market imperatives, and environmental destruction has continued. That process has extended its reach from the relations between exploiting and exploited classes to the relations between imperialist and subordinate countries. More recently, the spread of market imperatives has taken the form, for example, of compelling (with the help of international capitalist agencies like the World Bank and the International Monetary Fund) farmers in the Third World to replace strategies of agricultural self-sufficiency with specialization in cash crops for the global market. The dire effects of these changes will be explored elsewhere in this book.

But if the destructive effects of capitalism have constantly reproduced themselves, its positive effects have not been nearly as consistent. Once capitalism was established in one country and once it began to impose its imperatives on the rest of Europe and ultimately the whole world, its development in other places could never follow the same course as it had in its place of origin. The existence of one capitalist society thereafter transformed all others, and the subsequent expansion of capitalist imperatives constantly changed the conditions of economic development.

We have now reached the point where the destructive effects of capitalism are outstripping its material gains. No Third World country today, for example, can hope to achieve even the contradictory development that England underwent. With the pressures of competition, accumulation, and exploitation imposed by other more developed capitalist systems, the attempt to achieve material prosperity according to capitalist principles is increasingly likely to bring with it only the negative side of the capitalist contradiction, its dispossession and destruction without its material benefits, at least for the vast majority.

There is also a more general lesson to be drawn from the experience of English agrarian capitalism. Once market imperatives set the terms of social reproduction, all economic actors—both appropriators and producers, even if they remain in possession, or indeed outright ownership, of the means of production—are subject to the demands of competition, increasing productivity, capital accumulation, and the intense exploitation of labor.

For that matter, even the absence of a division between appropriators and producers is no guarantee of immunity (and this, by the way, is why "market socialism" is a contradiction in terms): once the market is established as an economic "discipline" or "regulator," which requires that economic actors remain market-dependent for the conditions of their own reproduction, even workers who own the means of production, individually or collectively, will be obliged to respond to the market's imperatives—to compete and accumulate, to let "uncompetitive" enterprises and their workers go to the wall, and to exploit themselves.

The history of agrarian capitalism, and everything that followed from it, should make it clear that wherever market imperatives regulate the economy and govern social reproduction there will be no escape from exploitation.

NOTES

1. This discussion of the particularities of English property relations is, of course, deeply indebted to Robert Brenner, and especially to his two articles in T.H. Aston and C.H.E. Philpin eds., *The Brenner Debate* (Cambridge: Cambridge University Press, 1985).

2. On regulation of production by the peasant community in France, see George Comninel, *Rethinking the French Revolution: Marxism and the Revisionist Challenge* (London: Verso, 1987).

3. See E.P. Thompson, "Custom, Law and Common Right" in *Customs in Common* (London: Merlin, 1991).

4. The discussion on Locke that follows here is drawn from my chapter on Locke in Ellen Meiksins Wood and Neal Wood, *A Trumpet of Sedition: Political Theory and the Rise of Capitalism, 1509–1688* (London and New York: New York University Press, 1997). For a detailed discussion of Locke and the "improvement" literature of the seventeenth century, see Neal Wood, *John Locke and Agrarian Capitalism* (Berkeley and Los Angeles: University of California Press, 1984).

5. On these early social critics, see Neal Wood, *The Foundations of Political Economy: Some Early Tudor Views on State and Society* (Berkeley and Los Angeles: University of California Press, 1994).

Chapter Two

LIEBIG, MARX, AND THE DEPLETION
OF SOIL FERTILITY: RELEVANCE FOR
TODAY'S AGRICULTURE

JOHN BELLAMY FOSTER AND FRED MAGDOFF

During the period 1830-1870, the depletion of the natural fertility of the soil through the loss of soil nutrients was the central ecological concern of capitalist society in both Europe and North America (only comparable to concerns over the loss of forests, the growing pollution of the cities, and the Malthusian specter of overpopulation). This period saw the growth of guano imperialism as nations scoured the globe for natural fertilizers; the emergence of modern soil science; the gradual introduction of synthetic fertilizers; and the formation of radical proposals for the development of a sustainable agriculture, aimed ultimately at the elimination of the antagonism between town and country.

The central figure in this crisis of soil fertility was the German chemist Justus von Liebig. But the wider social implications were most penetratingly examined by Karl Marx. The views of Liebig and Marx on soil fertility were to be taken up by later thinkers, including Karl Kautsky and V.I. Lenin within the Marxist tradition. Still, by the mid-twentieth century the problem seemed to have abated due to the development of a massive fertilizer industry and the intensive application of synthetic fertilizers.

Today, a growing understanding of the ecological damage inflicted by the reliance on synthetic chemical inputs, the scale of which vastly increased following the Second World War, has generated new interest in a sustainable agriculture in which soil nutrient cycling plays a central role. The need to devise an ecologically sound relationship of people to the soil is being rediscovered.[1] What follows is a brief outline of the evolution of this issue over the last hundred and fifty years.

LIEBIG AND THE NINETEENTH CENTURY CRISIS OF THE SOIL

In the 1820s and 1830s in Britain, and shortly afterwards in the other developing capitalist economies of Europe and North America, concern over the "worn-out soil" led to a phenomenal increase in the demand for fertilizer. The value of bone imports to Britain increased from £14,400 in 1823 to £254,600 in 1837. The first boat carrying Peruvian guano (the accumulated dung of sea birds) arrived in Liverpool in 1835; by 1841 1,700 tons were imported, and by 1847 some 220,000 tons arrived. So desperate were European farmers in this period that they raided the Napoleonic battlefields (Waterloo, Austerlitz) for bones to spread over their fields.[2]

The rise of modern soil science was closely correlated with this demand for increased soil fertility to support capitalist agriculture. In 1837 the British Association for the Advancement of Science solicited a work on the relationship between agriculture and chemistry from Liebig. The result was his *Organic Chemistry in its Applications to Agriculture and Physiology* (1840), which provided the first convincing explanation of the role of soil nutrients, such as nitrogen, phosphorous, and potassium, in the growth of plants. In England Liebig's ideas influenced the wealthy landowner and agronomist J. B. Lawes, who had begun experiments on fertilizers on his property in Rothamsted, outside London in 1837. In 1842 Lawes introduced the first artificial fertilizer, after inventing a means of making phosphate soluble, and in 1843 he built a factory for the production of his new "superphosphates."

Nevertheless, this technology was slow to diffuse outside of Britain. The first factories for the production of superphosphates were introduced in Germany only in 1855; in the United States only after the Civil War; and in

France only after the Franco-Prussian War. Moreover, the results obtained from the application of a single nutrient (such as phosphate) to the soil, although initially producing dramatic results, tended to diminish rapidly after that, since overall soil fertility is always limited by the nutrient in least abundance (Liebig's Law of the Minimum).

Hence, Liebig's discoveries at first only intensified the sense of crisis within capitalist agriculture, making farmers more aware of the depletion of soil minerals and the paucity of fertilizers. This contradiction was experienced with particular acuity in the United States—especially among farmers in upstate New York and in the Southeastern plantation economy. Blocked from easy, economical access to guano (which was high in both nitrogen and phosphates) by the British monopoly on Peruvian guano supplies, the United States undertook—first unofficially and then as part of a deliberate state policy—the imperial annexation of any islands thought to be rich in this natural fertilizer. Under the authority of what became the Guano Island Act, passed by Congress in 1856, U.S. capitalists seized ninety-four islands, rocks, and keys around the globe between 1856 and 1903, sixty-six of which were officially recognized by the Department of State as U.S. appurtenances. Nine of these guano islands remain U.S. possessions today. Yet guano imperialism was unsuccessful in providing the United States with the quantity and quality of natural fertilizer it needed.[3]

Meanwhile, Peruvian guano supplies had begun to run out in the 1860s and had to be replaced by Chilean nitrates. Although the potassium salts discovered in Europe gave ready access to that mineral, and both natural and artificial supplies of phosphates made that nutrient more available, the limiting factor continued to be fertilizer nitrogen (a synthetic nitrogen fertilizer was not developed until 1913).

The decline in natural soil fertility due to the disruption of the soil nutrient cycle accompanying capitalist agriculture, the growing knowledge of the need for specific soil nutrients, and limitations in the supply of both natural and synthetic fertilizers that would compensate for the loss of natural fertility, all contributed, therefore, to a widespread sense of a crisis in soil fertility.

In the United States this was further complicated by geographical factors. In upstate New York, which by 1800 had displaced New England as a center for wheat cultivation, the relative exhaustion of the soil was brought into

sharp relief by steadily increasing competition from new farmlands to the
West in the decades following the opening of the Erie Canal in 1825.
Meanwhile the slave plantations of the Southeast experienced dramatic declines
in fertility, particularly on lands devoted to the production of tobacco.

In New York farmers responded to the crisis by promoting a more rational
agriculture through the creation of agricultural societies. In 1832 the New
York Agricultural Society was formed. Two years later Jesse Buel, an Albany
newspaper editor, started the *Cultivator*, which sought to promote the kind
of improved farming already being introduced in Britain, concentrating on
issues such as manures, draining wet soils, and crop rotation. With the
publication in 1840 of Liebig's *Agricultural Chemistry* (as his *Organic Chemistry in its Applications to Agriculture and Physiology* is commonly known),
New York agriculturists turned to the new soil science as a savior. In 1850
the Scottish agricultural chemist, Professor James F.W. Johnston, whom
Marx was to call "the English Liebig," traveled to North America, and in his
influential work *Notes on North America* documented the loss of natural soil
fertility, demonstrating in particular the depleted condition of the soil in
New York as compared to the more fertile farmlands to the West.[4]

Many of these issues were reflected in the work of U.S. economist Henry
Carey, who throughout the 1850s laid stress on the fact that long distance
trade arising from the separation of town and country was a major factor in
the net loss of soil nutrients and the growing crisis in agriculture—a point
later developed further by Liebig and Marx. "[A]s the whole energies of the
country," Carey wrote of the United States in his *Principles of Social Science*
(1858), "are given to the enlargement of the trader's power, it is no matter
of surprise that its people are everywhere seen employed in 'robbing the earth
of its capital stock.' "[5]

These concerns of North American agriculturists were transmitted in turn
to Liebig, mainly through the work of Carey. In his *Letters on Modern
Agriculture* (1859), Liebig argued that the "empirical agriculture" of the
trader gave rise to a "spoliation system" in which the "conditions of the
reproduction" of the soil were violated. Soil nutrients were "carried away in
produce year after year, rotation after rotation." Both the open system of
exploitation of American farming and the so-called "high farming" of

European agriculture were thus forms of "robbery." "Rational agriculture," in contrast, would give "back to the fields the conditions of their fertility."[6]

Liebig looked forward to an eventual increase in the availability of fertilizers, both through discoveries of natural sources and the production of synthetic fertilizers. Yet he nonetheless generated what soil science historian Jean Boulaine has called a "great campaign to economize fertilizer use and to recycle nutritive elements on European farms." In this sense he was a "precursor of today's ecologists."[7] In his *Letters on the Subject of the Utilization of the Municipal Sewage Addressed to the Lord Mayor of London* (1865) Liebig argued—based on the condition of the Thames—that the two problems of the pollution of the cities with human and animal excrement and the depletion of the natural fertility of the soil were connected, and that organic recycling that would return nutrients to the soil was an indispensable part of a rational urban-agricultural system.[8]

MARX AND SUSTAINABLE AGRICULTURE

Marx relied heavily on the works of Liebig, Johnston, and Carey in his critique of capitalist agriculture. However, the root source for Marx's critique in this area was James Anderson, a Scottish agronomist, practicing farmer, and political economist who was a contemporary of Adam Smith.

In 1777 Anderson published *An Enquiry into the Nature of the Corn Laws* in which he introduced what was to become known as the Malthusian/Ricardian theory of rent. In Marx's view, Anderson's original model was far superior to the variant later offered by the classical economists Thomas Malthus and David Ricardo since it placed strong emphasis on the possibility of continuing agricultural improvement. Rent, Anderson argued, was a charge for the use of the more fertile soil. The least fertile soils in cultivation generated an income that simply covered the costs of production, while the more fertile soils received a "certain premium for an exclusive privilege to cultivate them; which will be greater or smaller according to the more or less fertility of the soil. It is this premium which constitutes what we now call *rent*; a medium by means of which the expence of cultivating soils of very different degrees of fertility may be reduced to a perfect equality."[9]

For Malthus and Ricardo the source of this differential fertility came to be seen almost entirely in terms of conditions of natural productivity independent of human beings. As Ricardo wrote, rent could be defined as "that portion of the produce of the earth, which is paid to the landlord for the use of the original and indestructible powers of the soil."[10] Moreover, they argued—with the presumed backing of natural law—that lands that were naturally the most fertile were the first to be brought into production, and that rising rent on these lands and diminishing agricultural productivity overall were the result of bringing lands of more and more marginal fertility into cultivation, in response to increasing population pressures.[11]

In contrast, Anderson had earlier insisted that continual improvement of the soil, through manuring, draining, and irrigating, was possible and that the productivity of the least fertile land could rise to a point that brought it much closer to that of the most fertile land; but also that the converse was true, and human beings could degrade the soil. It was such changes in relative productivity of the soil, according to Anderson, that accounted for differential rent—and not conditions of absolute fertility, as in the later arguments of Malthus and Ricardo.[12]

Where general fertility problems did arise in agriculture, this was, for Anderson, a consequence of the failure to adopt rational and sustainable agricultural practices. The fact that the land in England was owned by landed proprietors and farmed by capitalist tenant farmers, he argued, posed obstacles to rational agriculture, since the farmer tended to avoid all improvements, the full return for which would not be received during the duration of the lease.[13]

In *A Calm Investigation of the Circumstances that have Led to the Present Scarcity of Grain in Britain* (1801), Anderson contended that the division between town and country had led to the loss of natural sources of fertilizer. "Every person who has but heard of agriculture," he wrote, "knows that animal manure, when applied to the soil tends to add to its fertility; of course he must be sensible that every circumstance that tends to deprive the soil of that manure ought to be accounted an uneconomical waste highly deserving of blame." It was possible, he asserted, by the judicious application of animal and human wastes to sustain the "soil for ever after, without the addition of any extraneous manures." Yet London, with its gargantuan waste of such natural sources of fertility, "which is daily carried to the Thames, in its passage to which it subjects the people in the lower part of the city to the most offensive effluvia," was an indication of how far society had moved from a sustainable agricultural economy.[14] Armed with this critical analysis, and a historical perspective, Anderson strenuously attacked the Malthusian view that the crisis of agriculture and society could be traced to rising human population and its pressures on a limited supply of land.[15]

Marx's critique of capitalist agriculture drew upon both Anderson's original formulation of the classical rent theory and Liebig's soil chemistry in order to combat the influence of the Malthusian-Ricardian natural law doctrines of overpopulation and diminishing agricultural productivity. In the 1840s and 1850s Marx stressed the potential for "improvement" in agriculture if rationally organized through such means as the application of synthetic fertilizers.[16] Even in these early decades, however, he insisted that soil fertility was a historical issue, and that fertility could both improve and decline. The irrationality of capitalist agriculture, he argued, was bound up with the whole antagonism of town and country out of which bourgeois society had arisen.

But by the 1860s, based on his reading of such thinkers as Liebig, Johnston, and Carey, and in response to the soil fertility crisis, Marx began to focus directly on the soil nutrient cycle and its relation to the exploitative character of capitalist agriculture. Thus, in the first volume of *Capital* he wrote:

> Capitalist production ... disturbs the metabolic interaction between man and the earth, i.e. it prevents the return to the soil of its constituent elements consumed by man in the form of food and clothing; hence it hinders the operation of the eternal natural condition for the fertility of the soil.... All progress in capitalist agriculture is a progress in the art, not only of robbing the worker, but of robbing the soil; all progress in increasing the fertility of the soil for a given time is a progress towards ruining the more long-lasting sources of that fertility.... Capitalist production, therefore, only develops the techniques and degree of combination of the social process of production by simultaneously undermining the original sources of all wealth—the soil and the worker.[17]

This argument was developed systematically in Marx's analysis of capitalist ground rent in the third volume of *Capital*, where Marx also observed that, "In London ... they can do nothing better with the excrement produced by

4.5 million people than pollute the Thames with it, at monstrous expense."[18]
Such considerations on capitalist agriculture and the recycling of organic
wastes led Marx to a concept of ecological sustainability—a notion that he
thought of very limited practical relevance to capitalist society, but vital for
a society of associated producers.[19] The "conscious and rational treatment of
the land as permanent communal property," he wrote, is "the inalienable
condition for the existence and reproduction of the chain of human generations."[20] Further:

> From the standpoint of a higher socio-economic formation, the private property
> of particular individuals in the earth will appear just as absurd as the private property
> of one man in other men. Even an entire society, a nation, or all simultaneously
> existing societies taken together, are not owners of the earth, they are simply its
> possessors, its beneficiaries, and have to bequeath it in an improved state to
> succeeding generations, as *boni patres familias* [good heads of the household].[21]

Subsequent thinkers in the Marxist tradition, such as Kautsky and Lenin,
were to be deeply affected by the arguments of Liebig and Marx on agricultural sustainability and the necessity of recycling organic wastes, and argued
for the return of nutrients to the soil as a necessary part of a revolutionary
transformation of society—despite the increased availability of fertilizers in
their time. In *The Agrarian Question* (1899), Kautsky insisted that:

> Supplementary fertilisers . . . allow the reduction in soil fertility to be avoided, but
> the necessity of using them in larger and larger amounts simply adds a further
> burden to agriculture—not one unavoidably imposed on nature, but a direct result
> of current social organization. By overcoming the antithesis between town and
> country, or at least between the densely populated cities and the desolated open
> country, the materials removed from the soil would be able to flow back in full.
> Supplementary fertilisers would then, at most, have the task of enriching the soil,
> not staving off its impoverishment. Advances in cultivation would signify an
> increase in the amount of soluble nutrients in the soil without the need to add
> artificial fertilisers.[22]

Similarly, Lenin observed in *The Agrarian Question and the "Critics of
Marx"* (1901) that,

> The possibility of substituting artificial for natural manures and the fact that this
> is already being done (partly) do not in the least refute the irrationality of wasting

natural fertilisers and thereby polluting the rivers and the air in suburban and factory districts. Even at the present time there are sewage farms in the vicinity of large cities which utilise city refuse with enormous benefit to agriculture; but by this system only an infinitesimal part of the refuse is utilized.[23]

RELEVANCE FOR TODAY

The trends that were of concern to Anderson, Liebig, Marx, Kautsky, and Lenin only intensified as capitalism developed in the twentieth century. As mechanization and low prices for farm products forced people off the farms, workers concentrated first in cities and then in suburban communities. The continued development of employment opportunities in the urban industrial sector and then in the urban-suburban service and government sectors later in the century provided job outlets for the former farm families. (On the other hand, urbanization in most third world countries has taken place without commensurate increases in employment in the cities.) As an ever-higher percentage of the population lived off the farm, the break in the cycling of nutrients was even more complete than in the nineteenth century. This break in the return flow of nutrients to the land is illustrated in Figure 1.

As soils became depleted of nutrients and organic matter they became less fertile and there was much concern about what to do with "worn out" soils. At the same time that nutrients were depleted from farmland, sewage containing those nutrients fouled many lakes and rivers, while coastal cities dumped sewage into the ocean. Although sewage treatment systems installed since the 1970s have decreased the problem of water pollution in the United States, a new problem was created—how to get rid of the sludge that is produced. Currently sewage sludge is buried in landfills, incinerated, or applied to farmland, each of which has significant environmental consequences.

Two developments set the stage for a second break in the cycling of nutrients. First, the availability of inexpensive nitrogen fertilizers following the Second World War helped put in motion a number of changes. The production of nitrogen fertilizers uses the same process as the production of explosives, and the end of war production freed up a large capacity to make nitrogen fertilizers. (It is also important to note a further agrichemical connection to the military-industrial complex: many of the pesticides used in agriculture were originally developed for military purposes as defoliants and nerve agents.) With the widespread availability of nitrogen fertilizers, there was no longer a need to rely on legume crops, which convert atmospheric nitrogen into a form that plants can use, to supply non-legumes with sufficient fertility. The legume clover and alfalfa hay crops had previously been fed to ruminant animals such as beef and dairy cows and sheep. Once there was no need to grow those crops to supply nitrogen for non-legume crops (wheat, corn, barley, tomatoes), farms could more easily specialize as either crop or livestock operations.

Figure 1.

CHANGES IN THE SPATIAL RELATIONSHIPS OF PLANTS, ANIMALS, AND HUMANS

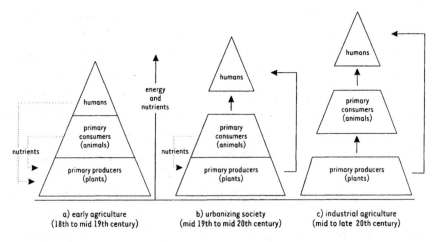

a) early agriculture
(18th to mid 19th century)

b) urbanizing society
(mid 19th to mid 20th century)

c) industrial agriculture
(mid to late 20th century)

Second, as concentration accelerated in agricultural production, processing, and marketing, corporations began to encourage production of animals near the few large processing facilities that they operated. They selected locations that offered certain advantages such as lax environmental laws, negligible threat of union activity, and low wages. The large processors were also increasingly marketing their products under brand names and, to have a uniform and predictable product, needed to control as much of the entire process as possible—either by producing the animals on their own corporate farms or under production contracts where the farmer might not even own the animals and had to follow strict instructions from their corporate employer. Thus animal production became concentrated in certain regions: beef feedlots in the southern Great Plains, poultry in Arkansas and on the Delmarva Peninsula (composed of parts of Delaware, Maryland, and Virginia) and hog production in certain parts of the Midwest and in North Carolina.

These two developments in the second half of the twentieth century have led to a new phenomenon that mirrors the separation of people from the farmland which so concerned Marx and others—the separation of agricultural animals from the cropland that produces their feeds (Figure 1c). The large-scale U.S. poultry and hog megafarms (aptly called factory farms) are owned almost exclusively by corporate integrators or by individual farmers under production contracts for corporations such as Tyson and Perdue. And beef feedlots with tens of thousands of animals are not uncommon. More than a third of cattle marketed in the United States come from just seventy feedlots, while 97 percent of U.S. poultry sales are controlled by operations that generate in excess of 100,000 broilers per year.[24] Even on dairy farms that produce a lot of their own feed, it is common to import about half of the animals' needs. This breakdown of the physical connection between the animals and the land producing their feeds has worsened the depletion of nutrients and organic matter from soils producing crops. Crop farms must use large amounts of synthetic fertilizers to compensate for the loss of vast quantities of nutrients as their products are sold.

In addition, as pointed out by Anderson and Marx, those renting land to produce crops have no economic incentive to make improvements for which they will not receive compensation during the life of the rental agreement. Fully 48 percent of all U.S. agricultural land in 1994 was rented from others.[25] In some sectors rental is especially common, with 60 percent of the land devoted to cash grain and 75 percent of all cotton land rented.[26] Land rental is also more common on larger farms, with 58 percent of the land operated by farms with annual gross receipts of $250,000 or more under rental agreements.[27] The great extent of rented land is another factor that increases the trend toward farm specialization and short-term approaches to maintaining soil fertility that rely on synthetic fertilizers rather than environmentally sound, long-term soil and crop management strategies.

ENVIRONMENTAL CONSEQUENCES

The lack of nutrient cycling resulting from the physical separation first of people and then of animals from cropland created the need to use ever higher levels of synthetic nutrients. And while the crop farms have too few nutrients, these very same nutrients accumulate in cities and on the large-scale animal factory farms. Because of the long distances involved, these accumulated nutrients are not returned to the major crop growing areas because the energy and financial costs are extremely high.

There are a number of severe environmental consequences of the developments described above:

(1) Large amounts of non-renewable energy sources are needed to produce, ship, and apply the fertilizers. Production of nitrogen fertilizer is very energy intensive. Of all the energy used to produce an acre of corn in the United States cornbelt—including fuel, wear and tear on machinery, seeds, and pesticides—nitrogen fertilizer accounts for the largest amount (double the next largest category), approximately 40 percent.[28]

(2) Another adverse consequence arises because the fertilizers used are soluble and are thus prone to cause groundwater and surface water contamination. In addition, the high concentrations of livestock produce more nutrients than the surrounding soils can safely absorb. A direct health hazard results as the groundwater many use for drinking is contaminated with high levels of nitrates. Excess nutrients from agricultural production are also implicated in the deterioration of estuaries such as the Chesapeake Bay, and marine environments such as the Gulf of Mexico's dead zone to the west of the Mississippi River's mouth, as well as many fresh water lakes.

(3) Even when cities are located near farms, the industrial contaminants, as well as chemicals in many of the products that people dispose around their homes, render most urban sewage sludges unsuitable for use on farmland. Although the U.S. Environmental Protection Agency considers most sludges safe for use on farmland, there are significant scientific concerns about the adequacy of these guidelines. U.S. standards are by far the most lax of all advanced industrial countries, with permitted levels of heavy metal eight times that of Canada and most European nations.[29] And there are potential contaminants in manures too—for example, routine feeding of copper to

hogs raised in confinement to enhance their growth results in manures that have excessive copper levels. Disposal of contaminated sludges and manures causes environmental problems that may affect the future productivity of soils or the quality of air and water.

(4) The lack of good rotations on most crop farms, partially caused by the availability of inexpensive synthetic fertilizers, has resulted in a loss of soil organic matter and a decrease in the diversity of organisms in the soil. This degradation of soil quality allows the growth of large populations of disease organisms and plant parasites that would have been held in check by a diverse community of competing organisms. Also, plants that are unhealthy tend to attract more insect pests than healthier plants. The upshot of this is that greater amounts of pesticides are used in an attempt to combat the increased pest pressures resulting from soil degradation. Thus much of the pesticide poisoning of farmers and farmworkers as well as the contamination of many foods and groundwater is a result of soil degradation.

(5) The cruel conditions under which animals are raised in large-scale production facilities create conditions in which disease can easily spread, necessitating frequent use of antibiotics. In addition, the routine use of low levels of antibiotics in feeds, which function somehow as a growth stimulant, accounts for most of the 40 percent of total antibiotics that are used on animals. The constant use of medicines causes both antibiotic contamination of food and the development of antibiotic-resistant strains of bacteria, which can then become a human health hazard.

(6) Mining operations undertaken to supply nutrients have resulted in substantial environmental damage. The fate of one of the victims of guano imperialism gives some indication of what can happen. The small South Pacific island nation of Nauru was under German control from 1888 to the First World War, after which it was under the control of Australia (except for Japanese occupation during the Second World War) until independence was gained in 1968. Strip mining of the phosphate-rich deposits began around 1908 and the deposit is expected to be exhausted within a few years. According to a *New York Times* article "four-fifths of the island has been mined out, leaving behind a pitted, ghostly moonscape.... The only habitable land is a narrow coastal fringe shaded by coconut palms. Because of the mining, even the weather has deteriorated. The waves of heat that rise from

the mined-out plateau drive away rain clouds, leaving the sun-baked island plagued by constant drought."[30]

EXPERIENCES OF THE NONCAPITALIST WORLD

The history of the noncapitalist world offers a few glimpses of other possibilities. The Soviet model, followed by most other countries in eastern Europe, offers no help on this issue because it closely copied many of the methods used in the United States, lack of attention to cycling of nutrients and care of the soil was partially offset by applications of fertilizers and pesticides. However, in China during Mao things were different. China has an extremely low amount of arable land per capita, but has had a long tradition of carefully cycling nutrients to maintain soil fertility (as noted by Liebig in the nineteenth century). Mao's emphasis on local food self-sufficiency in each region helped to reinforce these practices and, together with the encouragement of local industry, slowed down urbanization at the same time as impressive advances were made in agricultural production. But in the transition to capitalist relations that is now far advanced, nutrient cycling and careful soil management have decreased substantially, and there is a new emphasis on building fertilizer factories to supply the nutrient needs of agricultural production.[31] In Cuba, the economic crisis of the Special Period has been caused by the cancellation of favorable trade agreements with the collapse of the Soviet Union. Lack of funds to purchase fertilizers and pesticides from abroad created an interest in reducing the use of such materials, and organic production techniques have become a mainstay of Cuban agriculture with attention paid to nutrient cycling issues.[32]

WHAT CAN BE DONE?

What can be done to remedy the break in the cycling of nutrients in the advanced capitalist countries and the resulting environmental consequences? Without a major challenge to the structure of agriculture and corporate decision making, a profound change in the nature and sizes of cities and the curbing of suburban development, and a moratorium on the continued introduction of new synthetic chemical compounds until their environmental safety is proven beyond a doubt (all unlikely in the near future), there remain few options. These include encouraging the consumption of locally grown food and the recycling of clean food wastes from homes, restaurants, and markets back onto farmland. And seeking out of farmers that follow environmentally and socially sound practices at farmers markets and through the new Community Supported Agriculture farms (CSAs, where individuals and families buy shares in the production of the farm before the season starts) can help as well. A massive effort can also be undertaken to clean up sewage sludges by eliminating the contamination of sewage with potentially toxic wastes from industries as well as individual homes. This will be resisted by industry because of the large expenditures required for most to have zero discharge of toxic materials. Although such activities will not solve the problems, they will make a difference. And during the struggles, the mutual education of those interested in broader societal issues, on the one hand, and those concerned with sustainable agriculture and environmental issues, on the other, could lead to more permanent future alliances.

From a longer-term perspective, it is important to understand that neither a lack of technology nor a lack of understanding of ecological processes are standing in the way of sustainable agricultural systems today. Although there is plenty to find out, we already know how to design and implement agroecosystems that are biologically sustainable, taking into account soil nutrient cycles and other factors. But the mass of farmers cannot use this knowledge and survive under the current economic-social-political structure.

A humane and sustainable system, socialist and based on sound ecological principles, will concern itself with sustaining the earth, as Marx wrote, "as the inalienable condition for the existence and reproduction of the chain of human generations." To fail to take these more fundamental issues into account in our current struggles would be to ensure our failure not only in the cause of social justice, but also in fulfilling our obligations to the earth—understood as the ground we live on and the bio-geological processes that sustain us. One thing we can be assured of: future generations will only look at us askance if we allow ourselves to give in at any point to a system, such as the present one, run on the principle "Aprés moi le dèluge!." [33]

NOTES

1. See Kozo Mayumi, "Temporary Emancipation form the Land," *Ecological Economics*, vol. 4, no. 1 (October 1991), 35–56; Fred Magdoff, Les Lanyon and Bill Liebhardt, "Nutrient Cycling, Transformation and Flows: Implications for a More Sustainable Agriculture," *Advances in Agronomy*, vol. 60 (1997), 1–73; Gary Gardner, *Recycling Organic Waste: From Urban Pollutant to Farm Resource* (Washington, D.C.: Worldwatch, 1997).

2. Jean Boulaine, "Early Soil Science and Trends in the Early Literature," in Peter McDonald, ed., *The Literature of Soil Science* (Ithaca: Cornell University Press, 1994), 24; Daniel Hillel, *Out of the Earth* (Berkeley: University of California Press, 1991), 131–32.

3. J.M. Skaggs, *The Great Guano Rush* (New York: St. Martin's Press, 1994).

4. Margaret W. Rossiter, *The Emergence of Agricultural Science: Justus Liebig and the Americans, 1840–80* (New Haven: Yale University Press, 1975), 3–9; Karl Marx and Friedrich Engels, *Collected Works*, vol. 38, 476; James F.W. Johnston, *Notes on North America*, vol. 1 (London: William Blackwood and Sons, 1851), 356–65; Marx, *Capital*, vol. 3 (New York: Vintage, 1981), 808.

5. Henry Carey, *Principles of Social Science* (Philadelphia: J.B. Lippincott, 1867), vol. 2, 215, and *The Slave Trade Domestic and Foreign* (New York: Augustus M. Kelley, 1967), 199.

6. Justus von Liebig, *Letters on Modern Agriculture* (London: Walton and Mabery, 1859), 171–83, 220. Liebig's criticism of the "spoliation system" was made even more explicit in the revised 1862 edition of his *Agricultural Chemistry*, which influenced Marx. See William H. Brock, *Justus von Liebig: The Chemical Gatekeeper* (Cambridge: Cambridge University Press, 1997), 175–79.

7. Boulaine, "Early Soil Science," 25.

8. Brock, *Justus von Liebig*, 250–72.

9. James Anderson, *Observations on the Means of Exciting a Spirit of National Industry* (Edinburgh: T. Cadell, 1777), 376, *Enquiry into the nature of the Corn Laws; with a View to the New Corn Bill Proposed for Scotland* (Edinburgh: Mrs. Mundell, 1777), 45–50; J.R. McCulloch, *The Literature of Political Economy* (London: Longman, Brown, Green, and Longmans), 68–70.

10. David Ricardo, *Principles of Political Economy and Taxation* (Cambridge: Cambridge University Press, 1951), 67. Ricardo did not deny altogether the possibility of improvement in agriculture but gave it a very limited role. "Improvements in agriculture," he wrote, were "of two kinds: those which increase the productive powers of the land, and those which enable us, by improving our machinery to produce with less labour." The former type of improvement was mainly associated with "more skillful rotation of crops, or better choice of manure." *Ibid.*, 80. It seems

to have been a key assumption of the Ricardian rent theory that such improvements could have only a limited impact on fertility, and could in general be abstracted from altogether.

11. Karl Marx, *Theories of Surplus Value*, part 2 (Moscow: Progress Publishers, 1968), 114–17, 121–25.

12. Ibid., 241–44; James Anderson, *A Calm Investigation of the Circumstances that have Led to the Present Scarcity of Grain in Britain: Suggesting the Means of Alleviating the Evil and Preventing the Recurrence of Such a Calamity in the Future* (London: John Cumming, 1801), 5.

13. James Anderson, *Essays Relating to Agriculture and Rural Affairs*, vol. 3 (London: John Bell, 1796), 97–135; Karl Marx, *Capital*, vol. 3 (New York: Vintage, 1981), 757.

14. Anderson, *A Calm Investigation*, 73–75.

15. Ibid., 12, 56–64.

16. Karl Marx, *Grundrisse* (New York: Vintage, 1973), 527.

17. Karl Marx, *Capital*, vol. 1 (New York: Vintage, 1976), 637–38. Marx's argument was similar to that of Liebig in *The Natural Laws of Husbandry* (New York: D. Appleton and Co., 1863), 180 (this was the English translation of vol. 2 of the 1862 edition of Liebig's *Agricultural Chemistry*.)

18. Marx, *Capital*, vol. 3, 195.

19. On the relation of Marx's concept of sustainability to his vision of communist society see John Bellamy Foster, "The Crisis of the Earth," *Organization & Environment*, vol. 10, no. 3 (September 1997), 278–95.

20. Marx, *Capital*, vol. 3, 948–49.

21. Ibid., 911.

22. Karl Kautsky, *The Agrarian Question* (Winchester, MA: Zwan, 1988), vol. 2, 214–15.

23. V.I. Lenin, *Collected Works*, vol. 5 (Moscow: Progress Publishers, 1961), 155–56.

24. Gardner, *Recycling Organic Waste*, 43.

25. Judith Sommer, David Banker, Robert Green, Judith Kalbacher, Neal Peterson, and Theresa Sun, *Strucutal and Financial Characteristics of U.S. Farms, 1994*, (Agriculture Information Bulletin No. 735, Economic Research Service, U.S. Department of Agriculture), 79.

26. Ibid., 87.

27. Ibid., 84–85.

28. Pimentel, D., and G.H. Heichel. "Energy efficiency and sustainability of farming systems." In R. Lal and F.J. Pierce (eds.) *Soil management for sustainability* (Ankeny, Iowa: Soil and Water Conservation Society, 1991), 113–123.

29. Gardner, *Recycling Organic Waste*, 34.

30. New York Times, December 10, 1995, 3.

31. See Bill Hinton's chapter in this book for a discussion of the burning of crop residues in China.

32. See Peter Rosset's chapter in this book.

33. "*Aprés moi le dèluge!* is the watchword of every capitalist and of every capitalist nation. Capital therefore takes no account of the health and length of life of the worker, unless society forces it to do so." Karl Marx, *Capital*, vol. 1 (New York: Vintage, 1976), 381.

Chapter Three

CONCENTRATION OF OWNERSHIP AND CONTROL IN AGRICULTURE

WILLIAM D. HEFFERNAN

THE EVOLVING FOOD SYSTEM OF THE UNITED STATES

Native Americans and the European settlers who subsequently occupied the territory of the United States developed an agricultural and food production system that was largely self-sufficient. Most families produced, processed, and consumed their own food. Families made many of the tools and produced most of the seed they needed, and raised their own animal power. Few items were purchased for food production and processing, but there was very little surplus food or fiber to sell. The family controlled its food system from seed to plate—the ultimate integrated food system. The purpose of colonies, however, was to send raw materials, including food and fiber products, back to the mother country. The industrial revolution and the development of industrial cities, first in England and then in the United States, required that farmers produce a larger and larger surplus of food for the growing urban market. Government policy encouraged farmers to produce an ever greater excess of food and fiber and to do so with less and less labor. Thus agriculture evolved from a subsistence agriculture to a commercial agriculture in which the role of the farm family was to produce for the market.

In the evolving commercial agriculture system, farmers became separated from consumers. Increasingly, farmers sold their products to firms that would process and transport the food and fiber to the distant populations. These firms were eager to serve the function of linking the farmer to the consumer. Although relatively simple at the outset, the food system soon began to develop into many components, or stages, as a result of the specialization of function that is a characteristic of the industrialization model. As specialization evolved, the early "seed-to-plate" integrated food system developed into a multi-stage food system with hundreds of firms competing at the various stages. As the system developed more stages, the "middlemen," as they were often called in the farmers' movement literature, were not only the firms mediating between the farmer and the public, but also included those enterprises that provided a growing number of inputs such as credit and farm equipment. As the food and fiber products moved from one stage to the next within the processing-distribution sectors, information was available on the price of the product. Many farm products were auctioned at public events where anyone could observe or bid. This was the agriculture and food system which was held as a model of a competitive system in which (1) no firm bought or sold enough of the total goods or services to influence the price; (2) there was relatively easy entry and exit from any stage; and (3) information regarding the price of the goods and services along the total food chain was available to all. This food system in which the family farm structure was an important component was a good example of the early stage of capitalism. Later, the two processes of horizontal and vertical integration would begin altering the power relations among firms. This led to increased concentration of capital resources, and with it, increased concentration of control in the food system and the decline of the family farm structure.

CAPITAL CONCENTRATION AND LARGE COMMERCIAL AGRICULTURE

Although elements of the above ideal type of a competitive food system could be found in parts of the United States at various times, it was absent in many areas of the country. For an individual farmer, the question was not how many firms were involved in the different stages of the food chain across the country, but rather how much of this commodity chain was accessible to his (sometimes her) farm. As farmers moved west, one of their major problems was how to transport their products to markets in the eastern cities. The government, wishing to promote increased industrialization, also perceived the problem and subsidized the construction of transportation systems, especially railroads. This made the farmer dependent on a monopoly that could exploit him/her because of the unequal balance of economic power. If a farmer had access to only one railroad, the power relationship certainly favored the railroad. The farmer faced a monopoly regardless of how many other railroads existed in the country. Thus, many farmers faced the issue of limited market access from the time they became commercial farmers and began to be dependent on a single transportation system to move their products to the market.

Railroads in some parts of the country needed the business of farmers, but they had access to hundreds, if not thousands, of farmers. They were not dependent on any single farmer. Their only concern was that farmers might be successful in organizing a united stand against the railroads. Frank Norris' agrarian populist novel, *The Octopus: A History of California,*[1] was about a handful of farmers who attempted such a united stand, rising up in direct rebellion, only to be dispatched by the railroads. The whole history of the farmers' movement is largely about the unequal power balance between farmers and the railroads, and, more generally, between the farmers and all the "middlemen" they depended on for transportation, markets, and a host of inputs such as credit and farm equipment.

In southwestern Minnesota, for example, the selling of water fowl to cities to the East and later the selling of agriculture products, especially grain, all depended on the railroad for transportation. In the case of grain, the farmers usually had access to only one grain handling firm to store and to transfer the grain from farmers' wagons to the train.[2] Many of the transnational corporations (TNCs) of today, like Cargill, exercised economic power in many of the local markets in which they began operating. Most farmers' movements were not successful in establishing alternative economic systems or firms which benefited the farmers, but with the help of legislation to encourage farmer cooperatives, there were some successes. For example, Table 1, which lists the four largest firms in each of several commodity processing sectors in the U.S., shows that two cooperatives—Farmland Industries and Gold Kist—are major players in beef and broilers respectively. However, other cooperatives, like GrowMark, have developed joint ventures and other formal relationships with corporations like Archer Daniels Midland (ADM).

HORIZONTAL INTEGRATION

Most food firms started as relatively small, local firms, but as they became profitable they expanded their operations into other geographic areas. The expansions occurred through building new facilities, acquisitions, and mergers. The expansion of a firm within the same stage of the food system as their original operation is called horizontal integration. For example, the increase in size and decrease in the number of farms in the United States during most of this century is an example of horizontal integration. Horizontal integration also occurs at each of the other stages of distribution and processing. Although there are great variations among the different commodity sectors regarding the ways concentration of ownership and control have occurred in processing and distribution stages, the same general pattern of fewer and larger firms in each stage has been underway during the last half of the twentieth century in the United States, and has become most obvious during the last decade at the global level.

In some commodity sectors, one can point to significant concentration of the processing firms in even the first half of the century. For example, pork and beef slaughtering and processing were dominated by Wilson, Armour, and Swift as we entered the twentieth century. Opposition to their practices in the Chicago stockyards inspired Upton Sinclair's *The Jungle* [3] and led to the passage of the first Food and Drug Act that same year. And their collusion to set monopoly prices was largely responsible for the creation of the Packers and Stockyards Agency of the U.S. Department of Agriculture (USDA) in 1921 to monitor predatory practices. The Swift and Armour brand names exist today, but these firms were bought by ConAgra, which also bought Miller and Monfort. Some would argue that the fact that these firms do not exist today suggests that even firms with significant economic power can themselves be eliminated. But the important point is that they were absorbed within the larger agglomeration of capital. Still it is true that with the continuing trend toward concentration and centralization of capital no firm is safe from takeover or elimination in other ways. (This is often used as justification for why no government action should be taken to interfere with the free market.) The extent of the concentration of the processing stage of selected major meat and crop commodities is shown in Table 1.

Table 1. **THE FOUR LARGEST COMMODITY PROCESSING FIRMS AND PERCENT OF U.S. MARKET SHARE THEY CONTROL**

BROILERS (meat chickens)	55% of production	Tyson-Foods, Gold Kist, Perdue Farms, ConAgra
BEEF	87% of slaughter	IBP, ConAgra (Armour, Swift, Monfort, Miller), Cargill (Excel), Farmland Industries (National Beef)
PORK	60% of slaughter	Smithfield, IBP, ConAgra, Cargill
SHEEP	73% of slaughter	ConAgra, Superior Packing, High Country, Denver Lamb
TURKEY	35% of production	ConAgra (Butterball), Wampler Turkeys, Hormel (Jennie-0), Rocco Turkeys
FLOUR MILLING	62% of milling	Archer Daniels Midland, ConAgra, Cargill, Cereal Food Processors
SOYBEAN CRUSHING	76% of processing	Archer Daniels Midland, Cargill, Bunge, Ag Processors
DRY CORN MILLING	57% of milling	Bunge, Illinois Cereal Mills, Archer Daniels Midland, ConAgra(Lincoln Grain)
WET CORN MILLING	74% of milling	Archer Daniels Midland, Cargill, Tate and Lyle, CPC

Source: W. Heffernan, "A Concentration of Agricultural Markets," Unpublished paper, Department of Rural Sociology University of Missouri-Columbia (October,1997).

Forty percent or more of the processing of all agricultural commodities in the Midwest are controlled by the four largest firms. Although debate continues in the United States and in other countries on what constitutes an oligopolistic or near oligopolistic market, much of the economic literature suggests that when four firms control 40 percent of the market, they are able to exert influence on the market unlike that in a competitive system. In the meat sectors 87 percent (81 percent by the largest three) of the beef cattle are slaughtered by the four largest firms, and 73 percent of the sheep are processed by the four largest firms. The control of hog slaughtering by the four largest firms increased from 37 percent in 1987 to 60 percent today. Over one-half (55 percent) of the broilers (chickens produced for meat) today are produced and processed by the four largest firms, with Tyson now producing and processing almost one-third of the broilers in the United States. In the crop sectors, the four largest firms process from 57 percent to 76 percent of the corn, wheat, and soybeans in the United States.

Like the narrow opening of an hourglass which controls the flow of sand from the top to the bottom, the processing firms are positioned between the thousands of producers and millions of consumers in the United States and the world. These firms have a disproportionate amount of influence on the quality, quantity, type, location of production, and price of the product at the production stage and throughout the entire food system. The only stage in which a set of firms begins to equal the economic power of the food processors is the retail stage, which is also becoming more horizontally integrated. The interface between the processing and retail stages is currently where the giants of the food system interact. Certainly, it is not an area characterized by easy entry and exit. How many firms in the world have sufficient capital to face the economic power of these two sets of firms?

ADVANTAGES OF CROSS-SUBSIDIZATION
TO CONCENTRATED CAPITAL

In the food system, horizontal integration usually refers to expansion in the same stage of the same commodity sector. However, if one considers the sector to be meat, then horizontal integration would include the total meat sector. The data in Table 1 indicate that some firms are active in several different parts of this overall meat sector. For example, ConAgra ranks in the top four firms in the processing of beef, pork, broilers, sheep, turkeys, and seafood (which is not on the list). Spokespersons for the industry frequently highlight the competition for the public's dollar between different meats, such as the competition between beef and poultry. They frequently use the competition between meats to argue that the producers must update their production practices. This competition between commodities is also frequently used to justify the check-off system in which a per-animal fee paid by farmers is used primarily to support product promotion and research. The cost of the check-off system is borne by the producers, but there is growing concern as to who is benefiting. Currently the Livestock Marketing Association is leading a petition drive to force a beef producer recall referendum on the check-off programs. Their argument is that "after $1 billion spent in promotion and research over the first ten years of the program, beef demand is still declining."[4] They suggest the check-off funds are being spent directly or indirectly on projects that benefit processors and retailers rather than beef producers, and that the results are increased concentration and integration of the industry. One can ask how much competition exists between the different meat products when key decision-makers are involved in more than one part of the meat sector.

The movement of firms into the processing of several commodities may at one level be an extension of horizontal integration, but it also represents a major qualitative change in the economic power relationships. When a firm has a dominant position in several commodity systems, it can cross-subsidize. Firms operating in more than one commodity system gain economic power because they can survive a major loss in one commodity system over a long period of time if they are making significant profits in other systems. If a loss continues very long in a single-product firm's only commodity, it faces serious financial difficulty.

Lane Poultry was the largest broiler producer and processor in the United States following its purchase of Valmac Industries in 1980, but it was still a single-product producer. Lane lost Valmac Industries and then was itself purchased by Tyson Foods because of its economic losses in nine of eleven consecutive quarters in the late 1970s and early 1980s. Being the largest firm in a commodity sector, but a single-product producer, does not assure enough economic power to survive. Larger firms with profits in other sectors or systems have more economic power and may overtake them. Information we obtained from executives of a couple TNCs involved in broiler production at the time, indicated that the goal of their firms was to obtain a larger share of a growing market by overproducing, reducing prices and lowering profit margins so that small firms would have trouble surviving even during a market expansion. (This was a time when per capita consumption of poultry was increasing rapidly while beef consumption was decreasing in the United States.)

Planned overproduction and selling below cost of production also occurred in the farm-raised catfish sector early in the 1980s. Two major catfish cooperatives, Southern Pride and Delta Pride, experienced the problem of competing against ConAgra, Cargill, and Chiquita, the parent company of Morrill (now owned by Smithfield). The three TNCs were able to cross-subsidize. The cooperatives survived despite the fact that the annual report of one of the TNCs showed a loss in the catfish division for two years because of "overproduction" in the sector. Conversations with some of the TNC's personnel indicated the firm was prepared to extend this loss for another year or two. We concluded that because the five firms absolutely dominated the production and processing of farm-raised catfish at the time, the low prices were the result of overproduction and an effort on the part of the TNCs to gain market share at the expense of the members of the cooperatives.[5] In fact, Cargill, which has now exited the sector, entered the catfish sector during the time of negative profits with plans to increase catfish production.[6] Like the broiler and catfish sectors in the past, the hog sector is currently involved in a large increase in production even when prices are low and are predicted to stay low. During the last half of 1998 and the first half of 1999, the market price for hogs was below the cost of production. At times, the sale price for hogs was about one-fourth of the cost of production. However, many of the larger and diversified firms continue to construct new facilities as smaller single-product producers were forced out of business. The driving force is market share, not efficiency. Large firms that can cross-subsidize can operate in this arena, but smaller, nondiversified firms cannot survive. Economic power, not efficiency, predicts survival in this system.

VERTICAL INTEGRATION

The second major strategy of large firms seeking to reduce competition is vertical integration. Vertical integration occurs when a firm increases ownership and control of a number of stages in a commodity system. Just like diversifying into different commodity sectors (horizontal integration), this structure gives the firm more economic power. Data in Table 1 provide some indication of the extent of vertical integration when one notes that feed grain is very important in livestock production. A firm like Cargill is one of the three major global traders of grain (the major ingredient in animal feed), the second largest animal feed producer, and one of the largest processors of hogs and beef. Many livestock producers purchase their feed from the same firms to which they sell their animals.

Another example of the extent of vertical integration in the food system comes from ConAgra's annual report. ConAgra indicates that it is one of the largest distributors of agricultural chemicals and fertilizer in North America, and in 1990 it entered the seed business. Since then it has formed a joint venture with DuPont and formal relationships with some of the seed companies involved in biotechnology. ConAgra owns 100 grain-storage elevators, 2,000 railroad cars, and 1,100 barges. ConAgra is the largest turkey producer and second largest broiler producer. It produces its own poultry feed, as well as other livestock feed. It also owns and operates hatcheries. ConAgra hires growers to raise its birds and then it processes the birds in its own facilities. This broiler meat can then be purchased as fryers under the name of Country Pride or in further processed foods such as TV dinners and pot pies under the labels of Banquet and Beatrice Foods. From the basic raw materials for agricultural production to the retail store, a significant proportion of the food system is owned and controlled by ConAgra. ConAgra is the second largest food firm in the United States (behind Philip Morris) and the fourth largest in the world, with operations in thirty-two countries.

In the subsistence food system, the family controlled its food from seed to plate. In the emerging vertically integrated food system, a few food companies are gaining control of the country's food system by controlling it from seed to shelf. This system is being extended around the world by many of the firms that are headquartered in the United States.

Starting in the 1950s and 1960s, when feed companies and others started hatching their own baby chicks, hiring growers to provide labor, buildings, and land, and constructing their own processing facilities for broilers, the farm press and farm community began to focus on contract production.

Contract production is very different from forward contracting of a commodity product. Forward contracting is a sales agreement between a farmer and a buyer that involves an agreed upon price and other terms of the sale to be carried out at some future date. Contract production is an industrial model in which the integrating firm outsources a needed ingredient—the agricultural raw product.

In contract production, the growers are required to provide the land and the buildings, and equip the buildings to the integrating firm's specifications while providing all of the labor for the production stage of the system.[7] The growers are thus hired workers paid on a piece rate basis. They never own the birds or the feed, and have no knowledge of the genetics or the feed ration. The integrating firms provides the birds, feed, and medication. All of the major decisions are made by the integrating firm. The growers mortgage their land to raise the capital to build the buildings, which cost over $100,000 each. Typically their repayment schedule extends over a ten- to fifteen-year period, while the contract with the integrating firm goes from one batch of chickens to the next—a period of about six weeks. By the time the buildings are almost paid off, the equipment needs to be replaced and the buildings need to be modernized. As a consequence, few growers ever get out of debt. It is estimated that although about one-half of the capital in the broiler sector comes from the growers, all of the major decisions are made by the integrating firms. The growers are well aware that they can be cut off at any time.

In the early stages of vertical integration in the broiler industry, most growers had access to several integrating firms, but over time the numbers were reduced. For example, in 1969 in Union Parish, Louisiana, there were four integrating firms. Two were locally owned feed operations, and two were operations based out of state. By 1982, the two local firms were no longer integrating firms; they were now growers. The two outside firms were owned by ConAgra and Imperial Foods, one of the largest food companies of England. Within the following year, ConAgra bought the Country Pride broiler facilities from Imperial Foods. The growers report that they have had no price increase since 1982.

Two processes occur that alter the growers' opportunities. First, as the integrating firms in a given geographic area become fewer, the power relationships between growers and the firms become more unequal. Because of transportation and other costs, most integrating firms will send trucks out only about twenty-five to thirty miles from the processing site to deliver feed and to pick up poultry for processing. Today there are about forty firms producing about 97 percent of the broilers in this country. In total, they operate about two hundred and fifty processing facilities. Thus, there are very few growers who live close enough to more than one processing facility to even have an option to choose between integrating firms.

The second process that limits options for growers is that as the number of firms operating in the same geographic area declines to two or three, an informal agreement evolves between integrating firms that they will not raid their competitors' growers. If a grower gets cut off from one integrating firm, they cannot enter into a contract with another. My thirty years of observing the poultry sector suggest that in early capitalism when the growers have access to several integrating firms, the growers experience financial success, but when the system moves to monopoly capital the growers find themselves in financial crisis. The courts have also found that the growers are at the mercy of the integrating firms in other ways. Errors in the weighing of both feed and poultry have become so well documented that legislation has recently been introduced to address this issue. The USDA has also made a commitment to study this problem.

GLOBALIZATION

A third way TNCs can cross-subside and gain economic power is by operating in many different countries of the world. A firm like Cargill, which has operations in seventy countries, can absorb a loss in one or two countries over a few years as long they have good rates of return in other countries. It is easy to see how TNCs can gain footholds in new countries. They begin by producing or processing a commodity and thus increase the supply of the product which, assuming a given demand, drives the price down. In so doing, the price can drop below the cost of production. A local firm, especially if it is a single product producer, cannot absorb such a loss for long, but a TNC can absorb the loss for a relatively long time.

The food systems of the world are becoming so integrated by the TNCs that it makes little sense to speak of a food system in a single country. For example, not only do IBP, Cargill, and ConAgra process 81 percent of the beef in the United States, they also now have feedlots and slaughtering facilities in Canada and about the same market dominance there. With the passage of the North American Free Trade Agreement, beef can now easily travel back and forth across the border. It is possible for a 450-pound calf to be purchased by one of the three firms on one side of the border and be sent across the border to be grown to 800-pounds in a contract arrangement with a rancher. The firm may then decide to move the animal across the border again to be finished in their feedlot. If the firm does not have sufficient capacity in their slaughtering facility in that country, it may move the animal across the border again to be slaughtered. The meat may once again be moved across the border to be consumed. The question then is, in what country was the animal produced?

These same firms have beef operations in many other countries, including Australia, Mexico, Brazil, and Argentina. In such a system, the opportunity for governments to control their food systems is diminished and the role of TNCs is increased. As global trade barriers are reduced, it becomes increasingly difficult for relatively small local firms to compete with the economic power of the TNCs. Maple Leaf Foods, Canada's largest food processor, is currently struggling to survive in the pork sector. In order to survive, Maple Leaf has lowered wages, leading to labor strikes, in an effort to compete with the low wages paid by the U.S. slaughtering plants that have been obtaining live hogs from Canada.[8] Smithfield, the largest hog slaughterer in the United States, has indicated an interest in buying the Maple Leaf facility in Ontario, one of the facilities with major labor discord.

Many TNCs involved in the global agriculture/food system are conglomerates. Cargill, which is such an important player in meat and grain processing, also makes barges, operates barge and shipping lines, and processes pig iron, scrap iron, and other metals and petroleum products. Philip Morris, which most people associate with tobacco and cigarettes, is the largest food corporation in the United States and second largest in the world. It sells Kraft General Foods products (including Kraft cheese), Maxwell House coffee, Miller Beer, and Oscar Meyer meats. In 1996, Philip Morris had over $16 billion in revenues within the United States from its North American Food Division.[9] Many of the conglomerates regularly buy and sell various divisions. Purina Mills, the largest animal feed firm in the United States (with 10 percent of the market), has changed hands several times. Wishing to focus on its pet food segment, Ralston Purina (now the world's largest manufacturer of dry dog and cat food, batteries and flashlights) sold its Purina Mills Division in 1986 to British Nutrition, the largest livestock feed producer in Europe, which is owned by British Petroleum. In 1993, British Petroleum sold Purina Mills to the Sterling Group of the United States. Then in early 1998, the Sterling Group sold Purina Mills to Koch Agriculture Company, a subsidiary of Koch Industries. Koch Industries is a diversified energy and industrial firm ranked the second largest privately held company in the United States. Vertical integration, horizontal integration, integration among various segments of the food systems, conglomeration, and global integration all lead to increased economic power for the TNCs.

COMMUNITY CONSEQUENCES OF ABSENTEE CORPORATE OWNERSHIP

Capital that comes from outside the local community has major economic consequences for the local community. In small, locally owned businesses, such as family farms, family clothing stores, and family grocery stores, the family subtracts its annual expenses from its income to determine profits that are then allocated among labor, management, and capital. For the economic well being of the family and the rural community, it makes little difference how the profits are allocated among the three costs of production, because the family spends much of the profit in the local community. In the past, when family businesses were the predominant economic systems in rural agriculture communities, researchers talked about "multiplier effects" of three and four; money generated in the agricultural sector would circulate in the community, changing hands from one entrepreneurial family to another three or four times before leaving the rural community. This greatly enhanced the community's economic viability.

Giant corporations headquartered in distant places see labor as just another input cost to be purchased as cheaply as possible. Their profits are usually immediately taken out of the local rural community. They go to the firms' headquarters and on to stockholders or, if the corporation is a TNC, the profits are very likely invested in the food system somewhere else in the world. Only the return to labor, which was bought as cheaply as possible, remains in the rural community. Rural mining towns in Appalachia and the West show the adverse consequences of absentee ownership under a regime of concentrated capital. Today, the economic impacts of agricultural production on rural agricultural communities are perceived to be so small that few economic development specialists see any hope in expanding the economic base of a rural community by focusing on the production stage of the food sector. In some areas, attention is focused on the processing sector that is referred to as "value added."

These economic outcomes have major social consequences for communities, especially when combined with the social consequences coming from changing the workers' relationship to their work setting. Fifty years ago, Walter Goldschmidt's famous study in California showed a strong relationship between the structure of the food system and the social condition of the community, revealing that the well-being of communities dominated by large-scale, absentee-owned, corporate farms was greatly inferior to that of communities in which family farms predominated.[10] A host of studies building on Goldschmidt's work have confirmed these results when the focus was on family farm structures verses corporate structures.[11] But the social costs, often referred to as "externalities," are of no concern to TNCs, which see increasing the wealth of their stockholders as their major goal.

Perhaps the ultimate political power these giant food firms have is that— like some saving and loan associations, banks, automobile and airplane manufacturers—they are perceived to be so vital to the country that their bankruptcy would lead to major social disorganization. Given that food is a necessity, is there any doubt that the federal government would provide the resources to keep these firms from collapsing?

Large corporations do not behave differently in the food system than in any other segment of the economy. Agriculture is unique primarily because it took capital so long to dominate the sector. The fact that agriculture is losing its uniqueness is perhaps best revealed by the fact that Mitsubishi, among the largest automakers and the second largest bank in the world, is now one of the world's largest beef processors. The "mainstreaming" of the food system into the larger capitalist system is also revealed by the fact that

Pioneer Hi-Bred, DeKalb, Mycogen, and other seed companies which own the property rights to the new varieties created through the use of biotechnology have been merged with chemical firms (e.g., Novartis, Monsanto, DuPont, Dow) and with firms which ultimately process the genetically modified new varieties (e.g., ConAgra, Cargill, ADM) through joint ventures. One can predict that up against such power, the yeoman crop farmer will soon resemble the broiler grower.

NOTES

1. Frank Norris, *The Octopus: A Story of California* (Garden City, NY: Doubleday, 1956).
2. Andrew H. Raedeke, "Agriculture, Collective Environmental Action, and the Changing Landscape: A Case Study of Heron Lake Watershed," (Ph.D. Diss, University of Missouri, 1997).
3. Upton Sinclair, *The Jungle* (New York: Grosset and Dunlap, 1906).
4. Feedstuffs (March 2, 1998), 5.
5. William D. Heffernan and Douglas Constance, "Concentration in the Food System: The Case of Catfish Production," (Paper presented at the annual meeting of the Southern Rural Sociological Society. Forth Worth, Texas, 1991).
6. Bob Odom, "Louisiana Agriculture . . . Meeting the Challenges," *The Louisiana Market Bulletin* 74, No. 26 (December 1990), 1.
7. William Heffernan, "Constraints in the U.S. Poultry Industry," *Research in Rural Sociology and Development* 1 (1984), 237–260.
8. Feedstuffs, (March 23, 1998).
9. Richmond Times–Dispatch, April 19, 1997.
10. Walter Goldschmidt, *As You Sow: Three Studies in the Social Consequences of Agribusiness* (Montclair, NJ: Allanheld, Osmun, and Co., 1978).
11. William D. Heffernan, "Sociological Dimensions of Agricultural Structures in the United States," *Sociologia Ruralis* 12 (1972), 481–99; Linda M. Lobao, *Locality and Inequality: Farm and industry Structure and Socioeconomic Conditions* (Albany: State University of New York Press, 1990).

Chapter Four

ECOLOGICAL IMPACTS OF INDUSTRIAL AGRICULTURE AND THE POSSIBILITIES FOR TRULY SUSTAINABLE FARMING

MIGUEL A. ALTIERI

Until about four decades ago, crop yields in agricultural systems depended mainly on internal resources, recycling of organic matter, built-in biological control mechanisms, and natural rainfall patterns. Agricultural yields were modest but stable. Production was safeguarded by growing more than one crop or variety in a field as insurance against pest outbreaks or severe weather. Inputs of nitrogen were gained by rotating major field crops with legumes. Growing many different types of crops over the years in the same field also suppressed insects, weeds, and diseases by effectively breaking the life cycles of these pests. A typical corn-belt farmer grew corn rotated with several crops including soybeans as well as the clovers, alfalfa, and small grains needed to maintain livestock. Most of the labor was done by the family with occasional hired help, and no specialized equipment or services were purchased from off-farm sources. In these types of farming systems the link between agriculture and ecology was quite strong and signs of environmental degradation were seldom evident.[1]

The significance of biological diversity in maintaining such systems cannot be overemphasized. Diversity of crops above ground as well as diversity of

77

soil life below ground provided protection against the vagaries of weather, market swings, as well as outbreaks of diseases or insect pests.[2] But as agricultural modernization progressed, the ecology-farming linkage was often broken as ecological principles were ignored or overridden. Numerous agricultural scientists agree that modern agriculture confronts an environmental crisis. A growing number of people have become concerned about the long-term sustainability of existing food production systems. Evidence has accumulated showing that, while the present capital- and technology-intensive farming systems have been extremely productive and able to furnish low-cost food, they also bring a variety of economic, environmental, and social problems.[3]

Evidence also shows that the very nature of the agricultural structure and prevailing policies in a capitalist setting have led to this environmental crisis by favoring large farm size, specialized production, crop monocultures, and mechanization. Today as more and more farmers are integrated into international economies, the biological imperative of diversity disappears due to the use of many kinds of pesticides and synthetic fertilizers, and specialized farms are rewarded by economies of scale.[4] In turn, lack of good rotations and diversification take away key self-regulating mechanisms, turning monocultures into highly vulnerable agricultural ecosystems (agroecosystems) dependent on high chemical inputs.

THE EXPANSION OF FARM SPECIALIZATION
AND MONOCULTURES

Monocultures or near-monocultures have increased dramatically worldwide, where the same crop (usually corn, wheat, or rice) is grown year after year in the same field, or very simple rotations are used (such as corn-soybeans-corn-soybeans). Also fields that in the past contained many different crops, or a single crop with a high degree of genetic variability, are now entirely devoted to a genetically uniform single crop.[5] Available data indicate that the amount of crop diversity per unit of arable land has decreased and that croplands have also shown a tendency toward concentration in fewer hands. There are political and economic forces influencing the trend to devote large areas to monoculture, and in fact the economies of scale of such systems contribute significantly to the ability of national agriculture to serve international markets.[6]

The technologies that allowed the shift toward specialization and monoculture were mechanization, the improvement of crop varieties, and the development of agrochemical to fertilize crops and control weeds, insects, and other crop pests as well as antibiotics and growth stimulants for agricultural animals. United States government commodity policies over the last several decades encouraged the acceptance and utilization of these technologies. In addition, the largest agribusiness corporations have found that concentrating certain processing facilities for a given product (chickens, hogs, or wheat) in specific areas of the country produces more profits, which lead to more farm and regional specialization. As a result, farms today are fewer, larger, more specialized, and more capital intensive.

From an ecological perspective, the regional consequences of monoculture specialization are many-fold:[7]

(1) Most large-scale agricultural systems exhibit a poorly structured grouping of farm components, with almost no linkages or complementary relationships between crop enterprises, and among soils, crops, and animals.

(2) Cycles of nutrients, energy, water, and wastes have become more open, rather than closed as in a natural ecosystem. Despite the substantial amount of crop residues and manure produced on farms, it is becoming increasingly difficult to recycle nutrients, even within agricultural systems. Animal wastes cannot economically be returned to the land in a nutrient-recycling process because animal production is frequently geographically remote from where crops are grown. In many areas, agricultural waste has become a liability rather than a resource. Recycling nutrients from urban centers back to the fields is similarly difficult.

(3) Part of agroecosystem instability, and susceptibility to pests can be linked to the adoption of vast areas of crop monocultures or very simple rotations, which have concentrated resources for specialized crop-eating insects and have increased the areas available for the migration of pests. This simplification has also reduced environmental opportunities for natural enemies. Consequently, pest outbreaks often occur when large numbers of immigrant pests, inhibited populations of beneficial insects, favorable weather, and vulnerable crop stages happen simultaneously. The depletion

of soil organic matter has also reduced the food supply of soil organisms, leading to less diversity of soil life, and therefore to fewer natural checks on potential pest problems.

(4) As specific crops are expanded beyond their "natural" ranges or favorable regions to areas with high pest potential, or limited water, or low-fertility soils, intensified chemical controls are required to overcome such factors. The assumption is that the human intervention and level of energy inputs that allow these expansions can be sustained indefinitely.

(5) Commercial farmers witness a constant parade of new crop varieties as varietal replacement, due to biotic stresses and market changes, has accelerated to unprecedented levels. A variety with improved disease or insect resistance makes a debut, performs well for a few years (typically five to nine years) and is then succeeded by another variety when yields are threatened by pests or a more promising one becomes available. A variety's trajectory is characterized by a take-off phase when it is adopted by farmers, a middle stage when the planted area stabilizes, and finally a retraction of its acreage. Thus, modern agriculture relies on a continuous supply of new varieties rather than a patchwork quilt of many different varieties planted on the same farm.

(6) Although monoculture cropping requires increased use of pesticides and fertilizers, the efficiency of use of applied inputs is decreasing and yields of most key crops are leveling off. In some places, yields are actually declining. There are different opinions as to the underlying causes of this phenomenon. Some believe that yields are leveling off because the maximum yield potential of current varieties is being approached, and therefore genetic engineering must be applied to the task of redesigning crops. Agroecologists, on the other hand, believe that the leveling off is due to the steady erosion of the productive base of agriculture through unsustainable practices.

THE FIRST WAVE OF ENVIRONMENTAL PROBLEMS

The specialization of farms has led to the image that agriculture is a modern miracle of food production. However, excessive reliance on farm specialization (including crop monocultures) and inputs such as capital-intensive technology, pesticides, and synthetic fertilizers, has negatively impacted the environment and rural society. A number of what might be called "ecological diseases" have been associated with the intensification of food production and can be grouped into two categories. There are problems directly associated with the basic resources of soil and water, which include soil erosion, loss of inherent soil productivity and depletion of nutrient reserves, salinization and alkalinization (especially in arid and semi-arid regions), pollution of surface and groundwater, and loss of croplands to urban development. Problems directly related to crops, animals, and pests include loss of crop, wild plant, and animal genetic resources, elimination of natural enemies of pests, pest resurgence and genetic resistance to pesticides, chemical contamination, and destruction of natural control mechanisms.[8] Each "ecological disease" is usually viewed as an independent problem, rather than what it really is—a symptom of a poorly designed and poorly functioning system. Under conditions of intensive management, treatment of such "diseases" requires an increase in the external costs to the extent that, in some agricultural systems, the amount of energy invested to produce a desired yield surpasses the energy harvested.

The substantial yield losses due to pests, about 20 to 30 percent for most crops despite the increase in the use of pesticides (about 4.7 billion pounds of pesticides were used worldwide in 1995, 1.2 billion pounds in the United States alone), is a symptom of the environmental crisis affecting agriculture. Cultivated plants grown in genetically homogeneous monocultures do not possess the necessary ecological defense mechanisms to tolerate the impact of pest outbreaks. Modern agriculturists have selected crops mainly for high yields and high palatability, making them more susceptible to pests by sacrificing natural resistance for productivity. And as modern agricultural practices reduce or eliminate the resources and opportunities for natural enemies of pests, their numbers decline, decreasing the biological suppression of pests. Due to this lack of natural controls, an investment of about $4 billion in pesticide control is incurred yearly by U.S. farmers, which is estimated to save approximately $16 billion in U.S. crops. However, the indirect costs of pesticide use to the environment and public health have to be balanced against these benefits. Based on the available data, the environmental costs (impacts on wildlife, pollinators, natural enemies, fisheries, water, and development of resistance) and social costs (human poisonings and illnesses) of pesticide use reach about $8 billion each year.[9] What is worrisome is that pesticide use is still high and still rising in some cropping systems. Data from California shows that from 1991 to 1995 pesticide use increased from 161 to 212 million pounds of active ingredient. This increase was not due to increases in planted acreage, as statewide crop acreage remained constant during this period. Much of the increase is for particularly toxic pesticides, many of which are linked to cancers, used on such crops as strawberries and grapes.[10]

The reliance on pesticides to deal with crop pests has created the need to continually develop new pesticides. As a pesticide is used again and again, a certain percentage of the target pest is able to survive because of a natural resistance to the chemical. It doesn't take too long before a large portion of the target weeds, insects, or other pests become resistant to the pesticide. This keeps the farmer on a "pesticide treadmill" as the older pesticides lose their effectiveness and new ones need to be used.

Fertilizers have been praised as being responsible for the temporary increase in food production observed in many countries. National average rates of nitrogen applied to most arable lands fluctuate between 120-550 kg N/ha (110 to 490 lb N/A). But the bountiful harvests created at least in part through the use of synthetic fertilizers have associated environmental costs. Two main reasons why synthetic fertilizers pollute the environment are their wasteful application and the fact that crops use them inefficiently. A significant amount of fertilizer that is not recovered by the crops ends up in surface or groundwater. Nitrate contamination of aquifers is widespread and in dangerously high levels in many rural regions of the world. It is estimated that more than 25 percent of the drinking water wells in the United States contain nitrogen in the nitrate form above the safety standard of ten parts per million. Such nitrate levels are hazardous to human health, and studies have linked nitrate uptake to methamoglobinemia (low blood oxygen levels) in children and to gastric, bladder, and esophageal cancers in adults.[11]

It is estimated that about 50 to 70 percent of all nutrients that reach surface waters in the United States are derived from fertilizers. Fertilizer nutrients that enter surface waters (rivers, lakes, bays) can promote eutrophication, characterized usually by a population explosion of algae. Algal blooms turn the water bright green, which can prevent light from penetrating beneath surface layers, and therefore kills plants living on the bottom. Such dead vegetation serves as food for other aquatic micro-organisms, which soon deplete water of its oxygen, inhibiting the decomposition of organic residues, which accumulate on the bottom. Eventually, such nutrient enrichment of freshwater ecosystems can lead to the destruction of all animal life in the water systems. In the Gulf of Mexico there is a huge "dead zone," extending from the mouth of the Mississippi River to the west, where the excessive nutrients from farmland are believed to be responsible for oxygen depletion. It is also believed that excess nutrients may stimulate populations of the very toxic form of Pfiesteria, an organism that kills fish and is harmful to humans.[12]

Synthetic nitrogen fertilizers can also become air pollutants, and have recently been implicated in contributing to the destruction of the ozone layer and global warming. Their excessive use causes soils to become more acidic and also leads to nutritional imbalances in plants, resulting in a higher incidence of damage from insect pests and diseases.[13]

It is clear then that the first wave of environmental problems is deeply rooted in the prevalent socioeconomic system that promotes monocultures and the use of high-input technologies and agricultural practices that lead to natural resource degradation. Such degradation is not only an ecological process, but also a social and political-economic process. Therefore, the problem of agricultural production cannot be regarded only as a technological one; attention to social, cultural, political, and economic issues that account for the crisis is crucial. This is particularly true today where the economic and political domination of the rural development agenda by agribusiness has thrived at the expense of the interests of farmworkers, small family farms, rural communities, the general public, wildlife, and the environment.

THE SECOND WAVE OF ENVIRONMENTAL PROBLEMS

Despite that the awareness of the impacts of modern technologies on the environment increased as we trace pesticides in food chains and crop nutrients in surface waters and aquifers, some still argue for further intensification to meet the requirements of agricultural production in the twenty-first century. It is in this context that supporters of "status quo agriculture" celebrate the emergence of biotechnology as the latest magic bullet, which will revolutionize agriculture with products based on nature's own methods, making farming more environmentally friendly and more profitable for the farmer. Although certain forms of biotechnology hold promise for an improved agriculture, under the control of multinational corporations it is more likely that the results will be environmental harm, the further industrialization of agriculture, and the intrusion of private interests too far into public-interest sector research.

It is ironic that the biotech revolution in agriculture is being promoted by the same corporate interests (Monsanto, Novartis, DuPont) that championed the first wave of chemically-based agriculture. They now claim that by genetically modifying plants they can reduce chemically intensive farming and help develop a more sustainable agriculture. However, their practices to date do not instill great confidence in the supposedly benign effects of their products on the environment. The companies are developing products (various crop varieties) that produce immense profits while completely fitting in with the approaches which have been so harmful in the past. For example, two of the main thrusts of agricultural biotechnology have been the production of crop varieties that are either resistant to herbicides (so farmers will purchase and use more of the company's weed-killing chemicals) or contain a toxin that kills potential insect pests (in which case less insecticide is needed). The advantage claimed for the herbicide resistant crops is that the newer herbicides are less toxic than some of the older ones. USDA statistics show that in 1997 expanded plantings of Roundup Ready soybeans resulted in a 72 percent increase in the use of glyphosate, a worrisome trend given evidence that promoted herbicides such as Bromoxynil and glyphosate pose risks. Bromoxynil causes birth defects in laboratory animals, is toxic to fish and may cause cancer in humans. Because bromoxynil is absorbed dermally, and because it causes birth defects in rodents, it is likely to pose hazards to farmers and farm workers. Similarly, glyphosate has been reported to be toxic to some non-target species in the soil—to beneficial predators such as spiders, mites, carabid and coccinellid beetles and to detritivores such as earthworms, as well as to aquatic organisms, including fish.[14] Given that this herbicide is known to accumulate in fruits and tubers as it suffers little metabolic degradation in plants, questions about food safety also arise. Oncologists in Sweden have gathered some evidence that links exposure to glyphosate and the incidence of Non-Hodgkin Lymphoma. Given these problems, it is expected that, such biotechnological products will do nothing but reinforce the pesticide treadmill in agroecosystems, thus legitimizing the concerns that many scientists have expressed regarding the possible environmental risks of genetically engineered organisms. When genes for the insect toxin from the bacteria Bacillus thuringiensis (Bt) are incorporated into plants, the plants produce the toxin and feeding insects can be killed. Although less insecticide will be needed for Bt crops, their use can create other problems (see below).

So far, field research as well as predictions based on ecological theory indicate that the major environmental risks associated with the release of genetically engineered crops can be summarized as follows:[15]

(1) The trends set forth by corporations is to create broad international markets for a single product, thus creating the conditions for genetic uniformity in rural landscapes. History has repeatedly shown that a huge area planted with a single variety is very vulnerable to a new matching strain of a pathogen or insect pest.

(2) The spread of such crops threatens crop genetic diversity by simplifying cropping systems and promoting genetic erosion as older varieties become extinct.

(3) There is potential for the unintended transfer to plant relatives of the added genes with unpredictable ecological effects. The transfer of genes from herbicide resistant crops (HRCs) to wild or semidomesticated relatives (through cross-pollination) can lead to the creation of super weeds.

(4) Most insect pests will quickly develop resistance to the Bt toxin. Several moth species have been reported to have developed resistance to Bt toxin in both field and laboratory tests, suggesting that major resistance problems are likely to develop in Bt crops.

(5) Massive use of Bt toxin in crops can unleash potential negative interactions affecting ecological processes and non-target organisms. Studies conducted in Scotland suggest that aphid pests were capable of transferring the toxin from Bt crops to a beneficial beetle that feeds on the aphid. This decreased reproduction and longevity of the beneficial beetle. Similarly, studies in Switzerland show that mean total mortality of lacewing larvae (Chrysopidae) raised on Bt-fed prey was 62 percent compared to 37 percent when raised on Bt-free prey. These Chrysopidae raised on Bt-fed prey also exhibited prolonged development time throughout their immature life stage.

(6) Pollen from Bt crops carried by wind and deposited on wild plants can eliminate natural populations of insect herbivores, as suggested by a recent

Cornell study which showed that 44 percent of the monarch butterfly caterpillars eating milkweed leaves artificially dusted with BT corn pollen died after four days of exposure.

(7) Bt toxins can also be incorporated into the soil through leaf materials and litter, where they may persist for two to three months, resisting degradation by binding to soil clay particles while maintaining toxic activity, in turn negatively affecting soil organisms and nutrient cycling.

(8) A potential risk of plants containing introduced genetic material from viruses opens the possibility of new virus strains developing when viruses that infect the plant combine with the viral genes introduced by biotech companies.

(9) Another important environmental concern associated with the large-scale cultivation of virus-resistant, genetically modified crops relates to the possible transfer via flower pollen of virus-derived genes into wild plant relatives. The possibility that transgenic virus-resistant plants may broaden the host range of some viruses or allow the production of new virus strains through recombination and transcapsidation demands careful further experimental investigation.

Although there are many unanswered questions regarding the impact of the release into the environment of plants and micro-organisms containing genes from other organisms, it is expected that biotechnology will exacerbate the problems of conventional agriculture, and by promoting monocultures will also undermine ecological methods of farming such as rotations and polycultures (where two or more crops are grown together). Because genetically modified crops developed for pest control emphasize the use of a single control mechanism, which has proven to fail over and over again with insects, pathogens and weeds, these crops are likely to increase the use of pesticides and to accelerate the evolution of "super weeds" and resistant insect pest strains.[16] These possibilities are worrisome, especially when considering that in 1997 the global area devoted to genetically modified crops reached 12.8 million hectares. Seventy-two percent of the 25,000 genetically modified crop field trials were conducted in the United States and Canada, although some were also conducted, in descending order, in Europe, Latin America, and Asia.[17] In most countries, prudent safety standards to monitor such releases are absent or are inadequate to prevent or even predict ecological risks. In the industrialized countries from 1986-1992, over half of all field trials to test genetically modified crops involved herbicide tolerance. As Roundup (made by Monsanto) and other broad spectrum herbicides are increasingly used on cropland, the options for farmers for a diversified agriculture will be even more limited. In addition, the promises of spectacular yield increases by transgenic crops have not been realized. In 1998, yields were not significantly different in genetically modified versus non-modified crops in twelve of eighteen crop/region combinations according to USDA's Economic Research Service.

THE ARRAY OF ALTERNATIVES
TO CONVENTIONAL AGRICULTURE

Reduction and especially elimination of agrochemical use require major changes in management to assure adequate plant nutrients and to control crop pests. As was done not that many decades ago, alternative sources of nutrients can maintain soil fertility. These include manures, sewage sludge and other organic wastes, and legumes grown in rotations. The benefits of good rotations result from biologically fixed nitrogen and the interruption of weed, disease, and insect cycles. Livestock may be integrated with grain cropping to provide animal manures and to utilize better the forage produced. The maximum benefits of biological diversity on farms can be realized when livestock, crops, animals, and other farm resources are used (including good rotational designs) to optimize production efficiency, nutrient cycling, and crop protection.[18]

In orchards and vineyards, the use of cover crops improves soil fertility, soil structure, and water infiltration; prevents soil erosion, modifies the climate around the plants, and reduces weed competition. Orchards with ground cover vegetation have been shown to have fewer insect pests than clean cultivated orchards. This is due to a higher abundance and efficiency of predators and parasitoids (insects that lay eggs in other insects), enhanced by the rich floral undergrowth.[19]

Increasingly, researchers are showing that it is possible to provide a balanced environment, sustained yields, biologically mediated soil fertility, and natural pest regulation through the design of diversified agroecosystems and the use of low-input technologies. Many alternative cropping systems have been developed and evaluated, such as double cropping, strip cropping, cover cropping, and intercropping. More importantly, concrete examples from farmers themselves show that such systems lead to optimal cycling of nutrients and organic matter turnover, closed energy flows, water and soil conservation and balanced pest-natural enemy populations. Such diversified farming exploits the complementary relationships that result from the various combinations of crops, trees, and animals in spatial and temporal arrangements.[20]

The behavior of agroecosystems depends on the level of interactions between the various biological and non-biological components. By creating a functional biodiversity, processes occur that provide ecological services such as the activation of soil organisms, the cycling of nutrients, the enhancement of beneficial insects and antagonists, and so on. Today there is a wide selection of available practices and technologies, which vary in effectiveness as well as in strategic value.[21]

THE BARRIERS FOR THE IMPLEMENTATION
OF ALTERNATIVES

The agroecological approach seeks the diversification and revitalization of medium size and small farms and the reshaping of the entire agricultural policy and food system in ways that are economically viable to farmers and the general public. In fact, throughout the world there are hundreds of movements that are pursuing a change toward ecologically sensitive farming systems from a variety of perspectives. Some emphasize the production of organic products for lucrative markets, some land stewardship, while others promote the empowerment of peasant communities. In general, however, the goals are usually the same: to secure food self-sufficiency, to preserve the natural resource base, and to ensure social equity and economic viability.

Some well-intentioned groups suffer from technological determinism, and emphasize the development and dissemination of low-input or appropriate technologies. Somehow, it is believed, these technologies in themselves have the capability of initiating beneficial social changes. The organic farming school that emphasizes input substitution (i.e. a biological insecticide substituted for a more toxic synthetic one), but leaves the monoculture structure untouched, epitomizes those groups that have a relatively benign view of capitalist agriculture. Such a perspective has unfortunately prevented many groups from understanding the structural roots of environmental degradation linked to monoculture farming.[22]

The acceptance of the present structure of agriculture as a given condition restricts the real possibility of implementing alternatives that challenge such a structure. Thus, options for a diversified agriculture are inhibited by, among other factors, the present trends in farm size and mechanization. Implementation of such mixed agriculture would only be possible as part of a broader program that includes land reform and farm machinery redesigned for polycultures. Merely introducing alternative agricultural designs will do little to change the underlying forces that led to monoculture production, farm size expansion, and large-scale mechanization in the first place.[23]

Similarly, obstacles to changing cropping systems have been created by the government commodity programs in place these last several decades. The programs rewarded those who maintained monocultures of grain by assuring these producers a particular price for their product. Those who failed to plant the allotted acreage of corn and other price-supported crops lost area from their allowed "base," on which future subsidies would be paid. This reduced their potential income from the price-support program. Consequently the programs created a competitive disadvantage for those who used a crop rotation. Although the price-support system is being phased out, the pattern it helped to develop is very well established.

On the other hand, the large influence of transnational corporations (TNCs) in promoting sales of agrochemicals cannot be ignored as a barrier to sustainable farming. Most TNCs have taken advantage of existing policies that promote the enhanced participation of the private sector in technology development and delivery, putting themselves in a powerful position to scale up promotion and marketing of pesticides. Given such a scenario, it is clear that the future of agriculture will be determined by power relations, and there is no reason why farmers and the public in general, if sufficiently empowered, could not influence the direction of agriculture toward goals of sustainability.

CONCLUSIONS

The nature of the modern agricultural structure and contemporary policies have strongly influenced the context of agricultural technology and production, which in turn has led to numerous environmental problems. Given the realities of capitalism, resource-conserving practices are discouraged and in many cases such practices are not profitable for farmers. As the large-scale landscape homogenization with transgenic crops proceeds, environmental impacts will probably be substantial and it is expected that such massive deployment will exacerbate the ecological problems already associated with monoculture agriculture. Unquestioned expansion of this technology into developing countries is also undesirable. There is strength in the agricultural diversity of many of these countries, and it should not be inhibited or reduced by extensive monoculture, especially when consequences of doing so result in serious social and environmental problems.[24]

The expectation that a set of policy changes could bring a renaissance of diversified or small-scale farms may be unrealistic, because it negates the existence of economies of scale in agriculture and ignores the political power of agribusiness corporations and current trends set forth by globalization. A more radical transformation of agriculture is needed, one guided by the notion that ecological change in agriculture cannot be promoted without comparable changes in the social, political, cultural, and economic arenas that also constrain agriculture. Change toward a more socially just, economically viable, and environmentally sound agriculture will be the result of social movements in the rural sector in alliance with urban organizations.

NOTES

1. M.A. Altieri, *Agroecology: the Science of Sustainable Agriculture* (Boulder: Westview Press, 1995).

2. L.A. Thrupp, *Cultivating Diversity: Agrobiodiversity and Food Security* (Washington D.C.: World Resources Institute, 1998.)

3. Y. Audirac, *Rural Sustainable Development in America* (New York: John Wiley and Sons, 1997).

4. J.N. Pretty, *Regenerating Agriculture: Policies and Practices for Sustainability and Self-reliance* (London: Earthscan, 1995); and P. Raeburn, *The Last Harvest: the Genetic Gamble that Threatens to Destroy American Agriculture* (New York: Simon and Schuster, 1995).

5. R. Vallve, "The Decline of Diversity in European Agriculture." *The Ecologist* 23: (1993), 64–69.

6. P. Raeburn, *The Last Harvest: the Genetic Gamble that Threatens to Destroy American Agriculture* (New York: Simon and Schuster, 1995).

7. M.A. Altieri, *Agroecology: the Science of Sustainable Agriculture* (Boulder: Westview Press, 1995); and S.R. Gleissman, *Agroecology: Ecological Processes in Agriculture* (Michigan: Ann Arbor Press, 1997); and J.N. Pretty, *Regenerating Agriculture: Policies and Practices for Sustainability and Self-reliance* (London, Earthscan, 1995).

8. G.R. Conway and J.N. Pretty, *Unwelcome Harvest: Agriculture and Pollution* (London: Eathscan Publisher, 1991).

9. D. Pimentel and H. Lehman, *The Pesticide Question* (New York: Chapman and Hall, 1993).

10. J. Liebman, *Rising Toxic Tide: Pesticide Use in California, 1991–1995* (San Francisco: Report of Californians for Pesticide Reform and Pesticide Action Network, 1997).

11. G.R. Conway and J.N. Pretty, *Unwelcome Harvest: Agriculture and Pollution* (London: Earthscan Publisher, 1991).

12. H. McGuinnes "Living Soils: Sustainable Alternatives to Chemical Fertilizers for Developing Countries." (New York: Consumers Policy Institute, 1993).

13. Ibid.

14. J. Rissler and M. Mellon, *The Ecological Risks of Engineered Crops* (Cambridge, MA: MIT Press, 1996).

15. S. Krimsky and R.P. Wrubel *Agricultural Biotechnology and the Environment: Science, Policy and Social Issues* (Urbana, IL: University of Illinois Press, 1996); and A.A. Snow and P. Moran, "Commercialization of transgenic plants: potential ecological risks." *Bioscience* 47 (1997), 86–96.

16. J. Rissler and M. Mellon, *The Ecological Risks of Engineered Crops* (Cambridge, MA: MIT Press, 1996).

17. C. James, *Global Status of Trangenic Crops in 1997* (Ithaca, NY: ISSAA, 1997).

18. M.A. Altieri and P.M. Rosset, "Agroecology and the Conversion of Large–scale Conventional Systems to Sustainable Management," *International Journal of Environmental Studies* 50 (1995), 165–185.

19. M.A. Altieri, *Agroecology: the Science of Sustainable Agriculture* (Boulder: Westview Press, 1995).

20. M.A. Altieri, "Agroecological Foundations of Alternative Agriculture in California." *Agriculture, Ecosystems and Environment* 39 (1992), 23–53.

21. S.R. Gliessman, *Agroecology: Ecological Processes in Agriculture.* (Michigan: Ann Arbor Press, 1997).

22. P.M. Rosset and M.A. Altieri, "Agroecology Versus Input Substitution: a Fundamental Contradiction in Sustainable Agriculture." *Society and Natural Resources* 10 (1997), 283–295.

23. Ibid.

24. M.A. Altieri, "The Environmental Risks of Transgenic Crops: an Agroecological Assessment," In I. Serageldin and W. Collins (eds) *Biotechnology and Biosafety* (Washington D.C.: World Bank, 1999), 31–38.

Chapter Five

THE MATURING OF CAPITALIST AGRICULTURE:
FARMER AS PROLETARIAN

R.C. LEWONTIN

We are all familiar with the classical story of how capitalism came to dominate industrial production and how capitalist relations of production swallowed up the individual artisanal producer. We recognize the power that the capitalist mode has to infiltrate and finally transform other forms of the organization of production and exchange. We sometimes think that the power of that transformation is so great that all of the significant action already occurred in the past, at least in Europe and North America, and was essentially over by the end of the nineteenth century. In the society we inhabit, it is a *fait accompli*, whose dynamic we can only understand by reconstructing the past because it is not happening around us. On second thought we realize that the transition was still in progress until very recently in a few skilled domains like medical care and entertainment, where individual artisans were able to ply their trade throughout most of this century, but these fossils of early capitalist relations seem exceptional because of their requirement of special talents or of necessary skills acquired by long training. But the view that the transition to mature capitalism is essentially over except at the margins of the main body of commodity production is clearly wrong,

93

because it ignores an immense sector of basic essential commodity production, agriculture, which is still in the throes of the transition.

The penetration of capital into agriculture has been a long process of a different form than the classical case of industrial production usually exemplified by cloth weaving in the eighteenth and nineteenth centuries. Indeed, on the surface, agriculture would seem to have been resistant to capital. After all, despite a 72 percent drop in the number of of individual farm enterprises in the United States from 6.7 million in 1930, there are still about 1.8 million independent farm producers today. This means that even though only 6 percent of these establishments account for 60 percent of the total value of farm production, there are over 100,000 separate enterprises producing more than half of all the value of the output. In the industrial manufacturing sector the four largest enterprises account for an average of 40 percent of value produced, and even in a highly differentiated product like clothing, the top four companies produce over 15 percent of the value.

There has also been a major increase in the proportion of farmland that is leased to farmers who also own their own land. Roughly 55 percent of farmland is now operated by owner-renters who are for the most part small producers. Finally, despite the conventional wisdom that corporate farming is taking over, the proportion of farms and farmland operated by managers representing absentee owners has remained about 1 percent since the beginning of the century. Thus if we are to look for evidence of the capitalist transformation of agriculture, we will not find it in the classical industrial model. We do not find a concentration of more and more productive capacity in the hands of a very small number of farmers, employing a large wage labor force carrying out its tasks under close supervision and according to a tightly controlled schedule. There are, of course, some examples of a factory-like labor process in farming, especially in the harvesting of fruits and fresh vegetables, and these are often pointed to as evidence of a capitalist transformation to factory farming. However, the vast majority of farm enterprises do not employ a large labor force, but more typically have one or two hired laborers, usually for only part of the year.

In analyzing the process of the capitalist transformation of agriculture we must distinguish between farming and the agrifood system. Farming is the physical process of turning inputs like seed, feed, water, fertilizer, and pesticides into primary products like wheat, potatoes, and cattle on a specific site, the farm, using soil, labor, and machinery. The failure of classical capitalist concentration in farming arises from both financial and physical features of farm production. First, the ownership of farmland is unattractive to capital because it cannot be depreciated, and investment in farmland has very low liquidity as a consequence of the thin farm real estate market. Second, the labor process on very large farms is hard to control because farming operations are spatially extensive. Third, economies of scale are hard to achieve beyond what has already been realized by medium-scale enterprises. Fourth, risks from external natural events like weather, new diseases, and pests are hard to control. Finally, the cycle of reproduction of capital cannot be shortened because it is linked to an annual growth cycle in plants, or a fixed reproductive cycle in large animals. An important exception to this constraint has been in poultry, where there has been considerable success in shortening the reproductive cycle, and this has had important ramifications for the development of capitalist farming as we will see. For all of these reasons we do not expect to see, and have not seen, the wholesale direct takeover of farm ownership by large corporate enterprises employing large, well-controlled labor forces.

The agrifood system, however, is not simply farming. It includes the farm operation, but also the production, transportation, and marketing of the inputs to farming, as well as the transportation, processing, and marketing of the farm outputs. While farming is a physically essential step in the entire chain of agricultural production, the provision of farm inputs and the transformation of farm outputs into consumer commodities have come to dominate the economy of agriculture. Farming itself now accounts for only about 10 percent of the value added in the agrifood system, with 25 percent of the food dollar paying for farm inputs and the remaining 65 percent gained by transportation, processing, and marketing that converts farm products into consumer commodities. At the beginning of the century the value added on the farm was around 40 percent of the total food dollar, and many of the inputs were produced directly on the farm in the form of seed, draught animals, feed for the animals, manure and green manure for fertilizer, and family labor. For the most part these inputs are now purchased in the form of commercial seed, tractors, fuel, refined or synthesized chemical fertilizers, and machinery and manufactured chemical substitutes for labor. Thus, it is the production of farm inputs and the transformation of farm outputs that have provided an opportunity for industrial capital to capture profits in the agricultural sector.

Like any other industrial processes, the production of farm machinery, chemicals, and seeds, and the turning of threshed wheat into a box of breakfast cereal at the supermarket check-out counter are completely controlled by capital and its demands. The problem for capital, however, has been that sitting in the middle of the transformation of petroleum into potato chips is an essential step, farming, in the hands of two million petty producers. They cannot be dispensed with, they own certain essential means of production whose ownership cannot be concentrated (land in particular), and, while they are economically rational, they consume their surplus rather than turning it into capital. Agriculture is unique among all the sectors of capitalist production by possessing at its productive center an essential process organized around large numbers of independent petty producers. It is as if the spinning of yarn, the weaving of cloth, and the sewing of garments were in the hands of a few large capital enterprises (as they are), but the dyeing and finishing of the raw woven material were unavoidably the exclusive province of hundreds of thousands of home producers who bought the unfinished cloth and sold their product to clothing factories.

Farm producers have historically been in possession of two powers that stood in the way of the development of capital in agriculture. First, farmers could make choices about the physical process of farm production, including what was grown and how much, and what inputs were to be used. These choices, of course, were always constrained, partly because of local conditions of climate and soil, and partly because of the local nature of markets for farm products. Second, farmers were themselves traditionally potential competitors with the commercial providers of inputs, because they could choose to produce seed, traction power, and fertilizer themselves. The problem for industrial capital, then, has been to wrest control of the choices from the farmers, forcing them into a farming process that uses a package of inputs of maximum value to the producers of those inputs, and tailoring the nature of farm products to match the demands of a few major purchasers of farm outputs who have the power to determine the price paid. Whatever production risks remain are, of course, retained by the farmer. As the farmer loses any power to choose the actual nature and tempo of the production process in which he or she is engaged, while at the same time losing any ability to sell the product in an open market, the farmer becomes a mere operative in a determined chain whose product is alienated from the producer. That is, the farmer becomes proletarianized. It is of little import that the farmer retains legal title to the land and buildings and so, in some literal sense, is the owner of some of the means of production. There is no alternative economic use for these means. The essence of proletarianization is in the loss of control over one's labor process and the alienation of the product of that labor.

How has this transformation of farming been accomplished? In the first stages, in the century between the invention of reaping machines and the end of the Second World War, innovations in farming directly addressed that problem of the availability, cost, and control of farm labor through mechanization. No farmer could resist the arrival of the tractor, nor could one be home built. After the Second World War, refined and synthetic chemical treatments became the chief purchased inputs in the form of fertilizer, insecticides, and labor-saving herbicides. Again, these purchased inputs could not be resisted because of the large increase in yields and the reduction in labor. Herbicides, in particular, also reduced the requirement for tillage machinery, insecticides reduced the uncertainty of a successful crop, hormone sprays allowed for a close control of ripening time in fruit crops, and antibiotics prevented animal diseases. Once again there could be no competition between these industrial products and self-produced farm inputs.

The analysis of the growing role of capital inputs cannot be made, however, if a central feature of the productive process is lost sight of: *the concrete use of all these inputs is to produce living organisms.* The steps of mechanization and the use of chemicals were not possible in isolation from the nature of the organisms being produced. Unlike in other sectors of production, in agriculture living organisms are at the nexus of all input streams and are the primary sources of all output transformations. But living organisms are mortal, so their *production* requires their *reproduction*. That is, every cycle of farm production begins with seeds or immature animals to which value is added by on-the-farm operations, so seed (or the animal) is the central input into farming. The control of the biological nature of these seed organisms is a critical element in the control of the entire process of agricultural production, which puts the provider of this input in a unique position to valorize other inputs. For example, while a dramatic drop in the price of nitrogen fertilizer at the end of the Second World War made it economically possible for farmers to use this input in large quantities, for this input to be useful it was necessary to breed plants, corn hybrids in particular, that could, in fact, turn a massive nitrogen application into crop yield. The successful mechanization of tomato harvesting was only possible by a close cooperation of the machine designers with plant breeders. The breeders completely remade the biology of the tomato plant, turning a loosely branched plant that flowers and sets easily bruised fruit continuously over the growing season into a short, stout, Christmas tree-like plant whose tough fruits all ripen at about the same time.

The consequence of the central position of seed input in the production process is that seed companies are potentially in an extraordinarily powerful position to appropriate a large fraction of the surplus in agriculture. There is a barrier to this realization however. The seed of a desirable variety, when planted by the farmer, produces plants that themselves produce yet more seed of the variety. Thus the seed company has provided the farmer with a free good, the genetic information contained in the seed, that is reproduced by the farmer over and over again in the very act of farming. Some way must be found to prevent the farmer from reproducing the seed for next year's crop. The historical answer to this problem was the development of the inbred/hybrid method of breeding, using hybrid crosses between inbred lines, which makes it possible to sell seed that will produce hybrid plants, but which themselves do not reproduce hybrids. Because the second generation would not be true hybrids and thus would lose yield and be more variable, the farmer must go back to the seed company every year to buy new seed. As a result of the immense profits made by seed companies selling hybrid maize seed, the method was spread into other organisms such as tomatoes and chickens. Moreover major commercial hybrid seed and chicken breeders like DeKalb, Funk, and Northrup-King were at one time acquired by pharmaceutical and chemical companies like Ciba-Geigy, Monsanto, and Dow, although subsequently there have been divestments and realignments. Only the largest hybrid seed company, Pioneer Hi-Bred, remained obdurately independent until, in 1997, 20 percent of its equity and two seats on its board were purchased by DuPont.

Generally, the ability of commercial seed companies to control seed inputs by the inbred/hybrid method was severely limited. First, the method cannot be made economically workable in many important crops like soybeans and wheat, or in large animals. Second, while the inbred/hybrid method was successful for general yield increase, large numbers of important specific characters such as resistance to particular diseases, or resistance to herbicides, or increases in oil content in oil seeds, do not show hybrid vigor, but must be introduced by other breeding methods. Third, there are characteristics that would be desirable to introduce into an agronomically important species, but which are present in other organisms that cannot breed with the species under cultivation. The most famous example was the desire to make corn plants able to fix nitrogen from the atmosphere, as legumes are able to do, by making their roots hospitable to nitrogen-fixing bacteria. While this would reduce the market for nitrogenous fertilizers, it would place the provision of nitrogen in the hands of seed companies!

The limitations on what changes could be made to agronomic species that would be profitable to seed companies and their chemical company partners or owners meant that the penetration of capital into agriculture had reached its apparent limits in the 1970s. The introduction of major new forms of mechanization into farm production had come to an end, partly because of the dramatic change in the cost of fuel and partly because a steady supply of immigrant labor that could be deported stalled progress in agricultural labor organizing. The growing public consciousness of the polluting effects of fertilizers and pesticides and the development of OSHA regulations to protect farm workers against the deleterious effects of insecticide and herbicide sprays discouraged radical changes in the uses of chemicals or even continued growth in the use of older materials. In addition, these fertilizers and pesticides were being used at very high rates, probably higher than could be economically justified by the farmer. There was, for example, no growth in fertilizers after 1975 or in synthetic pesticide application rates beginning in about 1980. Any further possibility for input providers and output purchasers to increase their appropriation of the surplus in agriculture depended on 1) making some radical changes in the biology of agronomic species, and 2) guaranteeing that such changed biological systems would remain within their ownership and control. Moreover, that appropriation could be greatly increased by a greater consolidation of both input and post-farm production sectors (purchasing, processing, and distribution), to provide near monopoly control. Enter biotechnology.

BIOTECHNOLOGY AND THE CONTROL OF PROPERTY

The claim is being made here that the purpose of the commercial use of biotechnology is to extend the control of capital over agricultural production. To accomplish this purpose, biotechnological innovation should meet three criteria. First, the time and cost of its development must be within the limits set by capital investments in research. Thus, the attempt to introduce nitrogen fixation into non-leguminous plants has been largely abandoned by Agricetus, Agrigenetica, Biotechnica, and other biotechnology enterprises after spending over $75 million on the problem over more than ten years, despite the evidence that it ought to be possible, and despite the immense profits that could be made if it were successful. Second, the development must not provoke a significant challenge from politically effective forces concerned with health and environmental issues. All biotechnological innovations have been challenged on the basis of environmental and health risks, and this contributed significantly to the demise of at least one early biotech project. An important impetus for introducing biotechnology is that the resistance to yet further applications of fertilizer and pesticides was impeding further increase in the appropriation of the surplus in agriculture by input producers. Third, *ownership and control of the product of biotechnology must not pass into the hands of the farmer but must remain with the commercial provider of the input.*

The requirement that the biotechnological innovator maintain ownership and control over the altered variety creates a contradiction. As previously discussed, the farmer acquires a free good, the genetic information contained in the seed, when he or she purchases a new variety, and the breeder loses its ownership. The property rights protection offered by the inbred/hybrid method is limited to a few organisms and a few agronomic characteristics, and biotechnology has been introduced in precisely those instances where the inbred/hybrid method does not apply. How, then, can breeders appropriate a greater share of the surplus when they are giving away the critical material, the genes? The answer has been provided by a combination of legal and biological weapons in the hands of the breeders. These weapons are legal rights granted to breeders by the Plant Variety Protection Act and subsequent court decisions, in combination with the use of standard DNA "fingerprinting" that allows an unambiguous determination of the source of farm products. It is now standard that a farmer who wishes to purchase a bioengineered seed must sign a contract with the seed producer giving away all property rights in the next generation of seed produced by the crop. Not only does the farmer undertake not to sell seed from the crop to other farmers ("brown bagging"), but more revolutionary, *the farmer is prohibited from using the next generation of seed to produce next year's crop on his or her own farm*. All farmers who buy seed of Monsanto's Roundup Ready soybeans, or that company's seed potatoes for a special variety that makes "light" potato chips with low oil retention, must, by the terms of the contract, return to Monsanto in the next season if they wish to continue production of those varieties. (Monsanto is the producer of Roundup, a potent herbicide that kills all plants including soybeans. "Roundup Ready" soybeans, produced by genetic engineering, can be grown in fields heavily treated with Roundup without killing them and, presumably, without materially affecting their yield.) The enforcement of such a contract depends on the ability of Monsanto to identify a crop, and this can easily be done from a single plant or even a single seed because the DNA of the engineered variety contains certain characteristic sequences, placed there deliberately by the genetic engineers, that are unique to the variety. The assay of crops for such labeled sequences is called "genome control" by the biotechnology laboratories of seed producers, and a considerable laboratory effort has been put into developing these detection techniques. Nevertheless some brown bagging and replanting has been taking place. In reaction, Monsanto has placed full-page advertisements in magazines read by farmers, threatening and cajoling:

> When a farmer saves and replants Monsanto patented biotech seed, he understands that what he is doing is wrong. And that, even if he did not sign an agreement at the time he acquired the seed [that is, replanted or bought "brown bag" seed from a neighbor], he is committing an act of piracy.... Furthermore, seed piracy could cost a farmer hundreds of dollars per acre in cash settlements and legal fees, plus multiple years of on-farm and business records inspection.

It only takes a few widely publicized legal judgments to keep the rest in line.

But the story of property rights has yet one more chapter. The inbred/hybrid method only applies to a few organisms, and the contract system requires threats, monitoring, and litigation to make it work. It is biotechnology that has now perfected the solution to ownership in seed crops. It was announced on March 3, 1998, that a patent had been granted for a genetic manipulation that would allow plants to set seed and therefore make a crop, *but which would render those seeds unable to germinate.* Thus, at one blow, the problem of capitalist seed production, first addressed by the invention of the inbred/hybrid method at the beginning of this century, has been solved for all seed crops. As the inventors point out, there is still development to be carried out before this bit of biotechnology becomes a commercial reality, but there seems no bar to its transfer to any crop. And who are the inventors and owners of this patent? They are the Delta and Pine Land Company, a leading breeder and producer of cotton seed and soybean seed, and the Agricultural Research Service of the United States Department of Agriculture. Yet there is no suggestion that this development will be of any benefit to farmers or consumers. We could hardly ask for a more blatant case of state support of private property interests to the exclusion of any public benefit.

The use of the contract to enforce breeders' property rights allows us to make some predictions about the limitations of genetic engineering. At the present time the hormone BST, which causes dairy cows to direct more of their metabolism to milk production, is produced commercially by Monsanto in fermenters using genetically altered bacteria. But cattle normally produce their own BST, and there is no reason that the regulatory DNA that controls production of this protein in cows could not be altered to increase the amount. This would then make the purchase and administration of commercial BST unnecessary. We can predict, however, that this is unlikely. First, dairy herds have always been largely self-reproducing on small- to medium-sized enterprises, and there are no major commercial dairy herd breeders equivalent to major seed companies. Second, enforcement would be very difficult. It is easy for a representative of Monsanto to "acquire" a single potato or a few seeds from any farmer's field, or from a local elevator. It is considerably more intrusive to take the blood or tissue sample from a farmer's dairy herd that would be needed for "genome control." Moreover, since dairy herds are not all reproduced at one time but have overlapping generations, it would be impossible to say, except after a number of years, whether a cow was one of the originally purchased stock, or an offspring.

PRODUCTION CONTRACTS, BIOTECHNOLOGY, AND THE CONTROL OF FARMING

If the only effect of biotechnology and the contract system of guaranteeing property rights were to extend the domain of manufactured inputs into farming, nothing very revolutionary would have occurred. Farmers for a long time have been the purchasers of manufactured inputs. The major structural changes that are occurring in agriculture arise from a vertical integration of farm production in such a way that the purchasers of farm outputs take control of the entire production process. This vertical integration is made possible by 1) a technical linking of the inputs and outputs, 2) the dual function of a single capital enterprise as both the monopsonist (near monopoly) purchaser of outputs and the provider of critical inputs, and 3) a contract mechanism that links farmer into the loop of inputs and outputs. The use of such contracts predates biotechnology. Wherever the purchaser of farm outputs is also the processor of those outputs for the market, the possibility of vertical integration has existed. Contract farming has been a common feature of vegetable production for canning. Tomato canneries in Ohio were built in a location central to the farms, the canning company provided the seed and chemical inputs and collected the ripe tomatoes. The farmer provided the land and labor. But the system has evolved greatly since the first canning contracts. The critical role played by biotechnology has been in the material linking of inputs and outputs. In order to guarantee an efficient integrated system of production, the biological inputs into the chain of production, the organisms being raised, are engineered to fit the package of other inputs, the mechanics of the farming process, and the qualities that the final output is to have for the market. While some of these aims can be accomplished by conventional methods of breeding organisms, many of the needed qualities, such as specific disease resistance or qualitative changes in the composition of the organism, are best produced by biotechnological manipulations. Moreover various cloning and cell culture techniques make it possible to reduplicate large numbers of input organisms with desired heritable qualities, no matter how those qualities were originally produced.

An example of the nature of contract farming is in the production of broilers (chickens raised as meat) where the system is especially entrenched. A major supplier of chickens to supermarkets and fast food restaurants is Tyson Farms of South Carolina. Tyson chickens are produced, not by Tyson "Farms," but by small farmers, owning about 100 acres, producing an average of 250,000 chickens per year, with a gross income of about $65,000 and a net of around $12,000.

This production is under a four-year contract with Tyson (or other similar regional firms), a contract that makes Tyson the sole provider of the chicks to be raised, the feed, and veterinary services. The company is also the sole determiner of the number, frequency, and type of chicks provided. Tyson then collects the mature birds after seven weeks, at a date and time of their own determination, providing the scales on which the birds are weighed and the trucks to take them away. The farmer provides the labor, the buildings in which the chicks are raised, and the land on which the buildings stand. The detailed control of inputs and farming practices are entirely in the hands of Tyson. So, "The Producer (farmer) warrants that he will not use or allowed to be used . . . any feed, medication, herbicides, pesticides, rodenticides, insecticides or any other items except as supplied or approved in writing by the Company." Moreover, the farmer must adhere to the Company's "Broiler Growing Guide" and a failure to do so puts the farmer into "Intensified Management" status under the direct supervision of the Company's "Broiler Management and Technical Advisor."

The chicken farmer has ceased to be an independent artisan, buying materials, transforming them by his or her labor, and selling the product on a market. The contract farmer buys nothing, sells nothing, nor makes any decisions about the physical process of transformation. The farmer does own some of the means of production, land and buildings, but has no control over the labor process or over the alienated product. The farmer has then become the typical "putting out" worker characteristic of the first stages of capitalist production in the seventeenth and eighteenth centuries. What the farmer has gained is a more stable source of income, at the price of becoming an operative in an assembly line. The change in the farmer's position from an independent producer, selling in a market with many buyers, into a proletarian without options, is reflected in the nature of the recommendation in the 1998 report of the National Commission on Small Farms, that

> Congress should amend the AFPA [Agricultural Fair Practices Act] to provide the USDA with administrative enforcement and civil penalty authority that will, in turn, *enable growers to organize associations and bargain collectively without fear of discrimination or reprisal* [emphasis added].

The combination of biotechnological manipulation and contract farming can also have a catastrophic effect on third world economies. Much of the import of agricultural products from the Third World consists in qualitatively unique materials like coffee, flavorings, essences, and food oils with special properties. Moreover, the production of these materials is at a low technological level with high labor inputs, in countries with unstable political and economic regimes. As a result, the price and availability of, say, palm oil from the Philippines are unstable. These characteristics make such agricultural products prime targets for gene transfer into domestic species, which will then be grown as specialty crops under contract to processors. Calgene has engineered a high lauric acid canola (rape seed) strain for oils that are used for soaps, shampoos, cosmetics and food products that formerly required imported palm oils. These special canola strains are now produced in the Midwest under contract, displacing Philippine production on which a large fraction of the rural population depends economically. And the genes for the biosynthesis of caffeine have been successfully transferred to soybeans. If the essential oil genes for coffee flavor can also be transferred, then Central and South America and Africa will lose their market for beans destined for powdered coffee.

It would be a mistake to think that agriculture has followed the classical picture of the spread of capitalism. Unlike in industrial production, the first step in the capture of agriculture by capital was the immense flowering of input industries and output processors, who appropriated the surplus in agriculture by selling the petty entrepreneurial farmer what he needed, and buying what he produced. No parallel exists in the industrial sphere. It is only with the saturation of that possibility of appropriation that wholly new techniques have come into play. By concentrating on the central material link in farm production, the living organism, which at the same time was the most resistant to capitalization, biotechnology has accomplished two steps in the penetration of capital. First it widened the sphere of input commodity production by including a wide array of organisms that had previously escaped. Second, and more profound, it is making vertical integration possible with the accompanying proletarianization of the farmer. It is this second stage that is the capitalist agriculture of the future, because the physical nature of farm production, inevitably tied to the land, is such as to maintain its unique organization as a productive process.

Chapter Six

NEW AGRICULTURAL BIOTECHNOLOGIES:
THE STRUGGLE FOR DEMOCRATIC CHOICE

GERAD MIDDENDORF, MIKE SKLADANY,
ELIZABETH RANSOM, AND LAWRENCE BUSCH

In the contemporary global agrifood system, the emergence of a plethora of new agricultural biotechnologies[1] poses a series of far-reaching social, technical and ethical consequences and contradictions. These tools have radically merged questions of design at the molecular level with those of agricultural change. With more possible technological paths than ever before, the new biotechnologies have made technology choice central in the discourse over the future of agriculture. Implicit in the choice of these technologies is a redesigning of nature that could profoundly transform the agrifood system, ecosystems, and the social organization of agriculture. Indeed, global food production and consumption currently stand on the brink of a fundamental alteration in organizational form, which conceivably could surpass the redistributional outcomes of twentieth century industrialization of farming, agriculture and the food system.

Humans have for millennia been actively modifying nature to provide their sustenance. However, never before have the tools been available to redesign nature with the precision and speed that the new agricultural biotechnologies permit. For example, recombinant DNA techniques for

107

conferring insect resistance in crops are both more precise and much faster than conventional plant breeding techniques, which require repeated selection over many generations of plants. Similarly, DNA probes have been developed to allow for the identification of certain traits in animals, without going through the lengthy process of waiting for the offspring to be born. This will allow farmers to select out undesirable traits and add or enhance desired livestock traits with more speed and precision.

The new biotechnologies also allow the rapid movement of diverse genetic materials across previously insurmountable biological and chemical barriers to create microorganisms, plants, and animals in a manner intentionally desired and designed by humans. In essence, genetic material can now be exchanged among virtually all living organisms. This makes all of the world's genetic diversity into raw industrial material to be used in research and development. Moreover, expanded claims to intellectual property rights for genetic resources are privatizing what was once public domain.[2] Likewise, in a global agrifood system the implications of the new biotechnologies are no longer limited by geography. The ability to produce cocoa or vanilla in a laboratory using cell culture techniques, for instance, could virtually decouple the manufacture of these foods from land-based production systems, threatening the livelihoods of populations in developing countries.[3]

This compression of time and space raises problems for directing biotechnology policy. Much of the research and development in this area is being carried out in the private sector with little public input or oversight. Companies are striving to develop novel biotechnology products as quickly as possible, while simultaneously lobbying to reduce as much as possible the public regulatory processes. They hope this will get their products to market ahead of those of competitors. This greatly reduces the opportunities for those with concerns about biotechnology to have a voice in deciding which directions biotechnology should take.

Moreover, the discourse surrounding emerging biotechnologies is often inadequate, in part because of the shortcomings of current thinking concerning the separation of science and politics. It is time to move beyond these limitations by questioning the very boundaries between science and politics. First, let us review some of the current developments in agricultural biotechnology, and their social, technical and ethical consequences and contradictions.

NEW BIOTECHNOLOGIES IN AGRICULTURE

The biotechnology industry declares itself to be one of the "cornerstone industries of America's future economic growth,"[4] and promises new agricultural technologies that will feed the world. In contrast, some critics have warned that the primary fruits of agricultural biotechnology will be "Frankenfoods" and environmental havoc, spawned by technologies over which we will almost surely lose control.[5] Thus far the developments in the field support neither of these claims. Rather, the story is much more complex. What is clear is that agricultural biotechnology, and the debates surrounding it, will be with us for the foreseeable future.

Biological research in agriculture was traditionally in the public domain. However, most investment in biological research in agriculture is now being done by the private sector. Some analysts predict biotechnology crops will be worth $7 billion by 2005.[6] Thus, it is not surprising that industry leaders are betting heavily on agricultural biotechnology's commercial success, and industry is dominating the research agenda.

Before turning to a discussion of specific technologies and their implications there are two general issues which should be addressed. First, biotechnologies can increase market concentration. As with other products in a capitalist market, biotechnology developers rely on being the first to get their product to market so as to capture the largest market share. Thus, only countries in the forefront of biotechnology development are likely to reap the gains of investment in research and development. Also, due to the increasing scope and complexity of intellectual property rights on life forms, many companies avoid lawsuits by swapping patented material.[7] Companies that do not have many patents or are not connected into this network may be blocked from entering the market. Furthermore, the agricultural biotechnology industry is located primarily in Western industrialized countries. Only about ten developing countries have biotechnology programs. Thus, the inequalities that currently exist between developed and developing countries are further exacerbated.

Second, advocates of biotechnology focus on increasing productivity without questioning its distributional consequences. Typically, the argument that biotechnology will help feed the world is couched in humanitarian rhetoric and the (promised) results are presented as a means to legitimate the investment in research and development. However, these arguments ignore the multiple dimensions of food security. Biotechnology may address concerns such as the amount and quality of food available, but it does not deal with issues of access and distribution. Indeed, given its potential to displace large numbers of people and to deny them access to the means of subsistence, biotechnology could in some instances actually be detrimental to helping the world feed itself. Let us turn now to specific examples of plant, food, and animal biotechnologies and their implications.

Plants

The list of new plant biotechnologies on the market has grown extensively in the past few years (see Table 1 for a partial listing). In the United States alone, the area of transgenic crops planted increased from 8.1 million hectares in 1997 to 20.5 million hectares in 1998.[8] In plant biotechnology, herbicide resistant crops (HRCs) are one example of commercial developments. HRCs allow herbicide application after the crop has emerged from the soil, extending the period in which the chemical may be used. Expectations are that by 2000 the annual value of herbicide tolerant seed will be about $2.1 billion.[9] With the top four chemical companies controlling 53 percent of the market, it is not surprising that 30 to 50 percent of industry research and development spending is presently going towards HRCs.[10]

In 1997, an estimated 3 to 4 million hectares of herbicide-tolerant soybeans were planted—roughly 15 percent of the total soybean acreage in the United States.[11] This area grew substantially in 1998 worldwide, with the result that "more than one-half of the world soybean harvest and about one-third of the corn harvest now comes from plants engineered with genes for herbicide or disease resistance."[12] One brand of HRC soybeans on the market is Monsanto's Roundup Ready transgenic[13] soybean, which is resistant to the company's leading herbicide, Roundup, the largest selling weed killer in the world. Farmers who use the seed must sign a contract requiring them to use only Roundup and allowing Monsanto to inspect their fields at any time. Roundup accounts for about 17 percent of Monsanto's total annual sales.[14] For Monsanto, HRCs like Roundup Ready soybeans represent an opportunity for the company to increase its overall share of the agricultural

Table 1. **COMMERCIALIZED BIOTECHNOLOGIES IN THE U.S.**

Name of Product (Year Commercialized) – Brief Description

	Herbicide Resistant:	Identity Preserved:	Insect Resistant (Bt toxin):
PLANT*	Canola (NOM)** – resistant to herbicide glufosinate	Laurical (1995) – high lauric acid oil composition in canola	KnockOut (1995) – corn resistant to corn borer
	Roundup Ready Canola (NOM) – resistant to herbicide glyphosate	FlavrSavr (1994) – delayed ripening tomato (*taken off market*)	NatureGuard (1995) – corn resistant to corn borer
	BXN Cotton (1995) – resistant to herbicide bromoxynil	High Oleic Acid Soybeans (NOM): higher levels of oleic acid in the oil.	Bollgard (1995) – resistant to bollworm and budworm
	Roundup Ready Cotton (1996) – resistant to herbicide glyphosate	Terminator Genes (NOM) – sterilizes plant seed	NewLeaf (1995) – resistant to Colorado potato beetle
	Roundup Ready Soybeans (1995) – resistant to herbicide glyphosate	**Disease Resistant:** Freedom II (1995) – squash resistant to two viruses (*taken off market*)	
FOOD	**Modified Flavors:** High Fructose Corn Syrup (1980s) – corn sweetener used in soft drinks, etc.	New Processing Techniques: Chymogen (1990) – recombinant rennet used in cheese making	Biosensors (1980s) – detects biological activity in food
	Aspartame (1981) – high-intensity sweetener	**Rapid Detection Systems:** DNA probes (1980s) – evaluates authenticity of food ingredients	Polymerase Chain Reaction (1985) – used in early detection of bacteria and viruses in food manufacturing
ANIMAL	**Growth Hormones:** Bovine Somatotropin (1994) – growth hormone injected into cow to increase milk production	DNA probes (1982) – allows for the identification of certain traits	Dolly (NOM) – Lamb cloned using a non-reproductive cell nucleus taken from a ewe's udder
	Porcine Somatotropin (NOM) – injected growth hormone to increase average daily weight gain and lean tissue, while decreasing back fat in pigs	Embryo splitting (1980s) – produces identical animals. Not cost effective in the U.S., so not widely practiced in the industry.	**Transgenic "Pharming":** Rabbits that produce an enzyme (NOM) – used to treat a rare human genetic disorder.
	Reproductive Technologies: Embryo Transfers (1979) – one of first animal biotechnologies used, primarily for farm breeding	**Transgenic Animals:** Mice (1976) – first transgenic animal	Goats (NOM) – produce a drug called TPA

*For a more complete list of agricultural biotechnology refer to http://www.bio.org
For plant biotechnologies on the market refer to *The Gene Exchange*, Fall 1997.

inputs market by introducing genetically engineered seed that is tied to the use of its herbicides.

Today, all major seed companies have been bought or are tied to chemical companies. The consolidation of the chemical and seed industries has allowed a few companies to gain a large share of the agricultural inputs market. Concentration in the industry has generated considerable criticism of the control that agribusiness is gaining over the agrifood system. The concern is that, as fewer input suppliers increasingly dominate the market, the choices that farmers have before them will actually become more restricted. A few products will be heavily pushed as the industry standard. This can promote a narrower genetic base for agriculture as well as restrict the types of farm enterprises and narrow the range of choices available to farmers.

The commercialization of HRCs raises other long-term environmental issues as well. Some researchers have shown that herbicide tolerance engineered into crop plants can spread quite easily into weedy relatives of a crop.[15] Thus, widespread use of HRCs could lead to hardier weeds. Of course, everyone shares these consequences; they are not experienced solely by direct users of the technology.

The most recent plant biotechnology to create international controversy is the "Terminator technology." Co-developed by the USDA and seed company Delta and Pine Land, the Terminator technology encodes within each seed's DNA a gene that kills its own embryos, thereby sterilizing the seed and forcing growers to return to seed companies on a yearly basis to purchase new seeds. Grassroots organizations, particularly groups in parts of the world that struggle with food security, have vehemently opposed this technology. As one foundation research director explains, "engineering seed sterility is a logical goal for the multinational seed industry because around three-quarters of the world's farmers routinely save seed from their harvest for re-planting."[16]

While users of hybrid seed have long faced this same issue (i.e., having to return to seed companies annually), the Terminator technology is different in two fundamental ways. First, hybrids have only been successful with a few crops. In principle, all crops could be modified with the Terminator gene. In fact, if the gene works as expected, it will likely be licensed widely to seed companies, making it difficult for farmers to buy seed that does not contain the gene. Thus, farmers might well find that they have no choice in the matter.

Second, hybrids are relatively easy to produce by conventional breeding, so although the market is concentrated, there are many companies in the market. The Terminator technology could eventually allow a few chemical/seed companies to control all crop seeds worldwide. The serious inherent risk is the assumption of permanently stable institutions. If used on a large scale, it will make farmers fully dependent on seed companies for seed. If the seed is unavailable due to war, civil disturbance, natural disaster, etc. then farmers will suddenly discover that they have no seed to plant. This would obviously be catastrophic.

Another group of plant biotechnologies currently in use is identity preserved (IP) crops, which have been engineered with specific altered traits, such as tomatoes with delayed ripening (e.g., Flavr Savr), or canola with high lauric acid (an ingredient in cosmetics), such as Calgene's Laurical. IP crops are a way of adding value to a crop because the altered trait commands a premium in the market. Yet, for the developers to maximize profits they must maintain ownership or control of the product from seed to market. This encourages, and is certain to promote, contract farming. Contract farming has some advantages for farmers. For instance, farmers may not have to incur a large debt to finance the crop under contract. However, farmers entering contracts also lose autonomy as they no longer are permitted to make basic production and marketing decisions. Moreover, contract farming may also continue the shift toward larger and fewer farms, because the contracting company will face increased transaction costs as the number of contracts into which it enters increases. For example, if Calgene wishes to contract out one thousand hectares of its anti-sense tomato, it would likely seek out a larger, more capitalized producer for the full one thousand hectares, rather than enter into ten contracts at one hundred hectares each.

Food

Many food biotechnologies have been developed with little public awareness or discussion. In part, this is due to the fact that most consumers know very little about research and development in food processing. For example, researchers have produced chymosin, an enzyme used in cheese making, from genetically engineered organisms. The first commercial product, a recombinant chymosin called Chymogen, can be found in approximately 60 percent of all hard cheeses in the United States.[17] Yet, most people in the United States have never heard of this genetically engineered enzyme.

Food biotechnology also includes the use of enzymes in fermentation, as well as in starch processing. Today, the value of the world fermentation market is estimated at between $20 and $40 billion annually, while the market for starch enzymes is approximately $200 million annually.[18] One of the first products made with starch enzymes was High Fructose Corn Syrup (HFCS). HFCS is produced by using biotechnologically produced enzymes to convert corn into a sweetener. Corn converted by this method has attained widespread use in major food products such as soft drinks. Other products not yet commercialized include vanilla and cocoa produced in vitro.[19] In principle, any commodity that is consumed in a highly processed, undifferentiated form could be produced using these techniques. The result would be large batches of the commodity that are completely aseptic and require far less processing.

If successfully commercialized, *in vitro* biotechnologies will have an impact well beyond merely the technical aspects of their development. These technologies permit the global displacement of markets. Market displacement has always occurred due to product substitution, but biotechnology accelerates the process and leaves developing country populations in a precarious position. For instance, when HFCS attained widespread use it captured a large share of the cane sugar market from developing countries, threatening the livelihoods of an estimated eight to ten million people in the South.[20] Presently, vanilla and cocoa are still cheaper to import than to produce in factories. But, if such factory production can be done economically, people who depend on the export of these crops for their livelihood may see a significant loss of market share.

Animals

Unlike food biotechnologies, animal biotechnologies have created significant controversy. The fact that animals are sentient beings creates very different issues for biotechnology development. The issues are further complicated because the information about animal biotechnology research and development is not readily available. Almost all research on animal biotechnologies is funded by private industry. Furthermore, due to the controversy over the use of animals, much research is undisclosed. Often, only after research is completed do the results become public knowledge. Dolly, the lamb cloned in 1997, is a prime example of both the secrecy surrounding the industry and the controversy which animal biotechnology creates.

Early animal biotechnologies involved reproduction, particularly the ability to select certain desired livestock characteristics. Recent research has shifted towards (1) increasing the milk production of cows (i.e., bovine growth hormone), (2) improving or changing meat characteristics (e.g., porcine growth hormone), and (3) using animals to produce pharmaceuticals. Pharmaceutical manufacturing, also called "transgenic pharming," is the leading area of investment in transgenic animal[21] research and development. If successful, "pharming" will allow pharmaceutical companies to use an animal much like they would a laboratory. The animal would be engineered to produce a desired compound that would then be sold to treat various ailments. The first pharmed drug, likely to arrive on the market late in 1999, is an enzyme produced in the milk of transgenic rabbits for individuals who lack this enzyme due to a rare genetic disorder, known as Pompe's disease.[22] A list of other transgenic animals that have successfully produced a desired drug or drug ingredient includes pigs that produce human hemoglobin and sheep that produce an amino acid lacking in some humans. The intention is to eventually commercialize these products.

In addition to the issues noted above, certain concerns are specific to animal biotechnologies. Is it appropriate to treat animals as mere factories for human drugs? Will such animals suffer from their own health problems? Should we treat the patenting of animals in the same manner as we treat the patenting of a drug produced in a lab? Also, how will pharming impact the current structure of agriculture? These questions have received little public discussion.

The plant, food, and animal technologies discussed above and listed in Table 1 are merely the tip of the iceberg. In 1997 one of the largest agriculture biotechnology companies had 17 million hectares of genetically modified crops planted.[23] In addition, in the past three years there has been a dramatic increase in the use of biotechnology in production and processing of foods.

Today, foods that are produced or processed using biotechnology include breakfast cereals, taco shells, corn syrup, cooking oil, candy, margarine, milk, and cheeses, to name just a few. Indeed, there are many technologies still a few years from the market that will eventually reach commercialization.[24] These include transgenic fish, such as salmon, tilapia, and catfish, which are being engineered for industrial aquaculture production. Also, there are many more developments in pharming in both plants and transgenic animals. This makes it even more urgent that society begin to grapple with how and who will decide what directions biotechnology takes.

BIOTECHNOLOGY AS POLITICS BY OTHER MEANS

Despite the best efforts of advocates to portray biotechnology as the logical, inevitable, and unproblematic direction of agricultural research and development, it is a series of choices being made, each with associated consequences. The consequences of developing new technologies under the direction of corporations are substantial and extend throughout the global agrifood system. Thus, everyone is a participant in a global experiment with this new set of technologies that promises to create new winners and losers around the world, yet only a few have access to decision-making processes. Discussions of critical social, technical and ethical aspects of these technologies are currently suppressed by the view that science and technology are beyond the boundaries of conventional political discourse. The new biotechnologies are potentially beneficial to society, but not unless the institutional bases for technology choice are democratized. These technical and political dimensions can no longer remain separate if a socially just biotechnology is to emerge.

The rhetoric of neutrality embedded in the science of biotechnology masks a series of social contradictions. When closely examined, technical choices are simultaneously political choices not necessarily congruent with the fuller aspirations of a free, democratic society. The current developments in biotechnology reflect a decision-making process in which commercial interests override societal and environmental concerns. Moreover, while most scientists see themselves as searchers for truth, they remain largely oblivious to the *partial* character of what they "discover" or create. Similarly, corporate managers have a vested interest in promoting their own agenda even while claiming it serves merely to advance scientific knowledge. Given the increasing influence of corporate funding of and collaboration with university and government scientists, their research agendas are reshaped as well. This fundamental contradiction is at the heart of the politics of the new agricultural biotechnologies.

Biotechnology is one valid and reliable way of knowing, representing and manipulating nature. In principle, there is nothing inherently harmful about this new set of tools. However, within industrial capitalism biotechnology is tied to private profit, short-term control over nature, and neglect of short- and long-term social consequences. In part, this emerges from our society's faith in technological progress as the sole means to resolve human problems. At the same time, the institutional basis of industrial capitalism reinforces an increasingly illegitimate distinction between the political and technical. The legacy of this distinction can be traced back to the industrialization of agriculture and the industrialization of society.

In many respects, the production-oriented arguments utilized by biotechnology advocates echo sentiments exhibited in the post Second World War era development of industrial agriculture that produced the "green revolution." The green revolution focused on rapid production gains as a singular means to solve world food problems while stemming what was perceived as the advance of communism. Indeed, the application of new technological packages, corresponding infrastructure development, and the growth of export markets are all legacies of the green revolution. This approach did lead to significant production gains. However, the contradictions arising from these developments also led to exacerbated social, political and economic inequalities within localities, nation-states and regions of the developing and developed world.[25] Moreover, the debasing of tropical agricultural resources has led to negative long-term environmental consequences resulting in profound ecosystem alteration and, in some cases, severe degradation of the ability of the land to produce food. The green revolution provides an important lesson with respect to the application of the new agricultural biotechnologies: the ideology of inevitable technological progress excludes consideration of the distributional and environmental consequences of such efforts.

Marx was ambivalent about technological choice. On the one hand, he envisioned that new technologies could help achieve human emancipation and lead to a society of abundant production and consumption. On the other hand, Marx realized that technologies could also create routine drudgery that would alienate and demean those who use them. He foresaw the social conditions of industrial capitalism, which currently relate to how the new agricultural biotechnologies have emerged and are taking shape. However, there is nothing that necessitates this outcome.

NARROW OR STRONG OBJECTIVITY

Perhaps one of the primary sources of legitimacy for biotechnology is its connection to scientific objectivity—an association frequently highlighted by advocates in an effort to immunize their endeavors politically by attempting to draw a clear distinction between the scientific and the political. It is these very sources of legitimacy that require scrutiny. Acting on behalf of a "concerned public," proponents appeal to scientific objectivity to advance arguments for the best possible outcomes regarding support for new agricultural biotechnologies. This is not to say that biotechnology is not based on valid and even well intentioned science. What is problematic, however, is that early decisions about the direction of biotechnology become invisible after research is completed and technologies are produced. When choosing problems, scientists have a range of possibilities before them. For example, they could work on developing crops that more effectively shade out weeds, or intercropping and rotation systems for better weed control, or they could genetically modify plants to be resistant to herbicides.

Yet, after the direction of research and development has already been decided, the initial alternatives tend to disappear as scientists often portray the chosen path as the only viable one.[26] The chosen path then becomes, according to scientists, the only "accepted" objective view of the world. Hence, a *narrow objectivity* prevails in which a few scientists and corporate executives make early choices (i.e., when there are a number of viable alternative choices) about the direction of research and development, and then later define the chosen path as the standard measure for objectivity. They do so even as research is supported by corporations that have an obvious vested interest. This weaker form of objectivity can only be enhanced by increasing the number of perspectives—and the legitimate representation of those perspectives in decision making—that are included in making the initial choices.

The conventional stripping away of the social context of science facilitates the mystification of biotechnology. But, science and technology are political developments, with real constituencies and real social consequences. Democratizing science and technology policy is a necessary part of the process of addressing these contradictions. This requires developing new institutional mechanisms to promote the participation of those affected by new technologies. As a first step, the very definition of science and technology needs to be broadened to include activities that go on outside the laboratory, but that are fundamental to the scientific enterprise. Public and private funding agencies, instrument manufacturers, biotechnology firms and general farm and commodity organizations, among others, must all be recognized as essential social agents in science and technology development. Only when these intertwined components of science and technology are addressed can we speak of objective, socially responsible and ethically informed decision-making.

THE STRUGGLE TO DEMOCRATIZE SCIENCE
AND TECHNOLOGY

Increasing corporate control of the biotechnology research and development agenda raises a host of problems, not the least of which is a restricting of public access to decision-making in this arena. While opening the technology policy process to broad participation comes up against considerable structural constraints, a democratization of science and technology should not be seen as merely a utopian illusion. We are now accustomed to considering democracy as limited to party politics. However, there have been continuing struggles to extend it to technology choice. Several countries have made notable progress in this direction. While efforts in the United States have received limited support, in Western Europe the institutional innovations toward a more inclusive technology policy process are taking place. These initiatives should by no means be considered a panacea for dealing with technology development, but they are one approach to challenging corporate and state hegemony over technology choice.

For example, for more than a decade the Danish Board of Technology (DBT) has been running consensus conferences that have provided a forum in which ordinary citizens with diverse backgrounds are involved in technology assessment.[27] The results of these dialogues between citizens and a panel of experts are widely disseminated in the media, and are often acted on by legislative bodies. The DBT has held conferences on industrial and agricultural biotechnology (1987), irradiation of food products (1989), and genetically manipulated animals (1992). It appears that this model is now being more widely adopted in Europe.

In the United States the first promising efforts at proactively involving citizens in technically complex areas of policy are beginning to appear. In 1997 the Loka Institute, along with a number of other collaborating institutions, organized a pilot citizens' panel based on the consensus conference model. This particular panel dealt with issues arising from changes in telecommunications technologies and policy. Judging from the conference reports, the panel demonstrated that lay citizens are capable of meaningful participation in complex technical and public policy issues.[28] Both this approach and the work of the Danish Board of Technology warrant further exploration.

These are just two examples of mechanisms that attempt in some way to extend democracy to technology choice. While our purpose here is not to review the full range of extant examples, it is useful to consider some of their shared principles. In these efforts, the relationship between social priorities and technology choices is made explicit. A key feature of these strategies is that society must democratically define its priorities; only then should it ask how technologies might help to achieve those goals. This challenges the common assumption in science policy of a positive, linear relationship between scientific advance and social progress.[29] Another guiding principle is that since all citizens experience the effects of science and technology, and since citizens in democratic societies ordinarily expect to have a voice in decisions that will affect the way they live their daily lives, they must be involved in deciding the direction of science and technology policy.

These approaches also begin with the assumption that science and technology policymaking is an inherently political process, and that any constructive dialogue will necessarily bring together actors with divergent goals and values that often contradict each other. In the debates over biotechnology some might argue for values such as profitability or freedom from excessive regulation, while others might argue for safety, environmental soundness, or equity. There is no one decision rule with which to rank these competing values in a simple hierarchy. Rather, decisions must be accomplished through a process of debate, negotiation and compromise in which all stakeholders have a voice.[30]

In the United States, we have typically relieved ourselves from responsibility for the consequences of technical change by attributing them to the inevitable effects of technological advance combined with market forces. In this view, if undesirable consequences should result from technical change, not only can we develop new technical fixes, but also new products and additional economic activity. Yet, as the examples above suggest, it is not necessary to actually employ new technologies in order to determine their consequences. Such an approach leads to the never-ending search for technological fixes, even as it tears at the social fabric. Indeed, many of the negative consequences could be avoided if initial science and technology choices were made with better consideration of social priorities. We currently do not have these kinds of mechanisms in place—technical change has by far out-paced institutional innovation—but we do have the capacity in universities, non-governmental organizations, companies, and in our citizenry to direct science and technology in more democratic and socially desirable directions.

NOTES

1. Defined broadly to include techniques that use living organisms to improve plants, animals, or products, biotechnology in itself is not new. We use "new" to refer to technologies that use rDNA, cell fusion techniques, new bioprocesses, monoclonal antibodies, plant and animal cell and tissue culture, and embryo transfer, splitting and sexing.

2. Suri Sehgal, "Biotechnology Heralds a Major Restructuring of the Global Seed Industry," Diversity 12.3 (1996), 13–15.

3. Lawrence Busch, William B. Lacy, Jeffery Burkhardt, and Laura R. Lacy, *Plants, Power, and Profit: Social, Economic, and Ethical Consequences of the New Biotechnologies* (Cambridge, MA: Blackwell, 1991).

4. BIO (Biotechnology Industry Organization), BIO Web site, (1996). URL: http://www.bio.org/bio/2usbio.html (3/17/97).

5. Jeremy Rifkin, *The Biotech Century: Harnessing the Gene and Remaking the World*, (New York: Jeremy P. Tarcher/Putnam, 1998).

6. *Nature Biotechnology* ". . . Green is also the Color of Money," 16.11 (1998), 985.

7. Sehgal, "Biotechnology Heralds a Major Restructuring."

8. Anne Simon Moffa, "Toting Up the Early Harvest of Transgenic Plants," *Science* 282.5397 (1998), 2176–2178.

9. Thomas F. Lee, *Gene Future: The Promise and Perils of the New Biology* (New York: Plenum Press, 1993).

10. Ibid.

11. IFIC (International Food Information Council "Anticipating the Harvest of Food Biotechnology Crops." (1997). URL: http://www.ificinfo.health.org/insight/Sept Oct97/foodbiotech.htm (12/18/97).

12. Moffa, "Toting Up the Early Harvest."

13. A transgenic organism is formed by inserting foreign genetic material into the germ line cells of organisms.

14. Mark Arax and Jeanne Brokaw, "No Way Around Roundup," *Mother Jones* (January/February 1997), 40–41.

15. Thomas Mikkelsen, Bente Andersen, and Rikke Bagger Jørgensen, "The Risk of Crop Transgene Spread," *Nature* 380.6569 (1996), 31.

16. RAFI (Rural Advancement Foundation International). "Monsanto Terminates Terminator?" (1998) URL: http://www.rafi.org/pr/release25.html (1/29/99).

17. BIO, 1996.

18. BIO (Biotechnology Industry Organization), BIO web site (1998).   URL: http://www.bio.org/whatis/edito7.dgw (3/21/98).

19. In vitro production is an industrial process in which the cells of a multicellular organism are treated as if they were microorganisms. They are placed in a large vat where the environment (light, temperature, nutrients, etc.) is manipulated such that the cells multiply.

20. K. van den Doel and G. Junne, "Product Substitution Through Biotechnology: Impact on the Third World." *Trends in Biotechnology* 4:88–90 (1986).

21. Transgenic animals are animals into which foreign DNA is implanted into the fertilized egg.

22. "Phase II for Pharming." *Business and Regulatory News Briefs in Nature Biotechnology* 16.13 (1998), 1297.

23. Jeffrey L. Fox, "Monsanto Unaffected By Merger Halt?" *Nature Biotechnology* 16.13 (1998), 1307.

24. "Despite Opposition, Biotech Foods Ready for Primetime, Experts Say," *Food & Drink Weekly* 47.4 (1998), 1.

25. Harry M. Cleaver Jr., "The Contradictions of the Green Revolution," *American Economic Review* 2.62 (1972.), 177–186; John, H. Perkins, *Geopolitics and the Green Revolution: Wheat, Genes, and the Cold War*, (New York: Oxford, 1997).

26. This case has been made for the history of hybrid corn by Jack R. Kloppenburg, Jr. in *First the Seed: The Political Economy of Plant Biotechnology*, 1492–2000, (Cambridge: Cambridge University Press, 1988).

27. Danish Board of Technology, *Technology Assessment in Denmark: A Briefing* (Copenhagen: Danish Board of Technology, 1992).

28. The Loka Institute "First–Time U.S. Citizens' Panel: Telecommunications and the Future of Democracy, April 2–4, 1997." A report on The Loka Institute web site (1997), URL: http://www.loka.org/pages/results.htm (1/25/99).

29. Daniel Sarewitz, *Frontiers of Illusion: Science, Technology, and the Politics of Progress* (Philadelphia: Temple University Press, 1996).

30. Lawrence Busch and Gerad Middendorf, "Technology Policy in a Rapidly Changing World," in William Lockeretz (ed.), *Visions of American Agriculture* (Ames: Iowa State University Press, 1997), 205–217.

Chapter Seven

GLOBAL FOOD POLITICS

PHILIP McMICHAEL

THE URUGUAY ROUND AND AGRIBUSINESS IMPERIALISM

In the early 1990s, the U.S. Department of Agriculture estimated that Pacific Asia would absorb two-thirds of the over $3 billion increase in global demand for farm exports by the year 2000.[1] Pacific Asian imports would be assisted by $1 billion in U.S. Export Enhancement Program subsidies to American exporters. A portion of this lucrative market (much of which is tinned beef and processed foods sold in South Korea and Taiwan) would involve bulk wheat and corn imports by Indonesia, Malaysia and the Philippines. The USDA predicted:

> In the absence of sustained, aggressive investment in infrastructure and increased competitiveness for corn production, the Philippines could become a regular corn importer by the end of the decade. . . . U.S. corn may be able to capture a large share of this growing market.

Under the conditions of the 1994 agricultural agreement of the Uruguay Round, OECD projections predicted that U.S. corn exports would undercut local corn prices by 20 percent in the year 2000, depressing domestic corn prices, and threatening half a million peasant households with income declines of 15 percent. According to Kevin Watkins, this would result in high social costs such as reduced expenditure on education, increased reliance on child labor, nutritional decline, and the intensification of women's work outside the home to compensate. Comparatively speaking, the average subsidy to U.S. farmers and grain traders is roughly one hundred times the income of a corn farmer in Mindanao. As Watkins remarks, "In the real world, as distinct from the imaginary one inhabited by free traders, survival in agricultural markets depends less on comparative advantage than upon comparative access to subsidies." Noting that the government of the Philippines views this agreement as an instrument of economic efficiency, despite its implicit transfer of sovereignty over national food policy to an unaccountable trade body in Geneva, Watkins concludes: "Legal niceties aside, the Uruguay Round agreement bears all the hallmarks of an elaborate act of fraud. It requires developing countries to open their food markets in the name of free market principles, while allowing the United States and the EU to protect their farm systems and subsidize exports."[2]

The Uruguay Round's sleight of hand has been institutionalized in the recently formed World Trade Organization (WTO). The WTO presides over the most far-reaching attempt to level political, social and environmental protections in the name of efficiency and market freedom. But, as the above case indicates, the "level playing field" is not level—because the U.S. and the EU retain indirect agricultural subsidies by decoupling farm payments from commodity prices (encouraging agro-export "dumping"), and through extensive infrastructural supports. By externalizing these subsidies, U.S. and EU exports compete with artificially low prices. In market terms, then, Southern agricultures appear relatively inefficient. In privileging market prices as the criterion of agricultural competitiveness, free-trade rhetoric thereby justifies the use of institutional means to extend markets for agribusiness at the expense of small farmers across the world.

The market leveling view is a perverse legacy of the neoliberal project that emerged in the 1970s, initially as a hegemonic discourse of market rule and increasingly as a coercive policy deployed to institutionalize market rule to prevent backsliding. Institutionalization began with the debt management policies of the 1980s, when Third World political elites submitted to austere structural adjustment programs. In the 1990s, institutionalization of market rule has been generalized through international regimes such as the WTO and proliferating free-trade agreements.[3]

As I argue below, agribusiness imperialism is central to the coercive use of institutional mechanisms to monopolize control of world agriculture and flows of food. It primarily serves the interests of the corporate sector and a global minority of 600 million affluent consumers primarily concentrated in the triadic core of the world economy (Western Europe, North America and Japan). But the historical relations of production and consumption of food on a world scale have always been organized geo-politically. The following brief historical sketch of the geo-politics of food also interprets the process by which the U.S. has assumed a global "breadbasket of the world" strategy and sought to institutionalize its corporate "food power" via the current free trade regime.

AGRICULTURE AND CAPITALISM:
FROM AGRO-COLONIALISM TO AGRO-INDUSTRIALISM

Much of our political-economic understanding of global power relations is anchored in a binary view of the world expressed in the concept of the "international division of labor." In world capitalist history, the metropolitan, or European, world specialized in industry, while the "peripheral," or non-European, world specialized in raw material and food production. Development came to be understood as the process of overcoming this division, as Third World states sponsored domestic industrial sectors. In this scenario, agriculture is viewed as a specialization to be transcended.

The concept of the international division of labor reinforced the urban-industrial bias of the development paradigm, with agriculture cast as the residual. Moreover, it has obscured the parallel story of the politics of agribusiness in reshaping global political economy and power relations. One reason for this is that the history of development involves two divergent, and yet connected, historical threads that have been blended together in idealist constructions of "development." These two threads are the global movements of British and U.S. hegemony, each of which modeled two distinct forms of development. Let me address each in turn.

The former hegemony involved dividing the world along the classic lines of the *international* division of labor, expressed in the British slogan of "workshop of the world." British specialization depended on access to agricultural exports from tropical colonies and New World temperate regions (including the future American "breadbasket"). Indeed world capitalism emerged on the pedestal of colonial agricultures, where large-scale slave plantations prefigured the rise of the factory system. Not only did slavery anticipate proletarianization, but also the colonial system generated much of the early capital nurturing the rise of modern industry. More fundamentally, capitalist forms of production (and consumption) first emerged in agriculture, and the global food trade was, and remains, central to the organization of capitalism on a world scale.

In the nineteenth-century, Britain abandoned its Corn Laws (domestic farm protections) and imported its foodstuffs. The strategy was to fashion a global marketplace based on an international division of labor pivoting on a British "workshop of the world." This attempt to subdivide the world into a metropolitan industrial workshop and a peripheral agricultural hinterland was central to the political economy of the colonial system. Under Britain's "free trade" regime, rival European states and their investors consolidated their control over non-European regions, forcing them to specialize in export agriculture and extractive industry to supply the industrial world with dietary and raw material inputs (from sugar and meat to cotton and rubber).

Over the course of the nineteenth century the composition of agro-exports from the non-European world changed, as industrial commodities displaced luxuries such as silks and spices. The new agro-industrial and other raw material commodities entering world trade were for consumption by Europe's emerging industrial proletariat (sugar, coffee, tea, cocoa, vegetable oils) and expanding factories (cotton, timber, rubber and jute). As this European/tropical interrelationship deepened, another pattern of trade with the ex-colonial settler states (U.S.A., Australia, New Zealand, Canada) emerged which would transform the shape of world agriculture in the twentieth century. Exports of temperate products (grains, meat) from these regions supplemented, and then competed with, metropolitan agriculture, becoming the staple diets of European labor forces.[4]

In the twentieth century, the United States projected an alternative model of development based on the *national* integration of manufacturing and agricultural sectors. Whereas the British model was viewed as "outer directed," the U.S. model was viewed as "inner directed." However, obscured in this latter model is the powerful role of agribusiness and food power in the U.S.-centered global political economy of the twentieth century. In the late-nineteenth century, white settler farming (typified by family farming in the United States) formed the new agricultural core of the world economy, fueling industrialization in Europe as well as in the settler states. With the relatively low frontier person-to-land ratio, this strategic 'breadbasket' role generated a highly productive energy- and capital-intensive agriculture. In fact, this form of industrial agriculture became the model for agricultural development in the twentieth century, first in Europe and then in the post-colonial world.

The intensive agricultural model is significant because it required continual external inputs, provided through the market—whether technological inputs such as oil, inorganic fertilizers, hybrid seeds, machinery, and pesticides or specialty agricultural outputs such as corn and soy feeds for the new intensive meat sub-sector, for example. On a national scale, the model integrated industry and agriculture, fuelling post-Second World War prosperity within the terms of the Bretton Woods monetary regime (whose fixed exchange rates and controls on capital flows stabilized national economies). Meanwhile, on the transnational scale, large agribusiness corporations began coordinating exchanges of these inputs across national boundaries. Many of these exchanges originated in the postwar settlements in Europe and East Asia, whose reconstruction depended on U.S. trade and export credits. The Japanese livestock sector, for example, came to depend on feedstuffs such as imported corn from the United States and soy from Brazil. In other words, agro-industrial complexes (where agriculture is subjected to, and integrated with, industrial processes) were simultaneously nationally organized and internationally sourced.

In the meantime, agro-industrialization intensified the global division of labor associated with colonialism. While industrial uses of rubber, fibers and some vegetable oils (for soaps, lubricants and paint) had expanded since the late-nineteenth century, in the mid-twentieth century, diets of processed foods expanded dramatically, deepening the demand for certain tropical products such as vegetable oils and sugar. Such tropical exports underwrote post-colonial development projects, for a time. However, the strategic role of some tropical exports became increasingly precarious as agribusiness technologies matured. Following the metropolitan substitution of rubber and fibers, the search for substitutes for some tropical food products began as the agribusiness complex matured and corporations sought to use by-products of metropolitan agriculture such as corn syrup, soy oils as alternatives to sugar and tropical oils. These by-products became integral to the food processing industry.

Agro-industrialization thus eroded some of the agricultures fostered by colonialism, upon which Southern states came to depend for export earnings. In other words, the technologies and political power of the Northern agro-industrial complex have significantly shaped the structure of the global food economy. I shall now review briefly the political role of the U.S. agro-industrial complex in this process.

AGRIBUSINESS IN GLOBAL POLITICAL ECONOMY:
THE RISE OF AGRO-EXPORT DEPENDENCY

The U.S. agro-industrial complex stemmed from adjustments made during the interwar period in response to the Great Depression, which was particularly severe in agriculture. In 1935 the Agricultural Adjustment Act was amended to allow the Secretary of Agriculture to bar agricultural imports to protect the USDA price-support program, which set domestic prices above world market prices. Ironically, this neo-mercantilist policy of import controls eventually produced an agro-export program of global significance. Farm supports led American farmers to overproduce and the U.S. government disposed of these agricultural surpluses overseas via the Public Law 480 program of cheap food aid. It was within the context of this food regime disbursing food at concessional, and later, commercial, prices, that the huge grain traders, such as Cargill and Continental, prospered. They had traditionally marketed grains produced by American family farms, and had gained a captive market through the subsidized exports of the food aid program.[5]

In addition to cheap foodstuffs, U.S. exports of agribusiness technologies flourished through the facility of U.S. foreign aid programs, including the Marshall Plan and the green revolution, which targeted select Third World regions. These two particular programs spawned modernizing agricultural sectors replicating the capital and energy-intensive model of American agriculture, from Europe through Japan to Mexico. In South Korea four local firms formed joint ventures with U.S. agribusiness firms (including Ralston-Purina and Cargill) to introduce technical and marketing expertise to that country's food system. The 1970 PL-480 annual report stated that these enterprises had access to counterpart funds "to finance construction and operation of modern livestock feed mixing and livestock and poultry production and processing facilities. As these facilities become fully operational they will substantially expand the market for feedgrain and other feed ingredients." Two years later, the annual report concluded that "these firms were instrumental in accelerating the introduction of U.S. technology and were a major factor in the rapid expansion of . . . the increase in Korea's imports of U.S. corn, soybean meal, breeding stock and other supplies and equipment." [6]

This report illustrates how the U.S. agricultural model, including its specialized character, shaped the Korean livestock industry, which increasingly depended on foreign feedstuffs producers (e.g., in the U.S., Brazil, and Thailand). That is, agribusiness corporations not only had new domestic markets within which to sell their technologies, but also they integrated global commodity chains linking specialized agricultural sub-sectors across national boundaries.

The progression from multi-national markets to transnational complexes, as realms of corporate profiteering, did not derive from agribusiness specialization alone. It also grew out of geo-economic arrangements as global capitalism changed gears in the 1970s. The stable organization of nationally-regulated economies, with fixed exchange rates pegged to the dollar, gave way to an increasingly unstable organization of increasingly transnational economic relations governed by floating exchange rates, offshore money markets and financial speculation (in other words by financial globalization). As national controls on capital movements eased, transnational corporate activity expanded, and development agencies like the World Bank identified exporting to the global market as the preferred strategy for states and firms.

Interestingly enough, the U.S. government in the early 1970s adopted a "green power" agro-export strategy, to solve its growing imbalance of payments associated with the rising costs of empire (emanating in particular from the Vietnam war). Until the 1970s, U.S. farm policy focused on stabilizing the national farm sector, with exports and food aid as a by-product of the domestic management of surpluses. The 1973 Farm Bill, which removed production constraints on American farmers and encouraged commercial exports, was not simply a formal change in the mechanism of disposal of farm surpluses—it fundamentally altered the relation of American agriculture to the world economy.[7]

From the early 1970s, U.S. agriculture displayed a new export dependency, in which the production of more than one acre in three consisted of low-value primary products (wheat, corn and soybeans) destined for the export market. The green power strategy destabilized family farming throughout the world, and intensified export production and dependence on foreign markets, especially in the middle-income regions of the Third World, China, the Soviet Union, and Eastern Europe. Meanwhile, Western Europe, whose farm policies both mirrored those the U.S. and led to similar overproduction problems, was becoming a major grain exporter.

In the 1950s the Third World had accounted for about 10 percent of all wheat imports, but this proportion increased to 57 percent by 1980. A significant part of this food dependency arose from the United States' food aid program, which encouraged Western dietary habits on the one hand, and undercut local farmers' prices on the other. The food-dependent South became the site of intensified trade rivalry between the EC and the United States. This competition for markets, and the growing role of the transnational corporations in the global food economy, provided the context for GATT talks in the 1980s focusing on the liberalization of agriculture and trade in agricultural commodities.

FORMATION OF THE GATT AND NORTHERN EXCEPTIONS

The Uruguay Round's focus on agricultural liberalization broke new ground for GATT. As suggested in the case of the Philippines, liberalization is by no means a neutral matter of installing a "level playing field" in the global food economy. At the outset, liberalization embodied both a free trade demand by the Cairns Group of agro-exporting nations,[8] and a mercantilist, "breadbasket of the world" strategy pursued by the United States.

Interestingly, in the previous GATT Rounds, agriculture was always an exception to the liberalization of trade rules, at U.S. insistence. In 1955, agricultural trade was excluded from consideration in GATT codes, thus protecting U.S. farm supply policies from import competition. Since the mid-1980s, however, the United States has reversed this position, intending to deploy GATT against agricultural protection. Arguably, the immediate target is the European Common Agricultural Policy (CAP) of subsidizing cheap farm exports to enter markets once dominated by U.S. agricultural exports. Given the dependence of American agriculture on export markets, such rivalry has considerable domestic impact, on debt-stressed farmers and corporate exporters.

The American strategy evolved within this context: from a "green power" initiative in the world market in the 1970s, to a broader institutional initiative in the 1980s to enforce market power through a GATT free trade regime. Behind this liberalization initiative was the considerable restructuring, or economic polarization, of the farm constituency. The farm crisis of the 1980s ultimately favored the large producer and the food companies. By 1994, 50 percent of U.S. farm products came from 2 percent of the farms, while only 9 percent came from 73 percent of the farms. In the same year, 80 percent of U.S. beef was slaughtered by three packers: Iowa Beef Packers (IBP), ConAgra and Cargill.

The shift in farm credit delivery, from predominantly state-supplied credit in the 1970s to the Reagan policy of replacing Farmer's Home Administration loans with state-guaranteed private loans, marked an important change in farm policy. Not only did rural welfare policies shift towards socializing the cost of private expansion, this new policy climate also signaled the empowerment of private banks as suppliers of agricultural credit. The banks simultaneously benefited from U.S. monetarist policies which inflated the dollar, opening the door for Southern agro-exporting, and thereby facilitated a strategy of debt-repayment to the banks, but at the expense of American agro-exports.[9]

In response to rising farm prices after the mid-1980s farm crisis ceased, the newly- established Export Enhancement Program (EEP) subsidized agro-exports, particularly those competing with EC exporters. The United States sent the message: either "initiate policy reforms in accordance with

U.S. priorities, or the U.S. would use the EEP to subsidize exports to recapture world market shares for wheat, feed grains, and selected livestock products in direct competition with the Community."[10] To that end, EEP commodities have targeted markets in the Soviet Union, China, North Africa and the Middle East. The United States used the EEP as part of a negotiating strategy in the GATT Uruguay Round to challenge competitors' subsidies and other "unfair" trade practices. By 1994, agro-exports from the U.S. accounted for 36 percent of wheat trade worldwide, 64 percent of the corn, barley, sorghum and oats, 40 percent of the soybeans, 17 percent of the rice and 33 percent of the cotton. However, these trade challenges have not so much rewarded the United States (and other food exporting nations), as they have strengthened the grip of the food companies, which benefit from the free trade movement—for example, 50 percent of U.S. grain exports in 1994 were shared by two companies: Cargill and Continental.[11]

GATT, TNCS AND WORLD-AGRICULTURAL RESTRUCTURING

The current restructuring of world agriculture builds on a division within agriculture between low-value and high-value products. Trade in low-value temperate cereals and oilseeds has been historically dominated by the North, and trade in high-value products has fallen increasingly to corporate agro-exporters (or their contract farmers) producing in the South, for example Brazilian beef, Chinese and Hungarian pork, Brazilian, Hungarian and Thai poultry, Southeast Asian shrimp, and, generalized fruit and vegetable exports across the South. (Note that while some Southern countries—notably, Argentina, Thailand, and Uruguay—are net food exporters, the large majority are net food importers). The growth of agro-export "platforms" is an unstable strategy, signaling a more fundamental process at work: a widespread subordination of producing regions to global production and consumption relations organized by transnational food companies.

Under these conditions, agriculture becomes less and less a foundational institution of societies and states, and more and more a tenuous component of corporate global sourcing strategies. It increasingly anchors a system of global profiteering in food products, a system in which food travels from farm gate to dinner plate an average of 2,000 miles. Further, the corporate strategy of incorporating regions into global production and consumption relations simultaneously undermines the institutional bases of national farm sectors, in the North as well as the South.

Farm sectors have been so transformed that, for example, the U.S. government has been considering eliminating "farming" as a census category. This occurs in a context where 2 percent of the farms grow 50 percent of agricultural produce, the average family farm earns only 14 percent of its income from the farm, and 95 percent of American food is manufactured and sold by corporations (e.g., Philip Morris, which markets brand names such as Sungold Dairies, Lender's Bagels, Tombstone Pizza, and Kraft Cheese; and ConAgra, which markets Healthy Choice meals and desserts, Peter Pan peanut butter, Orville Redenbacher popcorn, Wesson oils, and Butterball, Armour and Hebrew National meats). The food industry is in fact the largest American industrial sector, even though it doesn't produce food security, as 30 million Americans do not get enough to eat. And it is dominated by huge conglomerates which virtually monopolize sales—ConAgra, for example, accounts for 25 percent of sales in foodstuffs, feed and fertilizer, 53 percent of sales of refrigerated foods, and 22 percent of grocery products.[12]

Centralization in a few mega-food companies also puts them in a commanding position vis-a-vis producers also. But the corporate takeover is not simply a question of the economic viability of family farming programs. It is also that these national farm-based institutions, which nurtured agribusiness by stabilizing national patterns of consumption of farm commodities, have now become *obstacles* to the transnational strategy and structure of the food companies. They are obstacles because domestic price supports, in raising prices of agro-industrial inputs, disadvantage food processors and grain traders in the world market.

For the South, the TNC strategy continues the neo-colonial project of undercutting local farmers with cheap food imports on the one hand, and extending the green revolution strategy to producing new agro-exports, on the other. The latter strategy (the "second green revolution") applies crop-breeding techniques and chemical inputs to crops geared to affluent markets in the cities or overseas. Either way, the threat to local food security, leaving aside potentially unhealthy dietary changes and the greater fragility of monoculture, is real. In Brazil, the world's third largest food exporter and

considered one of the "new agricultural countries," less than 1 percent of the
population owns about 44 percent of the fertile agricultural land, and 32
million people are officially considered destitute.

Transnational corporations stand to gain overall from a free trade regime,
since it will enhance and reward capital mobility and facilitate it by reducing
institutionalized costs. Cargill, for instance, is one such corporation that
views the world as its oyster. The largest private company and the eleventh
largest company in the world, Cargill employs 70,700 people in 800 locations
in sixty countries and over fifty different businesses—from grains to beef-
packing to fertilizer, peanuts, salt, coffee, transportation, steel, rubber and
fruits and vegetables. [13]

Global firms, and the agro-exporting states (the Cairns Group), were key
supporters of the GATT multilateral approach to liberalization. In fact, the
original U.S. proposal to the Uruguay Round was drafted by Cargill's former
senior vice president, also a former officer of the U.S. Department of
Agriculture. Cargill shares roughly 50 percent of U.S. grain exports with
Continental. Food companies, grain traders and the chemical industry all
generally favor using the WTO to phase out farm programs, eliminating
supply management and driving down prices by exposing producers to
world-wide differential labor costs. By reducing price supports, the corporations maximize their ability to structure comparative advantages in the world
market, sourcing their inputs from the variety of producing regions incorporated into the "free" world market.

The big grain traders (in order of size: Cargill, Archer Daniels Midland
[ADM], Continental, Louis Dreyfuss, Bunge & Borne, Mitsui, and Feruzzi)
have not only exerted their oligopolistic power in the world market to
structure supplies and control grain prices, but they have exerted advisory
power in the GATT negotiations regarding the content of the rules regarding
agricultural liberalization. For example, the GATT agreement is now used
at their behest to challenge agricultural supply management boards on the
grounds that they interfere with the free trade of agricultural products on the
world market. This has been particularly effective in Canada, where supply-
management agencies emerged during this century to protect farmers from
corporate food processors, only to be challenged by Cargill Canada. [14] Companies like Cargill have supported the NAFTA and GATT to institutionalize

a trade regime outlawing such "distortions" to global markets, despite sustained national and international protests by farmer organizations.

The corporate assault on national regulatory policies is both a trading as well as a production strategy. Companies are looking either to capture new markets through direct purchasing of crops and processed food, or to directly organize agricultural production. New forms of mass marketing of commodities produced under contract in multiple locations are emerging, especially in the global fruit and vegetable industry. The contractual relation integrates growers into an essentially industrial enterprise, in which hybrid seeds are combined with chemical inputs. The global coordination of multiple production sites, for a year-round supply of fresh produce, is achieved through information technologies. In Chile, now the largest supplier of off-season fruits and vegetables to Europe and North America, more than 50 percent of fruit exports are controlled by five TNCs. Not only do these "non-traditional" agro-exports reconfigure local agricultural landscapes, but also they affect agricultural labor—roughly two-thirds of the Mexican and Chilean agricultural labor forces depend on insecure, low wage employment. In Mexico, "workers on commercial farms are generally paid piece rates, are not entitled even to minimal social welfare protection such as sickness and maternity benefits and have no basic trade union rights."[15]

Capture of new markets also depends on liberalization, and is often achieved by purchasing existing enterprises, if only to capitalize on the brand name familiar to local populations. Thus corporations from the United States (Sara Lee/Douwe Egbert, Coca-Cola) and Europe (Nestlé, Unilever, Feruzzi, and Montedison) have made significant inroads into Hungary's food processing sector. Meanwhile the Thai-based Charoen Phokp (CP) has extended its feed, livestock, aquaculture and fast food empire from Southeast Asia into China, where CP, as the largest foreign agribusiness, aims to "put a chicken in every wok."[16]

Geopolitical relations figure in corporate market strategies too. Thus, firms like Nestlé Brazil use Brazil as a base from which to supply South America with biscuits. Meanwhile in Mexico, the food industry grew at an average annual rate in excess of all manufacturing through the 1980s. Moreover, growth in food processing was overwhelmingly concentrated in export production, growing faster than overall agricultural trade. Mexican economic liberalization offers new opportunities for foreign investors, often in joint ventures with Mexican capital, or with other foreign capitals. An example is the Trasgo group, a vertically integrated poultry operation, which combines Mexican, U.S. and Japanese capital and targets Japanese consumers. Del Monte, a vigorous supporter of the North American Free Trade Association (NAFTA), is currently experimenting with large scale commercial production of tomatoes via land companies managing the *ejido* lands.

Under increasingly liberalized conditions, companies from the United States (e.g., Bird's Eye, Green Giant, Pepsico, General Foods, Kellogg's, Campbell's, Kraft), Japan (e.g., Mitsui, Mitsubishi, C. Itoh, Sumitomo), and Europe (Unilever, Nestlé) have increased their rate of investment in food production and processing operations in Mexico, coinciding with changes in foreign investment regulations allowing 100 percent ownership. Presaging the 1990s, the Mexican Foreign Secretary proclaimed: "Mexico is one of the newer trading powers of the world that has helped to maintain the pace for bringing about an ambitious reform of the world trading system."[17]

THE WORLD FOOD ECONOMY IN A WTO REGIME

The endpoint of the Uruguay Round was the creation in 1994 of the World Trade Organization, in order to institutionalize freedom of trade, enterprise and property rights on a world scale. A WTO regime is not just a device for promoting the global circulation of commodities. It is also a new supra-national political form. It has a distinctive constitutional focus in enforcing rules regarding commodity circuits and national and sub-national regulations. Arguably, it will operate as an enforcement mechanism of market rules for the globally dominant states and corporations. Pressures to deregulate Northern farm sectors and to expand Southern agro-exporting involve a universal challenge to national economic organization (and institutions) by transnational firms. Global access by TNCs allows them to exploit the asymmetry between North and South, undercutting Northern entitlement structures and their institutional supports by optimizing global sourcing strategies.

The WTO is not only an agent of trade liberalization. It is also a tribunal for enforcing corporate rights to manage consumption. On the horizon is an intensification of agrochemical-corporate domination of world food production by six conglomerates involved in genetically engineered food (Monsanto, Novartis, AgroEvo, Dupont, Zeneca and Dow).[18] Their claim that there are now 60 million acres of genetically engineered crops, portends a controversial future. The companies argue that these new biotechnologies reduce the use of pesticides, and promise an end to world hunger. Critics dispute these claims, arguing also that these technologies will discriminate against small farmers, threaten public health and narrow available food choices. In this context, where agriculture broadly construed (farming, the farm-input and processing industries, and so on) still constitutes a large share of the global economy, it is not surprising to find lobbying to revise world food safety standards in favor of genetically-engineered foods, food disparagement laws gaining ground in the United States (witness the 1997 suit against Oprah Winfrey by the cattlemen for her allegedly disparaging remarks about hamburger), and global public relations firms structuring debate in favor of genetic engineering. The WTO is being deployed to challenge governments that oppose genetically engineered crops. For example, in September 1997 the WTO ruled against the EU's ban on imported beef and milk from cattle treated with one of Monsanto's recombinant growth hormones, Posilac.[19]

Behind the apparent multilateralism of the WTO stands the attempt to institutionalize rules of a neoliberal world order to match (and deepen) the corporate-led economic integration underway. This requires a formal codification of inter-state trade relations, much as we have seen occurring in the proliferation of regional free trade agreements. Free trade agreements like NAFTA mirror the asymmetry of the WTO regime. For example, quotas on duty free U.S. corn, wheat and rice imports into Mexico are being lowered in stages. In Mexico, 2.5 million households engage in rainfed maize production, with a productivity of two-to-three tons per hectare compared with seven-to-eight tons per hectare in the American mid-West. With an estimate of a 200 percent rise in corn imports under NAFTA's full implementation by 2008, it is expected that more than two-thirds of Mexican corn production will not survive the competition.[20]

A more far-reaching, substantive, power is anticipated in the negotiation over the terms of the WTO. In particular, the current dispute over the reach of the WTO regarding investment concerns the institutionalization of a global property regime. Through the TRIPS protocol, trade-related intellectual property rights of foreign investors have been strengthened by the possibility of patenting a variety of products and processes. Global corporations are empowered by this protocol, for example, to patent genetic materials such as seed germplasm, potentially endangering the rights of farmers to plant their crops on the grounds of patent infringement. This is an extraordinary form of expropriation of genetic resources developed by peasants, forest dwellers and local communities over centuries of cultural experimentation. Such biopiracy, or gene theft, has become a focal point of grass-roots resistance to the WTO regime. And resistance certainly quickened (and, arguably, was effective) when the so-called "terminator gene" was jointly patented by the USDA and Delta and Pine Land, the world's largest cotton-seed company. This gene can switch off plants' ability to reproduce, transferring monopoly power to licensed seed and chemical companies by forcing farmers to purchase new seeds annually. While the USDA views the terminator gene a vehicle of market creation for seed companies in the "developing" world, where farmers save seed for the next year's planting, critics point out that this transgenic technology threatens to eliminate plant breeding by millions of small farmers, seriously reducing food security. [21]

The WTO is as yet only empowered to rule on investments that are "trade-related," through the trade-related investment measures (TRIMS) protocol. However, the European Commission (backed by the U.S. and Japan) has a draft proposal for a Multilateral Agreement on Investment (MAI) that would relax all restrictions on foreign investment in any member state, grant the legal right for foreigners to invest and operate competitively in all sectors of the economy, and grant TNCs the same rights as domestic firms in signatory states.

Although stalled by considerable national and international resistance in the Spring of 1998, if implemented, the MAI (or a similar provision under consideration in the IMF) would seek to render domestic regulations transparent to investors and preclude restrictions on capital transfer across national borders. It would also restrict the right of governments to use investment policy towards social and environmental ends, and impose performance requirements on foreign investment. The draft code included proposals to institutionalize rights of corporations (and financiers) as investors, with a legal status equivalent to that of nation states, except that governments are not granted rights to sue such investors for damages on behalf of their citizens.

CONCLUSION

Agricultural liberalization is deeply symbolic of the attempt to legitimize world-economic integration, precisely because of agriculture's historic identification with place and nation. While greater integration transforms all states through economic liberalization, it also reinforces global power relations—in this case the relations of agribusiness imperialism. That is, what are presented as universal trade rules (to which states individually commit) really serve to reinforce *extant* geo-political and corporate interests.

Trade and investment liberalization restructures member states by privileging global circuits of money and commodities, and subordinating social policies to a global corporate regime that privileges efficiency over equity. The formalization of a global corporate regime is anticipated in the WTO's system of rules, which would use states as the vehicles of universal adherence to this regime at the expense of national political debate and powers. This is not to say that governments do not regulate and manage, but they do so increasingly within the framework of binding multilateral agreements, many of which privilege transnational corporate actors rather than national citizens and communities. When governments sign on to the WTO as member states, they agree to a package of rules and regulations that increasingly remove trade and investment decisions, and their social impacts, from citizen scrutiny and control. In effect, property rights displace citizen rights.

Within global agriculture, the institutionally driven process of liberalization undermines the ability of weaker, food importing states to protect local farmers, and transforms food into a new frontier of commodification. Global regulatory agencies like the WTO threaten to entrench (Northern) agribusiness power at the expense of farmers across the world, intensify the de-stabilization of rural communities and further compromise local food security. How far this process will go remains unresolved, especially as citizens and workers and farmers and peasants and indigenous movements are sensing that globalization is not so much a foregone conclusion as a political project delivering highly selective benefits to small fractions of the world's population.

NOTES

1. Pacific Asia accounted for 45 percent of U.S. export growth from 1991–1997. But recently, in the wake of the Asian financial crisis, short-term imports have declined. Crisis management, however, has enacted trade reforms that will boost American food exports in the longer-term. Meanwhile, the USDA has offered $2.1 billion in export credits to South Korea, Thailand, Malaysia, Indonesia and the Philippines to sustain American competition with Australian farm products. Martha Groves, "Asia's Woes Taking a Bite Out of U.S. Food Exports. Short-term drop-off in demand would be offest by reforms stemming from crisis," *Los Angeles Times*, 7 March 1998.

2. Kevin Watkins, "Free Trade and Farm Fallacies: From the Uruguay Round to the World Food Summit," *The Ecologist*, 26, 6 (1996), 244–255.

3. Philip McMichael, *Development and Social Change: A Global Perspective* (Thousand Oaks: Pine Forge Press, 2000).

4. See Sidney Mintz, *Sweetness and Power: The Place of Sugar in Modern History* (Harmondsworth: Penguin, 1986); and Harriet Friedmann and Philip McMichael, "Agriculture and the state system: the rise and decline of national agricultures: 1870 to the present," *Sociologia Ruralis* 29 (1989), 93–117.

5. Harriet Friedmann, "The political economy of food: the rise and fall of the postwar international food order," *American Journal of Sociology* 88S (1982), 248–286; Dan Morgan, *Merchants of Grain*, (New York: Viking, 1979).

6. Quoted in Susan George, *How the Other Half Dies. The Real Reasons for World Hunger*, (Montclair, NJ: Allenheld, Osman and Co., 1977), 171–172.

7. Alain Revel and Christophe Riboud, *American Green Power*, (Baltimore: The Johns Hopkins University Press, 1986).

8. The Cairns Group comprises Argentina, Australia, Brazil, Canada, Chile, Colombia, Fiji, Hungary, Indonesia, Malaysia, the Philippines, New Zealand, Thailand, and Uruguay.

9. Al Krebs, "Corporate agribusiness: seeking colonial status for U.S. farmers,"*Multinational Monitor*, July–August (1988), 19–21.

10. G. Ames, "U.S.–EC Agricultural Policies and GATT Negotiations," *Agribusiness*, 6, 4 (1990), 283–95.

11. Karen Lehman and Al Krebs, "Control of the World's Food Supply," in *The Case Against the Global Economy, and For a Turn Toward the Local*, eds., Jerry Mander and Edward Goldsmith (San Francisco: Sierra Club Books, 1996), 122–130.

12. Ibid; Barnaby J. Feder, "Cultivating ConAgra," *The New York Times*, 30 October (1997), D1, 1.

13. Brewster Kneen, *Invisible Giant: Cargill and Its Transnational Strategies* (London: Pluto Press, 1995), 10.

14. Ibid.

15. Watkins, "Free Trade and Farm Fallacies," 251.

16. Sarah Sexton, "Transnational Corporations and Food," *The Ecologist* , 26, 6 (1996): 257–8; Edward A. Gargan, "An Asian Giant Spreads Roots," *The New York Times* November 14 (1995), D1, D4.

17. K. Schwedel and S. Haley, "Foreign Investment in the Mexican Food System," *Business Mexico*, special edition (1992), 49; L.T. Kuenzler, "Foreign Investment Opportunities in the Mexican Agricultural Sector," *Business Mexico*, special edition (1991), 47.

18. A parallel trend is "food chain clustering," whereby these biotech firms form joint ventures with agribusiness firms, allowing the firms with transgenic interests access to production. As Heffernan observes: " . . . the Cargill/Monsanto cluster is now in the process of obtaining control of the "terminator gene" . . . . No longer will Monsanto have to depend on access to farmers' fields for collection of tissue samples to make sure farmers do not keep any seed from one year's crop to plant the following year." William Heffernan, with Mary Hendrickson and Robert Gronski, "Consolidation in the Food and Agricultural System," Report to the National Farmers Union, www.nfu.org/whstudy.html, February 5, 1999.

19. John Vidal and Mark Milner, "A $400bn Gamble with World's Food," *Manchester Guardian Weekly*, 21 December 1997, 1; George Monbiot, John Harvey, Mark Milner and John Vidal, "How Monsanto Reaps a Rich Harvest," *Manchester Guardian Weekly*, 21 December 1997, 19.

20. Kevin Watkins, "Free Trade and Farm Fallacies," 251.

21. John Vidal, "Mr Terminator ploughs in," *The Guardian*, 15 April, 1998, 4–5.

Chapter Eight

THE GREAT GLOBAL ENCLOSURE OF OUR TIMES: PEASANTS AND THE AGRARIAN QUESTION AT THE END OF THE TWENTIETH CENTURY

FARSHAD ARAGHI

"You take my life
When you do take the means whereby I live."
Shakespeare, The Merchant of Venice, Act 4, Scene 1

THE EMPTYING OF THE WORLD'S COUNTRYSIDE

Over the past five decades, a massive number of the world's people have been dispossessed, uprooted and displaced, "the means whereby they lived" having been taken in the name of development, modernization, industrialization, growth, globalization, progress, and profit. During this time, an enormous number of people who were involved in agriculture with direct access to the production of their means of subsistence were expropriated and displaced, creating huge urban masses of superfluous people. Between 1950 and 1990, the share of labor force in agriculture declined by 33 percent in the world and fell by 40 percent in the Third World. At the same time, world urbanization has proceeded on an unprecedented scale. In 1800, 98 percent of the world population was rural. By 1950, still 70 percent of the total world population, and 82 percent of the Third World population, lived in rural areas. But since 1950, and particularly since the 1970s, the proportion of the world's rural population as a percentage of total population has declined dramatically. Today 55 percent of the world population (27 percent in Latin America and the Caribbean, 45 percent in Middle East and North Africa, and 25 percent in the more developed regions) lives in rural areas.

As recently as 1950, the New York metropolitan area was the world's only megacity (with ten million or more inhabitants). In 1995, there were fourteen megacities in the world, ten of which were in the Third World. Between 1950 and 1995, the number of cities with a population of more than one million increased by more than 252 percent in the world and by 447 percent in the Third World. In 1950, 41 percent of the cities with a population of more than one million were located in the Third World. In 1995, more than 63 percent of such cities were in the Third World.[1]

In part, the staggering increase in the Third World's urban population is due to natural increase (the excess of births over deaths). In much larger measure, however, it is caused by a structural shift of people from rural to urban places of residence through migration. Globally, every year, twenty million to thirty million of the world's poor leave their villages for the cities of the Third World. For reasons that I will discuss later, global restructuring over the past two decades has led to the elimination of nonmarket access to the means of livelihood for millions of people; the share of the world population that relies on agriculture for food and livelihood has declined from 50 percent to 45 percent in just fifteen years. In China alone, eighty million peasants have migrated to the cities seeking employment—usually as construction workers, factory workers, or casual laborers—over the past several years, despite the Chinese state's attempt to manage this massive internal exodus through the development of "rural industries."

Since the late nineteenth century the debate on the future of peasant agriculture has focused on whether or not peasant owners can survive the growth of agrarian capitalism.[2] In this chapter, I propose an alternative analysis of the "peasant question," linking it to the social realities of our times. My analysis is based on distinguishing between two forms of dispossession of the peasantry: (1) dispossession through differentiation and (2) dispossession through displacement.

Depeasantization through rural differentiation prevails in eras when the state (and the class alliances it represents) attempts to prevent the liberalization of land by protecting the home market from world market forces as capitalism penetrates the periphery. To the degree that nation-states succeed in negotiating a level of protection for their home markets and national agricultures from global competitive forces, dispossession of the peasantry takes the form of a gradual rural differentiation within the home market context. This was the case, for example, in the late nineteenth-century continental Europe. The very concept of national "rural differentiation"—in which agricultural populations undergo differentiation into capitalists and proletarians—is a product of this era. This notion of rural differentiation largely dominated peasant studies from the 1950s onward and remains highly influential today.

By contrast, state policies that promote, to use Polanyi's words, the "mobilization of agricultural land," lead to depeasantization through displacement. Rural depopulation as a result of massive active displacement of peasants from the countryside to the city, and their proletarianization within the urban environment is the consequence. Historical examples of depeasantization through displacement are enclosure movements in Tudor and Elizabethan England, in continental Europe between 1850 and 1870, and, as I will argue here, the current waves of rural dispossession in most of the Third World, beginning in the 1950s and accelerating since the 1980s under the neoliberal trade regime.

In this paper I make two main arguments: First, global restructuring and market liberalization have increasingly rendered obsolete the premises of late nineteenth and the early twentieth century notions of rural differentiation (or the lack thereof) in a national context. The most relevant concept for the analysis of peasant dispossession today is not national rural differentiation, but rather rural displacement on a world scale. Second, in the early decades of this century the "peasant question" was a political question having to do with the role of the rural masses in a democratic or socialist revolution. After the Second World War, the "peasant question" turned into a concern with Third World "underdevelopment." The postwar debate on the peasant question and rural differentiation inherited the early-twentieth-century national frame of reference, but it also applied the "lessons" of the original debate to an altogether different purpose, that of Third World national development. To understand the peasant question(s) of our times, we need to restore its earlier political-economic dimension. I will discuss some of the implications of these points in the concluding part of this chapter.

SOCIALISM, CAPITALISM, AND THE "PEASANT QUESTION"

By the early 1960s, the United States had developed its first *programmatic* solution to the "peasant question," which basically was Lenin's agrarian question turned on its head: How could the Third World peasantries be "*de*mobilized," and their movements be *de*linked from the urban nationalist movements? Borrowing from America's own past, and drawing on the early postwar experience in Japan, South Korea, and Taiwan, the U.S. solution was to promote as part of its overall strategy the creation of family-sized farm units—that is, petty private ownership—which would, in Cold War rhetoric, "preserve the dignity of the individual" and ensure "the future of democracy in the world." Thus, for example, between 1950 and 1980 the number of "family farms" in Latin America, which averaged about two hectares each, increased by 92 percent. These reforms redistributed modest amounts of land while leaving most of the available land, and usually the most productive, in the possession of large owners. In 1980, for example, about 80 percent of petty land-owners in Latin America occupied 20 percent of cultivated area, while 20 percent of large commercial holders occupied 80 percent of the land area.[3]

As the new peasantries were being created and subsidized, however, two counter-forces undermined them. First, the reforms promoted further penetration of commodity relations into the countryside, increasingly exposing small owners to market forces. Second, the postwar food regime (1945-1972) depressed world grain prices and encouraged Third World food import dependency.[4] In the Third World as a whole, the ratio of food imports to food exports increased from 50 percent in 1955-1960 to 80 percent in 1980. Food imports contradicted the political ideals of "balanced national development" and expanding petty capitalist ownership in the Third World countryside.

In sum, during the post-Second World War period, national "peasantization" through land redistribution, and global "*de*peasantization" through urban displacement, proceeded simultaneously. There were two important consequences of these contradictory processes. First, class differentiation in rural Third World occurred at a sluggish rate, as peasant dispossession through displacement predominated over dispossession through differentiation. The number of Third World rural migrants increased by 230 percent between 1950 and 1975, as compared to the previous twenty-five years (1925-1950). Second, as massive as peasant dispossession through displacement was in this period, its effects were mitigated by national protection of agriculture through state financing of inputs, price supports, and subsidies. As a result, this period witnessed a *relative*, rather than absolute, decline of peasant populations in most of the Third World. The process of *absolute* decline of Third World peasantries began with global restructuring and denationalization of Third World agriculture.

GLOBALISM AND THE PEASANT QUESTION

With the U.S. defeat in the Vietnam War, in part due to the successful mobilization of the peasantry by the National Liberation Front, the efficacy of curbing socialist nationalisms through military means came into question. Before leaving the Pentagon for the World Bank, U.S. Defense Secretary Robert McNamara's strategy for winning the Vietnam War involved an enormous escalation in the commitment of troops and means of military destruction. By 1968, however, the failure of this strategy had become clear. As World Bank president (1968-1980), McNamara's policy became one of "poverty alleviation" in the South through the promotion of "rural development" and massive lending in general.

World Bank programs of assistance to the rural poor were based on neoclassical assumptions that ignored structures of inequality. Indeed, these programs were essentially the precursor of the agro-industrial export model that is now being zealously applied to Third World agriculture. Encouraging the use of green revolution technologies, these rural assistance projects (1) made small holders further dependent on chemical and biological inputs and industrial technologies, and (2) promoted cash cropping (especially production of animal feeds and fresh fruits and vegetables) and livestock production for export, at the expense of basic food cropping. These rural development projects contributed to undermining subsistence agriculture and led to large-scale peasant dispossession and displacement around the world.

The World Bank's lending on development projects increased from $953 million in 1968 to $12.4 *billion* in 1981.[5] This set the tone for commercial bank lending to the South, which increased by an amazing 4,400 percent between 1972 and 1981. The results, as we now know, were the massive indebtedness of the South (whose debt now stands at $1.5 trillion) and the so-called "debt peonage" that has become one of the cornerstones of global restructuring.

Global restructuring has two interrelated components: (1) the reorganization of the world division of labor, under the auspices of global finance capital and its agencies, to the advantage of transnational corporations, and (2) a radical redistribution of wealth from the global poor to the global rich. The first component involves the construction of a truly global division of labor within which the South (while differentiating) is subordinated to the North, while the North is subordinated to a regime of transnational regulation. Politically, for the first time since the Second World War, this has led to a restructuring of the neocolonial relation between Third World nationalisms and the wealthy capitalist countries of the North, and to a growing unification of the ranks of the propertied classes of the South and the North around a neoliberal program of trade liberalization.

The second component of globalization involves the rollback of the gains that the world's peasants, working and (increasingly) middle classes achieved between 1945 and 1975. "Policy lending," whereby the heavily indebted states receive further loans on condition of implementing "adjustment reforms," has been one important means of constructing the new world. Thus, the two components of the Structural Adjustment Loans—denationalization measures and austerity measures—correspond to the two components of global restructuring outlined above.

Of particular importance to the world's peasantries, global restructuring has involved the process of dismantling the "agrarian welfare state" which functioned in the first twenty-five years after the Second World War to counter the spread of peasant-based socialist/nationalist movements. Institutionalizing agro-exporting regimes, deregulating land markets, and drastically cutting farm subsidies and price supports are measures that have forced millions of subsistence-level rural petty producers to compete with (heavily subsidized) transnational food corporations and highly capitalized producers in the industrial world. That is, labor intensive local agricultures are pitted against globally organized agro-industrial corporations. Hence, as world market forces have increasingly become felt in the formerly protected home markets, the producers who are rendered redundant are either dispossessed or displaced, or essentially become part of what we may call "the reserve army of migrant labor."

To understand the significance of this notion of a reserve army of migrant labor, we need to distinguish between ownership of the means of production and "ownership" of the means of subsistence.[6] A peasant may own some of the means of production (e.g., title to a small plot of land) but may have lost his or her nonmarket access to the means of subsistence. This is the case with respect to peasants who maintain their land ownership, but who have lost control of the labor process. What they produce, how they produce, and for whom they produce are decided by the agro-food corporations (or their subcontractors). Here production is carried out *by* the peasantry (who may own a portion of the means of production), but not *for* the peasantry. These are the small holders who have nonetheless lost their nonmarket access to production, and are thus not able to engage fully in subsistence agricultural production. Precisely for the same reason, they are *partially* or *potentially* mobile and comprise the *reserve army of migratory labor*. Becoming *fully* mobile (through dispossession and displacement), however, requires the loss of ownership of the means of production (through sale, abandonment, or expropriation).

The significance of the renewal of rural displacement in the context of globalization and debt peonage can be gauged by a recent estimate that two billion people will become redundant worldwide if the neoliberal trade regime is fully implemented.[7] My own calculations indicate that currently about 65 percent of the growth in the world's urban populations is now attributable to rural-to-urban migration. More important, comparing the two periods 1950-1975 and 1975 to the present, the rate of increase in the urban population due to rural out-migration has been accelerating since 1975 (in Latin America this rate accelerated by about 14 percent, in Asia by about 10 percent, and in Africa by about 5 percent over a period of twenty-five years). Similarly, my analysis of the latest available data indicates that between 1950 and 1975, in the Third World as a whole, the average annual rate of rural population growth increased by 20.6 percent.[8] Between 1975 and 1995, however, in a dramatic reversal, the average annual rate of rural population growth declined by 38 percent. These data are clearly consistent with the analysis of the two periods outlined above.

THE "PEASANT QUESTION" OF OUR TIMES

An alternative interpretation of the "peasant question" is needed that can transcend the limits of twentieth century discourse on the "fate" of the peasantry. I have argued that "the peasant question" (or "agrarian question") cannot be fully understood without analyzing its politics, history, and geography, nor without seeing it within the context of a complex interplay among economic, political, and ideological forces at the local and global levels. Linking the "peasant question" to the question of the unit of analysis (nationalism or globalism), I have distinguished between two forms of peasant dispossession: (1) dispossession through class differentiation, and (2) dispossession through displacement. These two processes of peasant dispossession essentially imply two different types of "peasant questions." One type of peasant question is that which was posed within an essentially developmentalist frame of reference (Kautsky's *The Agrarian Question,* Chayanov's *The Theory of Peasant Economy,* and, arguably, a particular reading of Lenin's *The Development of Capitalism in Russia*). The second is that posed in the context of addressing the politics of transition to capitalism or socialism (Marx's analysis of primitive accumulation, Engels's *The Peasant Question in France and Germany,* and arguably, a political reading of Lenin's *The Development of Capitalism in Russia* and his other work on this topic).

Are any of these versions of the peasant question still relevant today? To answer this question, I suggest that we (1) restore the original political intent behind the peasant question, which dealt, in modern terms, with "alliance-building" possibilities, and (2) disentangle it from the home-market context of the late nineteenth century. Hence, if, by asking the "peasant question," we mean to ask whether the peasantry of an "underdeveloped nation" will differentiate into a rural proletariat and bourgeoisie (leading to national "development") or whether peasants will always resist differentiation, then the question has increasingly become irrelevant. But if we are pose the "peasant question" in its political and substantive sense to address the problem of alliance building informed by an analysis of global class formation in the post-GATT era, then I contend that the peasant question is more relevant than ever. If this is the case, then, what is the "peasant question" of our times? The "peasant question" has been transformed and differentiated into seven interrelated questions:

(1) The housing/homeless question

Peasant dispossession through displacement at the global level has resulted in an increasing concentration of masses of people in the urban centers of the Third World. Between 1950 and 1990, the urban populations of most countries in Africa, Asia, and Latin America increased by 300 percent. During the same period, the number of Third World cities with populations of more than one million increased from 34 to 174. Today, close to a billion people do not have adequate shelter. One hundred million people have no shelter at all, and an increasing mass of people, mostly new arrivals from the countryside, live in urban slums and shantytowns. The majority of the population in many Third World cities live in squatter settlements. Squatter settlements account for 90 percent of the population in Yaounde and Addis Ababa; 60 percent in Bogota, Mexico City, and Accra; 50 percent in Dhaka and Lusaka; and more than 30 percent in Manila, Nairobi, Istanbul, and Delhi. With the expansion of urban slums, a second kind of displacement is taking place in Third World cities in order to free valuable real estate land for commercial and industrial needs. Euphemistically referred to as "urban population relocation" in World Bank jargon, forced urban displacement has become a painful reality for millions of slum dwellers. According to a World Bank discussion paper, 425,000 people were the victims of "bank-financed urban and infrastructure projects entailing involuntary resettlement" between 1981 and 1990.[10] Every year worldwide, ten million people die due to housing shortages and poor housing conditions.[11] "Housing hunger" is no less severe, if not more severe, than "land hunger" was for the "differentiating" peasantry in the early twentieth century. The struggles of the homeless for housing are an essential aspect of the "peasant question" of our times.

(2) The informal workers question

Currently, there are 700 million unemployed people worldwide, 600 million of whom live in absolute poverty. In Mexico, for example, more than 50 percent of the population is currently unemployed or underemployed. Peasant dispossession via displacement is linked with the rise of informal economies in the Third World. Increasingly the displaced and uprooted people have been forced to make their living through informal work—a variety of economic activities that are not regulated by the state and enjoy no protection, continuous employment, or job-related benefits. Conceived as a political project, global restructuring could be seen as a process of dismantling the postwar wage-labor regime through *maquiladorization*, casualization of work, subcontracting and modern putting-out systems, feminization of cheap labor, and employment of child, bonded, and sweatshop labor.[12] The dismantling of the formal, urban (and relatively protected) wage-labor regime has been made possible by the existence of a massive and a global reserve army of migratory labor. One of the emerging peasant questions of our time thus is: what are the immediate demands of casual workers, and how could the spontaneous movements of casual workers be linked with urban/labor movements?

(3) The refugee/migrant question

The largest migration in world history is currently taking place. Unemployment, poverty, and overurbanization are driving millions of people out of their home countries. Between 1965 and 1995, the number of international migrants worldwide increased by 38 percent, reaching 125 million people by the mid-1990s. Of these, the ILO estimates that at least 42 million are "guest workers," a source of cheap, unskilled and semiskilled labor in the immigrant countries.[13] Legal labor migration accounts for only 25 percent of all Third World migrants. Between 1990 and 1995, international migration accounted for 45 percent of the population growth in the First World, with refugees now accounting for more than 30 percent of the total annual immigration of foreigners to Europe and America. Worldwide, there are 19 million refugees.[14]

(4) The "identity" question

Here I refer to a particular aspect of what Gayatri Spivak has called "identitarianism." With a mass of global working class people living a migratory life in "alien" (national or international) cultures and political contexts, the politics of essentialist identity formation (that is, "identitarianism") finds increasing importance. I have pointed out elsewhere that the rise of Islamic fundamentalism in Iran (as well as other forms of such fundamentalism elsewhere) cannot be accounted for solely as a response to the global politics of suppression and social control.[15] It also had an existentialist basis in the drastically migratory aspect of class formation in Iran in the late 1960s and 1970s. While working class movements around the world have yet to overcome their fragmentation based on sexism, heterosexism, national identity, religiosity, and traditional racism, the international mobility of labor, within the context of capitalism, generates a fertile ground for the development of new forms of racism and religious fundamentalism. The alienation of metropolitan workers from "foreign," immigrant laborers as a result of competitive pressures and cultural/ideological frictions tends to intensify essentialist identity formation on the part of migratory workers; this validates the estrangement of native workers from "foreign laborers," and thus reinforces the overall pattern.[16]

(5) The question of global hunger

With the rapid, massive, and global incorporation of formerly self-sufficient agricultural peoples into market relations, and with millions of people having lost their nonmarket access to the production of their means of subsistence, hunger has assumed a uniquely global character. "Hunger amidst scarcity" has given way to "hunger amidst abundance." The contemporary food problem is rooted in the increasing global commodification of food, rather than being a consequence of a lack of sufficient food. As every student of introductory economics learns, exchange of commodities under market relations depends on the willingness and ability of the participants to buy and sell. Currently there is a global surplus of food, and we can safely assume that people who are hungry are willing to eat; it is therefore people's inability to purchase food as a market commodity and the loss of their direct access to the production of their means of subsistence (i.e., depeasantization) that explains the global character of hunger today.

The global commodification of food, in other words, is the natural counterpart of the global commercialization of agriculture. Since the 1980s, the World Bank and the IMF have sponsored the latter, and have pressured the Third World states through their lending ("adjustment") policies to shift agriculture from local subsistence to export crops. Thus, Brazil's and Thailand's most productive lands are now producing millions of tons of soybeans and cassava—cash crop animal feeds for use in intensive livestock production in the North. Similarly, at the behest of the World Bank, IMF, and USAID, Zimbabwe, a "structurally adjusted" country, reduced corn cultivation from 895,000 acres to 245,000 acres to grow high-grade tobacco. With IMF advice, Zimbabwe sold much of its grain reserve to obtain cash. As a result, a country that used to be the breadbasket of Africa now faces major famine.[17] The pursuit of structural adjustment policies, one author points out, "turned one of Africa's best health and education records into a virtual shambles" while paying out $50,000 an *hour* in gross *interest* payments between 1986 and 1991.[18] In Costa Rica, structural adjustment is encouraging the planting of flowers, melons, strawberries, and red peppers for export instead of growing rice, beans, and corn. Similarly, Kenya and Botswana, located in a continent whose name evokes images of emaciated children with swollen bellies, are major beef exporters to Europe. And Lesotho has become a major exporter of asparagus, while its people suffer from severe malnutrition. Since the 1980s, food consumption per person has been steadily declining for most Africans. The data produced by the joint effort of the World Health Organization and Food and Agriculture Organization show that an estimated 786 million Third World people were chronically undernourished in the 1990s.[19] As the food riots from Algeria to Jordan demonstrate, the food question is another dimension of the "peasant question" of our times.

(6) The "green question"

The global commercialization of agriculture and commodification of food have involved a progressive conversion of arable land to cattle pasture. In the past few decades, more than 25 percent of Central American forests have been cleared to develop pastures for grazing cattle. Over the past few decades Kenya has lost 50 percent of its forests and Thailand's forest cover has declined by 40 percent. Overcropping, overgrazing, deforestation, and desertification are devouring cropland at an alarming rate. Between 1950 and 1990, the amount of grainland in the world per person declined by 50 percent. The rise of an international cattle complex in response to increasing demand for meat by the world's more affluent classes and societies has resulted in land concentration and displacement of the world's peasant populations. As Jeremy Rifkin has pointed out: "While American consumers saved, on the average, close to a nickel on every hamburger imported from Central America, the cost to the native environment was overwhelming and irreversible. Each imported hamburger required the clearing of six square yards of jungle for pasture."[20]

Much of this environmental destruction in recent decades can be traced to international agencies' policies and lending practices. Bruce Rich has documented not only the serious social and environmental consequences of the World Bank lending policies, which mostly affect the masses of poor and powerless people, but also the growing social movements of the same people and their advocates who have created, as the World Bank's Vice-President for external relations put it in 1986, the "most important image problem" for the World Bank.[21] A leaked internal World Bank report indicated that in order to make way for various World Bank projects in the South four million people were to be forced off their lands by 1996. Dam projects, most of which are justified at least in part in terms of meeting the water and electrical power needs of intensive farming and growing urban populations, account for the bulk of this forced relocation. The "greening" of the World Bank has taken place after years of protest by millions of people who, as Chico Mendez put it, "became environmentalists without even knowing the word."[22] As the rise of international grass-roots environmental movements demonstrates, the green question has become an aspect of the "peasant question" of our era.

(7) The indigenous/landless question

Worldwide, an estimated one billion rural people (180 million households) are landless or near-landless. In Central America as a whole, 94 percent of all farms use only 9 percent of the farmland. In Guatemala an estimated 1.2 million hectares of land owned by large owners lie idle, either for speculative purposes or because cash crop prices are too low to justify cultivation. In Costa Rica, the 2,000 richest cattle owners occupy more than 50 percent of the nation's arable land, while 55 percent of all rural households are landless.[23]

In the Philippines, of the 10 million people in the agricultural rural force, 6.5 million are landless workers. In Brazil, 45 percent of the arable land is owned by the top 1 percent of landowners; the bottom 80 percent holds 13 percent of the land and there are five million landless families. In Mexico the dismantling of the *ejido* system (communal farm lands that included 70 percent of all Mexican farmers and 7 percent of Mexico's remaining forests), along with the implementation of NAFTA, will make an estimated one million farmers landless every year, with as many as 15 million peasants projected to abandon agriculture in the next two decades. Free trade agreements, globalization/denationalization of agricultures, and global competition are likely to increase the widespread destitution and bankruptcy among subsistence owners on the one hand, and reinforce land acquisition and concentration by the propertied classes on the other. Such class warfare waged from the above has already generated a vigorous response from the dispossessing peasantries, notably in Brazil (the Landless Rural Workers' Movement which has succeeded in repossessing 7.2 million hectares of land), Mexico (the Chiapas movement which has explicitly linked local poverty with the global free trade regime), and Guatemala (where squatters hold some 22 percent of farms). [24]

CONCLUSION

The eminent historian Eric Hobsbawm has remarked in his panoramic history of the twentieth century, *The Age of Extremes*, that of all the convulsive social changes of this century—two massive world wars, decolonization and the rise of the interstate system, the astounding spread of industrialization, the rise and fall of state-socialism, the extraordinary development of technology, the communications revolution, and so on—the most fundamental change has been the passing of peasant and rural life. [25] At the beginning of the century, the vast majority of the world's peoples were peasants or lived in rural areas. By the end of the century, peasant life was rapidly disappearing, and the world had become overwhelmingly urban.

The passing of peasant and rural life, however, does not mean that the world can be understood completely or accurately through a metropolitan lens. Though tens of millions of rural people experience dislocations of one sort of another each year, billions of rural people remain, albeit increasingly as migratory and casual/informal laborers, refugees, threatened indigenous peoples, homeless and landless, or as smallholder peasants holding on against the tide of the global commodification of food.

These dramatic and fundamental changes signal the fact that the form of the early twentieth century peasant or agrarian question has been transformed. However, the substance of the peasant or agrarian question, which was always a programmatic effort to link diverse manifestations of the ongoing progressive social movements, is still relevant today, precisely due to its world wide character.

NOTES

1. Calculated from data in United Nations, *World Urbanization Prospects: The 1996 Revision* (New York: United Nations, 1998), 20–29, 88–94, 104–110.
2. For a review and critique of this debate see Farshad Araghi, "Global Depeasantization: 1945–1995," *The Sociological Quarterly* 36 (Spring 1995), 337–368; Philip McMichael and Frederick Buttel, "New Directions in the Political Economy of Agriculture," *Sociological Perspectives* 33 (1990), 89–109.
3. Araghi, "Global Depeasantization: 1945–1995," 347.
4. Harriet Friedmann and Philip McMichael, "Agriculture and the State System: The Rise and Decline of National Agricultures: 1870 to Present," *Sociologia Ruralis* 29 (1989), 93–117.
5. This practice dovetailed with the rapidly increasing mass of international finance capital spurred by the breakdown of the Bretton Woods system.
6. In other words, while the loss of ownership of the means production is at the same time the loss of nonmarket access to means of subsistence, the reverse is not always the case. That is, the loss of nonmarket access to the means of subsistence does not necessarily require the loss of ownership of the means of production. This distinction will clarify some of the issues raised by R.C. Lewontin in chapter 5 of this book.
7. James Goldsmith, *The Trap* (New York: Carroll & Graf Publishers, 1994), 39.
8. United Nations, World Urbanization Prospects.
9. World Health Organization, "International Year of Shelter for the Homeless: Shelter and Health" WHO Features, No. 108 (June 1987), 1.
10. Calculated from data in Michael Cernea, "The Urban Environment and Population Relocation" World Bank Discussion Papers (Washington, D.C. :The World Bank, 1993), 25.
11. United Nations, "Habitat II: City Summit to Forge the Future of Human Settle-

ments in an Urbanizing World," *UN Chronicle* 33, No. 1 (September 1996), 40–48.

12. Philip McMichael, "The Global Crisis of Wage-labour" *Studies in Political Economy* 58 (Spring 1999), 11–40.

13. International Labor Organization, "As Migrant Ranks Swell, Temporary Guest Workers Increasingly Replace Immigrants," ILO Press Release, 18 April 1997.

14. United Nations, "Your Papers, Please: International Migration: What Prompts It? What Problems Arise?" *UN Chronicle* 34, No. 3, (1977), 15.

15. Farshad Araghi, "Land Reform Policies in Iran: Comment." *American Journal of Agricultural Economics* 74 (1989), 1046–1049.

16. Relatedly, the rise of identitarianism also questions the old "national question." In the era of "denationalization" and decomposition of formerly multiethnic societies (e.g., Yugoslavia) what may appear as the "national question" may in reality be an aspect of identitarianism. The national question as such, similar to the "peasant question" of the early twentieth century, has increasingly become irrelevant.

17. There are historical parallels, notably the Great Irish Potato Famine. While the immediate cause of crop failures was a blight, the dependence of the Irish peasants on the potato was a creation of British colonialism. We may here distinguish between the "visible colonialism" of the Irish case (where Britain controlled its colonies by the "visible hand" of the state) and the "invisible colonialism" of the late twentieth century (when the transnational corporations and their agencies control the weaker states by the "invisible hand" of the market and the debt regime).

18. Susan George and Fabrizio Sabelli, Faith and Credit: *The World Bank's Secular Empire* (Boulder: Westview Press, 1994), 61–67; Jim Naureckas, "The Somalia Intervention: Tragedy Made Simple" *Extra!* 26, No.2 (March 1993), 10–13.

19. World Health Organization, "Malnutrition and Diet-Related Death Rates Remain Rampant in Some Nations," *WHO Press* 20 (November 1992), 1–5.

20. Jeremy Rifkin, *Beyond Beef* (New York: Plume), 192.

21. Bruce Rich, *Mortgaging the Earth: The World Bank, Environmental Impoverishment, and the Crisis of Development* (Boston: Beacon Press, 1994), 160–181.

22. Marlise Simons, "Brazilian Who Fought to Protect Amazon Is Killed," *New York Times*, 24 December 1988, 1.

23. Nicholas Hildyard, "Too Many for What? The Social Generation of Food, Security, and Overpopulation,' *Ecologist* 26 (November/December 1996), 282–289.

24. Ibid, 285.

25. Eric Hobsbawm, *The Age of Extremes* (New York: Pantheon, 1994).

Chapter Nine

ORGANIZING U.S. FARM WORKERS:
A CONTINUOUS STRUGGLE

LINDA C. MAJKA AND THEO J. MAJKA

There have been two periods of intense union activism among U.S. farm workers, both of which were accompanied by considerable protest, public involvement, and eventual governmental support, at least at the state level. The first was the Depression era of the 1930s in which first the Communist Party and later the Congress of Industrial Organizations (CIO) took up the cause of farm workers. These activities, however, came to an abrupt conclusion as the expansion of jobs in urban areas in preparation for United States entry into the Second World War drained the enormous agricultural labor surplus and stimulated the importation of *braceros* (farm workers) from Mexico.

The second, and by far most successful, was the UFW-led farm worker movement that flourished in California from 1965 to around 1980. In California in 1975, after ten years of organizing, strikes, protest marches, consumer boycotts, inter-union rivalries, and expired union contracts, the California Agricultural Labor Relations Act (ALRA) was passed which gave farm workers the right to unionize. In 1979, the United Farm Workers (UFW) under its president Cesar Chavez won an important contract-renewal strike settlement in the lettuce and vegetable industry in California that significantly increased wages for field workers and stipulated union-management negotiations over mechanization. In addition, during the 1980s, after a boycott of Campbell-owned products, the Farm Labor Organizing Committee (FLOC) under its president Baldemar Velasquez signed three-party contracts, involving the union, large processors/food corporations, such as Campbell and Heinz, and many tomato and cucumber growers in Ohio and Michigan, which covered around 7000 workers. Farm labor organizations and advocacy groups appeared to be building momentum in other states during the 1970s and early 1980s.

During its upward trajectory, the UFW signed contracts with 80 percent of California's table grape growers and a sizable proportion of the state's lettuce and vegetable growers and wineries. In addition, its successful consumer boycotts stimulated the passage of the ALRA mentioned above. The California law filled a legal gap in a major state that had been caused by the lack of NLRA rights and stipulated guidelines for union-recognition elections among field workers. It created the Agricultural Labor Relations Board (ALRB) to oversee elections and enforce the ALRA's guidelines. Through its organizing campaigns and the terms of its contracts, the UFW attempted to transform the status of agricultural labor by altering many of the conditions of work and employment that have characterized farm work in California and elsewhere for over a century. The union sought to eliminate the use of farm labor contractors (FLCs), reduce worker migrancy, and stabilize the farm labor force so that fewer new immigrants were necessary. In fact, the resolution of the 1979 lettuce and vegetable strike signified for many, including a number in the grower community, a significant step towards institutionalization of farm labor unionism in California.

In the early 1980s the UFW entered a defensive stage and began to decline. Internal UFW disputes resulted in the departure of key personnel, including many organizers and members of the legal staff. Also, a change in governors— from Democrat Jerry Brown to Republican George Deukmejian in 1983— resulted in a decline in enforcement of the ALRA and encouraged more intense grower resistance. The consequence was a plummeting of UFW influence and the number of workers under union contracts.[1] Progress has mostly stalled in the 1990s and many of the gains have been reversed. At the time of Chavez's death in March 1993, the UFW held only a handful of contracts covering about 5000 workers, down from over 60,000 workers covered by 120 contracts during the early 1980s. FLOC, while holding onto their Ohio and Michigan contracts, has yet to expand their base beyond the Upper Midwest. Both unions are currently (as of spring 2000) involved in major organizing drives, among strawberry workers in California (UFW) and migrant cucumber harvesters in North Carolina (FLOC). However, largely because of the circumstances described below, tangible results have been difficult to achieve.

Historically, there has been a close connection between rising wages and/or organizing campaigns and the influx of new immigrants which, in turn, led to reversals of progress.[2] New immigration is a major contributor to continued difficulty for renewed organizing in the fields. During the past two decades, the farm labor supply in much of the country has become increasingly composed of new or recent immigrants, primarily from Mexico. During this time, wages and conditions of agricultural work have declined significantly.

Changes in the composition and circumstances of agricultural labor have accentuated the status of farm workers as belonging to the proletarian class but not fully part of it, marginalized by immigrant and sometimes citizenship status as well as by very low wages, difficult working conditions, and uneven employment. In some ways, farm workers are similar to garment workers— both early in the twentieth century, and more recently as the latter occupation has once again become populated again by recent immigrants. However, unlike most occupations, agricultural labor has been further marginalized by minimal levels of unionization and continued exclusion from the protections of the National Labor Relations Act (NLRA). All of these characteristics serve to perpetuate farm workers as a "super-exploited" segment of the U.S. working class. Much of the driving force behind the patterns treated in this chapter is a search for profit maximization by increasing absolute surplus value.

THE HISTORICAL ROLE OF IMMIGRATION

The demand for a seasonal supply of low-wage labor for California's specialized, large-scale farms has been filled since the 1870s by a steady supply of immigrants. These migrant streams included, at various times, Chinese, Japanese, Asian Indians, Mexicans, and Filipinos, to mention the most numerous. It is no exaggeration to say that all these groups were economically exploited and racially oppressed. During the late nineteenth and early twentieth centuries, racial segregation excluded many immigrants, such as the Chinese, from skilled urban employment. Instead, immigrants settling in urban areas served as a reserve army of labor available for seasonal work in the fields at low wages. The harvest labor market maintained conditions of a chronic labor surplus, and sometimes placed groups of diverse ethnic backgrounds and languages in competition with each other for available jobs. Workers lived in deteriorated camps under the scrutiny of employers or their agents, and their low incomes and racial-ethnic status segregated them from alternative housing and services. If field workers attempted some form of coordinated resistance, their employers often joined into collective opposition in order to maintain an unorganized, union-free labor market. Growers and their supporters as well as local police frequently used violent tactics to curtail organizing and break strikes. Authorities sometimes used threats of deportation against noncitizens (particularly Mexicans), and some growers even manipulated inter-ethnic tensions and hostilities to prevent worker solidarity.

There have been three consequences arising from this succession of immigrants in agriculture. First, each stream of new immigrants looking for work created downward pressure on wages and sustained the wage gap between farm workers and those in urban jobs. Second, new immigrants undercut attempts at collective bargaining and, in fact, were often used to replace previous immigrants who were becoming organized. Third, acreage increased in labor-intensive crops because of the continued availability of low-wage labor, and mechanization of harvest and other activities was postponed.

Yet, as persistent and prominent as these patterns and strategies have been, it periodically appeared as if this system could not be sustained, and that it might even be on the verge of extinction. Sometimes, ethnic solidarity would facilitate successful collective bargaining in particular localities.

RECENT TRANSFORMATIONS OF THE AGRICULTURAL LABOR FORCE

Throughout the 1980s, economic difficulties, reforms and dislocations in Mexico, and political upheavals in Central America brought hundreds of thousands of new immigrants into the United States, especially California. Under the Carlos Salinas administration, the Mexican government adopted economic reforms that privatized a number of public enterprises and emphasized market forces in ways that resulted in the loss of tens of thousands of jobs from the economy. Agricultural modernization in Mexico reduced the need for farm work, made it more difficult for peasants to own land, and eroded the ability of small landowners to compete on the international market. Meanwhile, neoliberal reforms in 1992 increased the amount of land corporations could operate under "*ejidos*" (a state-protected form of communal land tenure) to as many as 2500 hectares (6000 acres), while peasant access to state credit and technical assistance declined dramatically.[3] These consequences of economic change undercut the incentives of rural Mexicans to remain in their villages, and reinforced migration as an important strategy for providing sufficient family income. These and other factors, combined with a population boom, difficulties in finding work in Mexico's cities, and the dislocations caused by NAFTA, insured that large numbers of people continually sought entry into the United States.

In California in particular, many new immigrant farm workers are not from the traditional "sending communities" in the six western states of Mexico centered around Guadalajara, but instead are from Mexico's three southwestern states. Most notable have been Mixtec Indian immigrants from Oaxaca and surrounding states, places that contain large concentrations of poverty and high rates of unemployment. Most Mixtecs are undocumented single males, and some speak very little Spanish. Mixtecs are on the bottom of the ethnic hierarchy in Mexico as well as in the United States, creating further divisions among the agricultural labor force.[4]

In some areas of the United States, a seemingly endless supply of low-wage immigrant labor has stimulated increased acreage devoted to labor-intensive agricultural production. For example, California's fruit and vegetable sector has expanded its harvested acreage by 41 percent since 1988, and fruit and vegetable production has doubled from 15 million to 30 million tons over the past twenty years. There is also a high rate of worker exodus from agriculture due to relatively poor compensation and working conditions as well as job instability. In addition, the volume of Mexican workers who have been recruited specifically for farm work in the United States by contractors or employers has increased during the last fifteen to twenty years. Despite the need for greater numbers of workers compared with two decades ago, during the 1990s there has been an even greater imbalance between the numbers of those looking for work and the jobs available in the chronically oversupplied agricultural labor market. In fact, many growers hire more workers per acre as a hedge against too many workers quitting, but this has also resulted in a reduction in the average time each worker is employed. Reduced work hours have contributed to a sharp drop in the average annual earnings of farm workers and resulted in an increase in the poverty rate among farm workers nationally from 50 to 61 percent between 1990 and 1994-95.[5] The increase of poverty among farm workers in California during the same years has been almost identical, from 48 in 1990-91 to 61 percent in 1994-97.[6]

Since 1988 the Department of Labor's National Agricultural Workers Survey (NAWS) project has carried out a series of interviews with randomly selected people employed in "seasonal agricultural services" (SAS) throughout the United States three times each year. The surveys— the best source of data on the changing circumstances of farm workers is the United States—have demonstrated that among agricultural workers in the United States, the number of foreign born, particularly Mexican born, has continued to surge with a steady flow of new immigrants. Both nationally and in California, the farm labor force has become increasingly composed of Latin American immigrants, particularly young Mexican men, including the steady influx of those who are undocumented.

Data from interviews during fiscal years 1994-95, the latest national data to be published, indicated that 69 percent of workers interviewed were foreign born, with 65 percent born in Mexico. Only 10 percent of workers were United States-born Hispanics, and another 18 percent were United States-born whites. (NAWS interviews during 1989-91 put the percentage of foreign-born at 60 percent, with Mexican-born accounting for 53 percent of the total SAS. Among first-year farm workers, a full 88 percent were foreign-born in 1989-91, giving further evidence of a labor force in transition.) In addition, of the farm workers who migrate to find work within the United States, 85 percent were foreign-born, almost all from Latin America. There is also a striking gender dimension of the farm worker population. The

1994-95 interviews indicated that the percentage of women in agriculture declined from 25 to 19 during the surveys period. Among the foreign-born, only about 13 percent were women.

Nationally, recent estimates of undocumented workers in agriculture range from 30 to 50 percent depending on the crop and region. The proportion of undocumented workers among those interviewed for the NAWS surveys climbed steadily and dramatically from 7 percent in 1989 to 37 percent in 1994-95. Among the 18 percent of farm workers who were employed in United States agriculture for the first time in 1994-95, a full 70 percent were undocumented.[7]

Data from California indicate similar trends, with even higher levels of recent immigrants and undocumented. NAWS interviews of California SAS workers during fiscal years 1995-97 showed that a full 95 percent were foreign born, with 53 percent residing in the United States less than 10 years. In addition, 42 percent of workers indicated they were undocumented.

The increasing proportion of Mexican-born workers is especially apparent in agricultural areas where farm work and similar occupations had been traditionally performed by African Americans and whites. This pattern has spread as far as the eastern seaboard—for example, to states like North Carolina, Virginia, Delaware, Maryland, Georgia, and South Carolina. In addition, Mexican-born workers are an increasingly proportion of the labor force in other occupations in rural areas, such as meatpacking in the Midwest, poultry processing in southern states and on the Delmarva Peninsula, seafood processing on the East Coast, and construction in California, the Southwest, and the South.

Farm worker wages remain very low. For 1989-91, the average annual personal income for SAS workers nationally was $6500.[8] In California, for 1994-97 the median annual personal income for crop workers was between $5000 and $7500, with 75 percent earning less than $10,000. The median annual income for undocumented workers was lower, between $2500 and $5000.

Nationally, both recently-legalized and undocumented farm workers have fewer employer-provided benefits than farm workers who are legal permanent residents or U.S. born. For agricultural workers given temporary visas under the terms of the 1986 Immigration Reform and Control Act (IRCA),

18 percent are provided medical insurance and 14 percent vacation pay. Only 5 percent of undocumented workers are provided medical insurance and 4 percent vacation pay. The comparable percentages for legal permanent residents are 30 percent and 20 percent, while for the U.S. born they are 32 percent and 27 percent.

THE LABOR CONTRACTOR SYSTEM

The farm labor contractor system, which arose in the nineteenth century in California, has historically reflected the emergent industrialization of agriculture, with its treatment of harvest labor as an input to be bought as cheaply as possible. The persistence of this system throughout the twentieth century reflects a further capture of agriculture by capital—large-scale growers gain more control over their labor force and sustain profits by delaying the economic and social progress of farm workers. Employer resistance to most forms of worker organizations means that the labor contractor system provides an important method of getting jobs and workers together for a migrant labor force. Until recent decades virtually all groups employed for harvest labor required some type of intermediary between the large-scale grower and individual worker. Contractors found their niche as entrepreneurs who collect fees from growers to supply workers as well as service fees from workers. The grower and the contractor set the wages, hours, and conditions of work for the farm laborers. The contractor stood in the place of the employer in all dealings with field workers: he or she paid the workers wages and received their grievances if any were tolerated.

The labor contractor system has created a self-perpetuating cycle. It operates in the employers' interest by keeping wages low and causes workers to be migrants in order to secure enough days of work to get a livelihood. As the migrant labor force has become more widely scattered, the agricultural employer has an even greater need for the services of a labor recruitment agent such as the contractor. Contractors primarily identify with the employer. As agents for the growers they are in business for themselves and commonly regard union organizers as troublemakers. The grower retains control over such aspects as the timing of work, job location, amount of production, and overseeing and general surveillance. The contractor is responsible for the supervision and discipline of the work crew. The crew leader arrangement creates an ambiguity in the employment relationship which, on the whole, functions to the advantage of growers. While the grower retains fundamental control over the labor process, the contractor is treated as the employer and is the most visible source of authority and responsibility to the workers. Grievances have no place to be voiced except to the contractor, but the conditions that generate grievances are usually matters that had been settled by prior agreement with the grower. Resolution of most complaints is thus out of the contractor's power.

A further advantage to agribusiness is that under the labor contractor system, the term "contract" has is essentially a euphemism. The agreements between grower and contractor do not necessarily take the form of a written contract. The bargain generally exists as a set of oral and tacit understandings. Even when the agreement is put into writing, both parties can take a nonlegal view of the document. Negotiations can be treated not so much as legally binding responsibilities as a set of "clear understandings" in which farm workers took no part.

From the point of view of the worker, contractors secure employment, carry out all dealings with the grower, collect the wages, pay individual workers, make a profit from selling them provisions and other necessities, and even make loans and keep their accounts. While representing workers to some degree with the employer, the contractor's livelihood depends on being able to secure an agreement with the grower. At times contractors agree not to intrude on each other's territory in order to prevent them from underbidding one another.

Historically, there have been many opportunities to further exploit farm workers in the labor contractor system. Contractors often retained sums paid by the grower as an end-of-harvest "bonus" and pocketed the shares of those workers who were unable to finish the harvest through illness or injury. Various means of profiteering arose because of the exclusion of some immigrants from the housing market, and the contractors typically had a monopoly over the supply of board in the labor camp, and food and drink in the fields. Contractors required overflow containers when field laborers were paid by volume and short-weighed the produce when payment was made by weight. By far the most costly fraud perpetrated by contractors was to disappear with the payroll or fail to pay earnings in full. Even if workers found the legal resources to sue the contractor, little restitution was gained from suing an individual who owned few productive assets.

The very structure of the labor contractor system has limited the types of worker demands that could be determined collectively. The system allows growers to claim that they did no hiring, and that FLCs are the actual employers. Because alternative sources of field workers are available to supplant organized workers, growers and contractors have little incentive to respond to any worker demands over issues basic to the work situation. Even during the most favorable periods for farm worker cohesiveness, the contractor system yielded only limited wage increases for specific jobs, and even then at the cost of protracted farm worker militancy.

The presence of the labor contractor system within a modern agro-industrial chain of production reflects the profoundly contradictory forces of material abundance combined with intense exploitation. Inequality and poverty are exacer-bated, and a whole array of social, environmental, and economic problems become intermingled. Under the labor contractor system, farm workers have endured low wages, pesticide dangers, deplorable living and working conditions, and little protection from racial discrimination.

Resistance by field workers to the conditions of their labor is as old as the contractor system itself, but only two recent farm worker unions, the UFW and FLOC, made sufficient gains in union recognition and agricultural labor agreements to challenge successfully the exploitative practices inherent in the labor contractor system. The struggle to humanize the conditions of work in agriculture has presupposed union organizing. The demand to eliminate the labor contractor in employment negotiations was basic to farm worker attempts to regain control over work and resist the pattern of low-wage labor and migrancy, of which the contractor was an integral part. In crops and regions where these unions had become established the labor contractor system eroded and began to disappear. However, as soon as unionization waned, FLCs became reestablished as the central means to supply workers for the agro-industrial system.

RESURGENCE OF THE FARM LABOR CONTRACT SYSTEM

Recent Mexican immigration has created a dramatic comeback by FLCs in California and elsewhere as the intermediaries who match workers with jobs.

A report published by the Urban Institute concluded that "FLCs are the major immigration story in U.S. agriculture in the 1990s."[9] Many growers today prefer contractors since this arrangement allows growers to avoid the paper work, and sometimes the legal liability, of complying with immigration laws and labor regulations, such as paying the minimum wage and adhering to the terms of the ALRA and IRCA. In addition, during periods of expanded oversupply of both workers and intermediaries, as has been the case for several decades, competition among FLCs is heightened and can reduce growers' production costs and transfer costs to workers. But contractors are more than employers: They are essentially private agents channeling new immigrants into the farm labor market, both in the United States in general and California in particular. FLCs in California typically command a crew of thirty to fifty workers, furnish their transportation to fields, and sometimes arrange for their housing and board as well as for other services. Naturally, new immigrants, particularly the undocumented, are those most in need of contractors' services. While it was the case that under most UFW contracts FLCs were prohibited, contractors still were prominent, since large portions of harvest operations in California's agriculture were never covered by UFW contracts. In addition, most contracts by rival unions, primarily the Teamsters, left intact the employer option of utilizing contractors. After the decline of unionization, FLCs rapidly proliferated in agricultural operations, showing up even where they had previously been absent. For example, Salinas Valley vegetable growers have increased their use of contractors, and contractors now dominate the supply of peak-season labor for fruits and vegetables in the San Joaquin Valley. The growing importance of FLCs accompanied the increased use of farm management companies as employment intermediaries, as well as reorganization of a number of unionized enterprises in which the company declared bankruptcy and then reconstituted themselves with a nonunion work force.

FLCs are now the single most important agricultural employer in California; they supply more than one-third of the 900,000 workers who have farm jobs at some time during the year, and over half of the 600,000 with seasonal farm jobs. The California share is considerably greater than the nationwide average of 11 percent of SAS workers who are employed by FLCs.[10] In California, the annual payrolls of FLCs have gone up steadily, from $160 million in 1978 to $540 million in 1990. FLCs are currently the major factor influencing the structure and functioning of the farm labor market.

The expanded usage of FLCs is important for several reasons. First, labor costs for growers are reduced considerably from those under union contracts. A study of compensation of workers under UFW contracts signed after 1976 showed that wages and fringe benefits increased while the number of contracts declined. Statewide, the hourly salary for workers classified as "general labor" under 108 UFW contracts was $3.38 in 1978. This increased to $6.20 in 1985, but the number of contracts was only twenty-eight. Fringe benefits consistently added another 15 to 18 percent.[11] However, during this period, farm worker wages in general fell precipitously. Estimates of their drop during the 1980s have typically ranged from 20 to 35 percent depending on the crop and geographical area, and this reduction has continued during the 1990s. Nationally, the NAWS report on the 1989-91 interviews showed that average hourly wages (in 1989 dollars) for farm workers hired by contractors were $4.92 compared to $5.14 for non-FLC employees.

Expanded use of contractors is important for a second reason. Compared to workers hired directly by individual growers, a greater proportion of those channeled into the fields by contractors are new immigrants, particularly undocumented ones. The results are predictable. Studies by agricultural economists indicate that workers employed by FLCs have lower earnings, less experience with the same grower, less consecutive employment with the same grower, fewer hours at work when employed, and more time without work than other farm workers in California. The increasing importance of FLCs has resulted in a downward pressure on wages, already lowered after union contracts expired. Benefits, such as health care, retirement pensions, disability plans, paid vacations, and sick leaves that were either instituted by the UFW or rival unions such as the Teamsters or by growers seeking to avoid unionization, are now far less common. Contractors also reduce the take-home pay of workers because they often charge more for housing, meals, and/or transportation than do growers when they directly hire workers and furnish these services.

CONCLUSION

Both high levels of immigration channeled directly into migrant agricultural labor and the accompanying farm labor contractor system create enormous difficulties for those attempting to improve wages and conditions for agricultural labor. FLCs, in particular, sustain poor employment conditions and stimulate high turnovers. But with continued high levels of immigration, FLCs and/or labor recruiters are one way to connect potential workers with jobs. In addition, new immigrants, generally more desperate and with fewer alternatives than established workers, are less likely to take the risks that supporting unionization often involves. Migratory employment patterns also mean that gains made via collective bargaining at one work site may only apply to a small portion of one's annual income. These factors make it particularly difficult for farm labor unions.

Historically, however, farm worker strikes and organizing attempts have also involved immigrants, particularly those who had been in the United States for a number of years. One may expect current immigrants to be similarly inclined when opportunities arise, but continued worker turnover and replacement by still newer immigrants do not facilitate acts of resistance. In California, nevertheless, the ALRA has established a mechanism for union certification elections, and the UFW has been slowly increasing its membership over the last four years by winning elections and signing contracts. Moreover, FLOC has demonstrated its staying power in the Upper Midwest, and its achievements include substantially curtailing the use of FLCs by growers under contract and the elimination of exploitative sharecropper arrangements.

Successful past efforts have also relied on considerable public support, since the structural position of agricultural labor by itself is comparatively weak. Public support was the basis for the successful UFW consumer boycotts of the 1960s and 1970s and FLOC's boycott of Campbell products during the 1980s. Unfortunately, institutionalization of positive changes has proven elusive, and similar kinds of public attention will most likely be needed again to reverse the patterns of the past two decades.

NOTES

1. Theo J. Majka and Linda C. Majka, "Decline of the farm labor movement in California: Organizational crisis and political change," *Critical Sociology* 19 (1993), 3–36; Patrick H. Mooney and Theo J. Majka, *Farmers' and Farm Workers' Movements: Social Protest in American Agriculture* (New York: Twayne Publishers, 1995).

2. Linda C. Majka and Theo J. Majka, *Farm Workers, Agribusiness, and the State* (Philadelphia: Temple University Press, 1982).

3. Alain de Janvry, Gustavo Gordillo, and Elisabeth Sadoulet, *Mexico's Second Agrarian Reform: Household and Community Response* (La Jolla, CA: Center for U.S.–Mexican Studies, University of California, San Diego, 1997).

4. Carol Zabin, Michael Kearney, Anna Garcia, David Runsten, and Carole Nagengast, *Mixtec Migrants in California Agriculture: A New Cycle of Poverty* (Davis: California Institute for Rural Studies, 1993).

5. Richard Mines, Susan Gabbard, and Anne Steirman, *A Profile of U.S. Farm Workers: Demographics, Household Composition, Income, and Use of Services* (Washington, D.C.: U.S. Department of Labor, Office of Program Economics, Research Report No. 6, April 1997).

6. Howard R. Rosenberg, Anne Steirman, Susan M. Gabbard, and Richard Mines. "Who Works on California Farms? Demographic and Employment Findings from the National Agricultural Workers Survey"(Washington, DC: U.S. Department of labor, Office of Program Economics, 1998).

7. Richard Mines, Susan Gabbard, and Anne Steirman, "A Profile of U.S. Farm Workers: Demographics, Household Composition, Income, and Use of Services." (Washington, D.C.: U.S. Department of Labor, Office of Program Economics, Research Report No. 6, April 1997).

8. Richard Mines, Richard, Susan Gabbard, and Ruth Samardick, *U.S. Farmworkers in the Post-IRCA Period* (Washington, D.C.: U.S. Department of Labor, Office of Program Economics, Research Report No. 4, March 1993).

9. Philip L. Martin, and J. Edward Taylor, *Merchants of Labor: Farm Labor Contractors and Immigration Reform* (Washington, D.C.: The Urban Institute, 1995).

10. Richard Mines, Susan Gabbard, and Jimmy Torres, "Findings from the National Agricultural Workers Survey (NAWS), 1989: A Demographic and Employment Profile of Perishable Crop Farm Workers"(Washington, D.C.: U.S. Department of Labor, Office of Program Economics, Research Report No. 2, November 1991).

11. Philip L. Martin, Daniel Egan, and Stephanie Luce, "The wages and fringe benefits of unionized California farmworkers: 1976–1987." Davis: Department of Agricultural Economics, University of California, 1988.

Chapter Ten

REBUILDING LOCAL FOOD SYSTEMS
FROM THE GRASSROOTS UP

ELIZABETH HENDERSON

The grassroots movement for a sustainable food and agriculture system has been gaining momentum over the past decade. From a scattering of isolated individuals practicing alternative farming methods and small, local organizations, sustainable agriculture is swelling into a significant social movement with a national network and an effective policy wing. Populist in spirit, with strong feelings for civil rights and social justice, and an underlying spirituality, this movement is not linked with any political party or religious sect. It is firmly grounded in every region in the country, encompassing organic and low-input farmers; food, farming, farmworker, community food security, and hunger organizations; animal rights activists; and environmental, consumer, and religious groups.

The restructuring of the world food system under corporate control since the Second World War has resulted in a crisis with environmental, economic, and social dimensions. The symptoms of the crisis include loss of farmland and farmers (and in the United States, especially minority farmers), impoverishment of rural economies and the decline of small towns, shrinking of the farmer's share of the food dollar, erosion of the soil, pollution of air and water with synthetic pesticides and farm run-off, the spread of monoculture and the correspondent decline of biodiversity—the litany of problems goes on and on. In the absence of a unified organizational response, a wide variety of individuals and groups have tackled different aspects of these problems and have proposed solutions.

Around the world, people have responded by resisting, nowhere so clearly or eloquently as the Zapatistas rallying for land and against Mexican participation in the North American Free Trade Agreement (NAFTA). In the United States, resistance to the corporate restructuring of the world food system has focused on protecting the family farm, saving the environment, and promoting food safety. These three strands come together in consumer desire for organic food. There has been new research aimed at helping family farms in their struggle to survive in often hostile environment, new efforts to rebuild rural communities, attempts at finding ways to reduce total reliance on the "free (global) market," and increased commitment to saving the genetic resources of the Third World from patenting by agribusiness. Yet, in focusing on single issues, many organizations have not always grasped the systemic nature of the problems they face or the need for an integrated analysis and multifaceted response. Worse yet, groups have been pitted against one another because they failed to see their shared interests. For example, some major environmental organizations joined with corporate interests to resist targeting price supports for small farmers in the deluded belief that it would be easier to control pollution from a few large farms. Failing to see that low prices for farm commodities were linked with the low wages paid to farmworkers, some small farmers have joined in attacks against better conditions for farmworkers. The history of the growth of the movement for a sustainable food and agriculture system is the complex story of how a growing number of these separate groups are discovering their interconnections and common interests.

The very decentralization and lack of hierarchical leadership that has impeded the convergence of this movement is, at the same time, the source of its great populist vitality and increasing strength. Like a vast jigsaw puzzle dropped in a dark closet, the pieces have had to discover one another and figure out how to fit together. Many of the pieces have joined in the National Campaign for Sustainable Agriculture. The Campaign has a broad definition of sustainable agriculture as a food and agriculture system that is economically viable, environmentally sound, socially just, and humane. Or, in the words of Wendell Berry, "an agriculture that does not deplete the land or the people." Berry has been one of the moving spirits in the movement, writing poems, novels, and essays from his farm in Kentucky. He articulates a fierce critique of the irresponsibility of the impersonal relations of the industrialized, corporate, global food system, while lifting up the homely values of steward-ship of the land and respect for the local people, their farms, businesses, and living web of interdependencies. (See *The Unsettling of America: Culture and Agriculture*, 1977, and *The Gift of Good Land, Further Essays*, 1981).

By the end of the lobbying effort directed at Congress in relation to the 1996 Farm Bill, over 500 groups were associated with the National Cam-paign. An ongoing task for the Campaign steering committee is to broaden the circle continually by reaching out to new groups, help heal wounds from old battles, and reveal deeper connections. This brief introduction can only give a taste of the vitality and diversity of the expanding network that makes up the movement for a sustainable food and agriculture system. The discussion below is arranged by the major goals the organizations are striving to achieve.

ORGANIZATIONS WITH DIRECT FARM IMPACT

The main goal of a number of organizations is to provide farmers with help using more environmentally sound practices, while managing their farms better in order to survive in the hostile economic system dominated by corporate agribusiness.

Fighting the Decline of the Family Farm: The Center for Rural Affairs

Founded in 1973, the Center for Rural Affairs (CRA) in Walthill, Nebraska, has taken the lead in creating effective local farm programs while spreading understanding of the realities of farm policy. The Center was formed by rural Nebraskans who were concerned about the decline of family farms and rural communities. Introducing the Center's Annual Report for 1997-1998, Chuck Hassebrook and Don Ralston write:

> We are at a critical juncture whereby people everywhere can choose to foster justice, opportunity and stewardship in rural America. The Center for Rural Affairs flatly rejects the "inevitable" decline of family farms and rural communities. The decline

we see around us is not inevitable. It is the result of decisions made by people, that can be reversed by people—with the right combination of community initiative, passion, citizen involvement, and perseverance. The Center for Rural Affairs is committed to this work...!

The Center provides technical assistance in replacing expensive off-farm inputs with renewable resources, such as solar dryers for grains and legume cover crops instead of nitrogen fertilizers. To save small-scale hog production for the family-sized farm, the Center has worked with farmers on using hoop houses, a cheap new technology for raising hogs, while heading up a regional attack on corporate hog production and a national attack on the monopolization of hog slaughter and marketing. To support the local farm economy, the Center sponsors the Rural Enterprise Assistance Project (REAP) which offers training and support to farmers and other rural residents who want to run small businesses. The Center's Beginning Farmer Sustainable Agriculture Project takes a comprehensive approach in helping beginning farmers get started while learning to farm in environmentally and socially sound ways.

While working with local initiatives, the Center takes an active role in state and federal policy advocacy and development. It is a founding member of the Midwest Sustainable Agriculture Working Group (MWSAWG), a coalition of farming and environmental organizations, and Program Director Chuck Hassebrook was one of the original co-chairs of the National Campaign for Sustainable Agriculture. The Center's monthly newsletter is probably the best single source for analysis of farming issues.[1]

The Struggle of Black Farmers:
The Federation of Southern Cooperatives/Land Assistance Fund

Community organizations and leaders who had been molded and forged in the Civil Rights Movement of the 1960s created the Federation of Southern Cooperatives to save and enhance the land resources owned by its primarily black membership. Currently, there are over seventy active cooperative member groups with over 20,000 member families in Mississippi, Alabama, Georgia, and South Carolina. The member cooperatives engage in agricultural production and marketing, community development credit unions, and consumer, worker, and housing issues.

The main objective of the Federation has been to help black landowners keep their land. Attorneys and over one hundred trained volunteers give legal support. Ongoing technical assistance helps farmers manage their farm businesses more effectively and move away from traditional crops to specialty vegetables, organic production, and livestock that are more suitable for making a living on small acreage. One of the farmer cooperatives in Georgia is developing a shared vegetable packing facility so that members can pool their produce and sell to bigger markets. A Mississippi co-op is facilitating direct marketing to black neighborhoods in Chicago.

The Federation has worked since the 1980s to create a "minority farmers rights bill" to assist family farmers of color across the country. In 1992, the Federation sponsored a "Caravan of Black and Native American Farmers" to Washington, D.C., which culminated in demonstrations at the Capitol and the U.S. Department of Agriculture (USDA). Advocacy by the Federation resulted in the inclusion of Section 2501 in the Farm Bill of 1990, which recognizes the problems of minority farmers and authorized $10 million for an outreach, education and technical assistance program for socially disadvantaged farmers. In 1997, the Federation helped organize a series of "Listening Sessions on Civil Rights" which brought hundreds of farmers to tell their stories of neglect and discrimination at the hands of USDA. Out of these hearings came the formation of a Civil Rights Action Team in the USDA to deal with the issues of agricultural credit and the backlog of civil rights complaints, and the formation of the Commission on Small Farms. Both the Federation and the National Campaign were well represented on this Commission. Its historic report, *A Time to Act*, (January, 1998), calls for the implementation of effective policies designed to protect small farmers' access to fair markets and for the redirection of existing federal funding programs skewed toward serving the interests of agribusiness.

Organic Farm Movement: Northeast Organic Farming Associations

The Natural Organic Farmers Association (later to become the Northeast Organic Farming Association, NOFA) was started in 1971, and brought together farmers, gardeners, and consumers of organic foods. Inspired by the writings and publications of J.I. and Robert Rodale, the Soil Association founded by Lady Balfour in England, and the writings on soil and health by

Sir Albert Howard, the people who joined NOFA wanted to eat healthy food grown on healthy soils. Because the agricultural universities and the extension services were busy with chemical agriculture, NOFA became a primary regional focus for hands-on learning through workshops, farm tours, demonstrations, and conferences. Farmers and gardeners taught one another, and shared what in another context might be considered trade secrets on nontoxic methods of cultivation and pest control. Branching out from a single organization in Vermont and New Hampshire, in the early 1980s, autonomous chapters formed in seven northeastern states. In Maine, a sister organization, the Maine Organic Farmers and Gardeners Association (MOFGA), holds sway. Although a few of the chapters have been able to hire staff, most NOFA activities depend on volunteers. An Interstate Council loosely coordinates the state chapters, publishes a quarterly newspaper, *The Natural Farmer*, and sponsors an annual summer conference and celebration of rural life.

By 1998, the northeast organic programs were certifying close to 750 farms in eight states. Never quick to turn to government agencies, the NOFAs were less than enthusiastic about the Organic Foods Production Act of 1990 that established the National Organic Program in the USDA. While recognizing the value of a consistent, nationally accepted definition of organic in the marketplace, most NOFA members consider the USDA a tool of conventional agribusiness and dread the bureaucratization of organic certification.

The growth of the market for organic foods over the last five years has brought an influx of imports from western states and points south of the border. To survive the competition, northeastern organic farmers have been turning more and more to direct sales through farmers markets, farm stands, and community supported agriculture projects (CSAs).

Forging a Farmer-Community Alliance: Community Supported Agriculture

Introduced to this country for the first time in 1985, the concept of CSA has been snatched up enthusiastically by organic farms, especially in the northeast.[2] In a CSA project, a group of consumers form a sort of cooperative with an individual farm or small group of farms. The members agree to share the risks of farming with the farmers. If the crop is abundant, the sharers get more food; if there is a crop failure, they get less. Unlike other fresh market vegetable sales, CSA sharers sign a contract to pay in advance, or in regular installments, for the entire season. The farmers develop a budget and divide their annual costs by the number of shares to arrive at the approximate price of a share. To include lower income members, many CSAs either charge on a sliding scale or invite more affluent members to contribute to a scholarship fund. Most CSAs contribute food to the emergency food supply. While no two CSAs are alike, most of them ask the members to help administer the project or join in the farm work, and most use either organic or biodynamic growing methods.

Farmers who have adopted CSA find that selling their food directly to people with whom they have a long-term relationship makes farming more satisfying. For some sharers, CSA is an economical way to get fresh, organic produce and support a local farm. For others, CSA encompasses both political and spiritual significance, as expressed by Josh Tenenbaum, a member of the Genesee Valley Organic CSA connected to my farm:

> Although there are many terrible things happening in the world—war, poverty, environmental degradation—even simple gestures, right here, today, can have much effect. When we dig our hands into the brown, damp soil, does not the entire earth tremble? We see that planting and weeding, building a community around sustainable agriculture is the most fundamental peace work, on so many different levels. By joining the CSA, we directly reduce the toxins normally used in food production, with the farmer, the soil and water healthier as a result. With the small amount of time most of us have, it is good to support an endeavor which embraces not only our families and communities, but the entire world.

GUARANTEEING ACCESS TO FOOD

The Battle over Food Inequality: Community Food Security Coalition

"Food security represents a community need, rather than an individual's plight," writes Andy Fisher, one of the founders of the Community Food Security Coalition. With Mark Winne of the Hartford Food System and Bob Gottlieb of the UCLA Department of Urban Planning, Fisher invited activists and academics working on food- and agriculture-related issues from around the country to form a network and advocate for legislation to help low-income communities become food secure. As they define it, community food security means "all persons in a community have access to culturally acceptable, nutritionally adequate food through local non-emergency sources at all times."

Working together with the National Campaign for Sustainable Agriculture, the CFS Coalition was able to pass the Community Food Security Act as part of the 1996 Farm Bill. The Coalition has focused on training and technical assistance for groups seeking funding under this legislation, while shaping its network into a national organization.

The work of the Hartford Food System (HFS), a nonprofit organization in Connecticut, is a model for the systemic approaches the Coalition encourages. Since 1978, HFS has worked to plan, develop and operate local solutions for the city of Hartford's food problems. To help save area farmland by improving the earnings of local farmers while increasing the supply of fresh, nutritious food for city people, HFS worked with Hartford city agencies and community organizations to establish the Downtown Farmers Market, the first farmers market in the state. The number of farmers markets in Connecticut has since swelled to forty-eight. To enable more low-income people to shop at these markets and increase sales from local farms, HFS developed the Connecticut Farmers Market Nutrition Program which annually provides over 50,000 low-income state residents with $396,000 in special vouchers which they can only spend to purchase fresh produce from area farmers markets. Since he helped initiate it in 1987 in Connecticut, Mark Winne has facilitated the spread of the Farmers Market Nutrition Program all over the country with funding from the USDA.

In 1994, HFS linked up with Holcomb Farm, a town-owned farm thirty minutes away in Granby, Connecticut, to establish a CSA. Half of the produce from the farm is sold as shares to suburban residents, while the other half goes to low-income community groups in Hartford. One of these groups brings teenagers to pick at the farm and then trains them to run farm stands where they sell their shares of the produce. HFS Program Director Elizabeth Wheeler is working with the public schools in Hartford on Project Farm Fresh Start to find ways to incorporate locally grown organic foods into the school lunch program. HFS has also helped bring new supermarkets to inner city neighborhoods, and initiated city- and statewide food policy councils to plan for greater food security.

Making Farmworkers into Farmers: The Rural Development Center

Training farmworkers to become independent farmers is the main focus of the Rural Development Center (RDC), founded by Jose Montenegro in 1985. Located on 112 acres of farmland in the Salinas Valley in California, the center provides training and education to low-income people to give them the skills and experience they need to run their own farms. Upon completion of a five-month course on agricultural production and farm management, participants can use RDC land, water, equipment, and continuing technical support for up to three years. Staff member Luis Sierra assists them in finding markets for their crops. María Inés Catalán was one of the first trainees to try organic production methods and, with Sierra's help, in 1997 started a CSA with thirty shares. Seventy to eighty families take part in RDC programs each year, and 84 percent of the graduates leave to become independent farmers.

RESEARCH FOR SUSTAINABILITY

Against the Commodification of Nature: The Land Institute

Located in the midst of the prairie in Salina, Kansas, the Land Institute is an independent research center for sustainable agriculture. Founded by Wes and Dana Jackson in the late 1970s, the Sunshine Farm Project of the Land Institute devotes itself to the development of agriculture based on renewable energy technologies. Through careful observation of the natural prairie and the selection of promising varieties, Wes Jackson and his colleagues seek to develop perennial grains so as to eliminate the need for the annual plowing and cultivation which open up the soil to erosion. Initially, regarded with great skepticism by the agricultural research establishment in the early years, Jackson's work is taken seriously today.

From his podium in the prairie, Jackson speaks out as one of the most respected intellectual leaders of the sustainable agriculture movement. In his essays and speeches, he enunciates a critique of reductionist science and the industrial mind, and calls for the rule of humility over technology. His constant theme is the inadequacy of the knowledge upon which science bases its decisions. A deeply spiritual man, Jackson upholds food as a cultural, rather than an industrial, product, and fulminates against "the commodification of nature." (See *New Roots for Agriculture*, 1980, and *Meeting the Expectations of the Land: Essays in Sustainable Agriculture and Stewardship*, 1984).

POLICY ADVOCACY AND ANALYSIS

Uniting Family Farms: The National Farmers Union

Representing over 300,000 farmers in 24 states, the National Farmers Union (NFU) is second in size only to the Farm Bureau. Like the Farm Bureau, the NFU puts a lot of energy into policy development and lobbying for its members in Washington. Unlike the Farm Bureau, however, the NFU stands clearly for the interests of the family farm and against the agribusiness multinationals. The NFU annually brings farmers to Washington to lobby against concentration in the food industry and such initiatives as NAFTA and GATT, and for a floor price and the Northeast dairy compact to raise milk prices to farmers, country-of-origin labeling, and a fair bargaining law that would help farmers negotiate better terms from corporate integrators like Tyson and Perdue.

Back in the countryside, the NFU has taken a lead in organizing a number of the "new wave" farmer cooperatives. Operational since 1993, the Dakota Growers Pasta Company in North Dakota has more than 1,000 member-growers from three states. This co-op provides jobs for 200 residents and represents cumulative investments valued at $51 million. The Mountain View Harvest Cooperative held its grand opening in 1997. Two-hundred-and-twenty Colorado wheat producers pooled $5 million in resources to purchase a bakery and a grain elevator. This year, the Wisconsin Farmers Union is launching a specialty cheese cooperative. Following a European model, the project will produce a wide variety of premium-priced cheeses.

Opposing GATT and NAFTA: The Institute for Agriculture and Trade Policy

Founded in 1986, the Institute for Agriculture and Trade Policy (IATP), more than any other organization, was responsible for alerting the agricultural community to the significance of GATT and NAFTA. According to Institute President Mark Ritchie, the progressive farm movement took the trade issue to a lot of other movements, including the environmental movement, the labor movement, consumers, and others. The Institute really helped catalyze and build a broader trade movement. Working with the NFU and other agricultural groups, the Institute initiated the Fair Trade Campaign, and produced a tireless barrage of information, which came very close to tipping the scales against the NAFTA.

Alongside its work as a resource center on trade policy, IATP's staff of eighteen coordinate a national "Farmer-led Watershed Protection" network, work on the follow-up activities of the Rio de Janeiro Earth Summit and the World Food Summit, and run a computer-based marketing program for sustainable farms. Their basic assumption, according to Ritchie, is that "if farmers can make a good living, they can farm sustainably and the community can thrive." IATP also operates a for-profit business that imports organic and small-producer grown coffee from Chiapas, Mexico, and Guatemala, in conjunction with the Rigoberta Menchu Foundation. Since the 1970s, Mark Ritchie has been one of the clearest voices analyzing the destructive agricultural policies of this country's public institutions. His little pamphlet, *The Loss of our Family Farms: Inevitable Results or Conscious Policies?* has opened many eyes to the role of corporate interest groups in decimating the farming population.

THE NATIONAL CAMPAIGN—FARM BILL STRUGGLE

To complement their concrete local organizing, most of the groups mentioned in this article are also involved in public policy. Their successful collaboration resulted in the passage of the Low Input Sustainable Agriculture Program (LISA) in 1985, and encouraged farming and environmental groups to cooperate more actively on federal farm policy. (The LISA Program was later renamed the Sustainable Agriculture Research and Education [SARE] Program.) Formed in 1987-88, the Midwest Sustainable Agriculture Working Group (MSAWG) set the pattern for the other regions. By the time that work was started in Congress on the 1996 Farm Bill, there were four regional and several state SAWGs. MSAWG is a network of thirty-five organizations established to create policy proposals for agricultural research and extension, commodity programs, marketing and rural development, and conservation and the environment. The members sign on to the policy proposals of their choice. Education on these proposals and lobbying for them is done by the member organizations; the network itself has no staff. A subset of twelve MSAWG member organizations willing to commit more dollars to direct policy work in Washington also formed the Sustainable Agriculture Coalition. They employ Fred Hoefner as their lobbyist in D.C. to represent the formal positions of the Coalition to Congress.

After the 1990 Farm Bill, members of MSAWG called upon organizations from other parts of the country to form a National Coordinating Council for Sustainable Agriculture. Hal Hamilton, a former dairy farmer and rural development organizer from Kentucky, joined Chuck Hassebrook as co-chair. The council took as its main task the coordination of a National Dialogue, a highly participatory process to create policy proposals for the 1996 Farm Bill. The Council invited appropriate organizations all over the country to submit proposals for discussion at grassroots meetings. These diverse gatherings of farmers, environmentalists, academics, and food system activists of all kinds reworked the proposals for a second, larger round of similar meetings. Representatives of each regional SAWG and many national groups came together in Washington to finalize the proposals and set priorities for a National Campaign for Sustainable Agriculture.[3] Participants voted according to how much work their organizations could be expected to put forth on each policy. The proposals for which the most work was pledged became the top priorities for the National Campaign. About equal weight was given to structure of agriculture issues, preserving and enhancing the family farm, rural development, local control and empowerment, and con-servation and the environment.

Despite the unfriendly climate in Congress, the campaign was successful during the 1996 Farm Bill negotiations in coordinating enough grassroots lobbying through telephone trees, action alerts, and organized group visits to preserve existing sustainable agriculture programs. These included SARE, the outreach program for socially disadvantaged farmers, the Farmers Market Nutrition Coupon Program, and the Alternative Technology Transfer for Rural Areas program (ATTRA). A surprising victory was the addition of the Community Food Security Act. The congressional rush to phase out all price supports to farmers swept aside the Campaign's attempt to capture the big money by transforming commodity payments into a system of green payments, similar to current experiments in Europe. However, elements of campaign proposals survived in the Fund for Rural America and the Conservation Farm Option. With the passage of the 1996 Farm Bill, the Campaign restructured for the long run as a national policy network committed to keeping up the pressure on Congress and the USDA at the level of both appropriations and close oversight of implementation.

CONCLUSION: TOWARD A WIDER MOVEMENT

From an initial focus on farm production, the movement's vision has broadened. Sustainable agriculture ripples out in ever-expanding circles from the soil of a single field to the whole farm, to the watershed and community around it, and to the economic relations and quality of life of everyone involved in the food system. The people in this movement see local control of food production as basic to sustainability as a whole and to the survival of democracy. A few of those involved feel so powerless that they turn their backs on broader issues and take refuge from the troubles around them by cultivating their own gardens. But many more see two possible pathways ahead. If people choose obedience to the commercial catechism and vote with their dollars for convenience in the supermarket, the bread on our tables will be manufactured from grains genetically engineered and patented by Monsanto, shipped by Cargill from wherever it is cheapest to grow, and sold to those of us who can afford it under a familiar label actually owned by Philip Morris, Archer Daniels Midland, or Mitsui-Cook. By this path, the multinationals will maximize their profits regardless of the immediate and ultimate costs to family farmers, low-income families, or the environment.

The movement for sustainable agriculture offers an alternative path. If enough people organize to take control of local resources, a local or regional food system becomes possible. This will be a system based on farms and gardens, of many sizes, growing food in the most ecologically sensitive way, compensating farmers and farmworkers with decent wages, respect, and safe working conditions, and distributing its benefits fairly so that everyone can enjoy fresh, nutritious, safe food regardless of their ability to pay. Seen in this context, food becomes political. Every direct purchase from a local farmer becomes an act of fair trade, and every square foot of home garden, every family-owned farm, and every value-adding cooperative becomes a small piece of liberated territory in the struggle for a just and sustainable society.

Although most on the left would find resonance in the second vision, they may think that the key tactics chosen by activists at the grassroots are insufficient to mount a systemic critique of corporate agriculture and liberal capitalist economics as a whole. By adding value to their products through cooperative efforts or on individual farms (producing pasta from wheat, cheese from milk, etc.) and by direct marketing to the public, farmers will in a sense have partially withdrawn from the current system and captured more of the value of their products. And by making direct connections between farmers and urban residents and through a variety of efforts, the poor will have better access to nutritious foods. Activists must help people confront immediate day-to-day problems in their lives. Yet a left analysis would question whether this pathway is really a solution to the problems or rather something that will produce only a minor irritant to corporate dominance of the food system. A complete transformation of the agriculture and food system, it might be argued, requires a complete transformation of the society. Certainly, any attempt to create a more humane, just, and ecologically rational society will have to embrace the struggle for sustainable agriculture.

—The Editors

NOTES

1. National Campaign for Sustainable Agriculture can be reached at P.O. Box 396, Pine Bush, N.Y. 12566, (914) 744-8448, FAX: (914) 744-8477; e-mail: Campaign@magiccarpet.com.
2. The NOFA-sponsored *CSA Farm Network* for 1997, funded by NE SARE, lists over 200 CSAs in the ten northeast states. *CSA Farm Network* is available from NOFA-NY, P.O. Box 21, South Butler, NY 13154, for $10, plus $2 postage. The Biodynamic Association (P.O. Box 550, Kimberton, PA 19442) maintains a national database of CSAs with over 600 listings nationwide. You can get the listing for your state by calling 1-800-516-7797.

Chapter Eleven

WANT AMID PLENTY: FROM HUNGER TO INEQUALITY

JANET POPPENDIECK

"Scouting has some unacceptables," the Executive Director of the Jersey Shore Council of the Boy Scouts of America told me, "and one of them is hunger."[1] We were talking in the entrance to the Ciba Geigy company cafeteria in Toms River, New Jersey, where several hundred Boy Scouts, their parents, grandparents, siblings, and neighbors were sorting and packing the 280,000 pounds of canned goods that the scouts of this Council had netted in their 1994 Scouting For Food drive. The food would be stored on the Ciba Geigy corporate campus, where downsizing had left a number of buildings empty, and redistri-buted to local food pantries to be passed along to the hungry. The scouting executive was one of several hundred people I interviewed as part of a study of charitable food programs—so called "emergency food" in the United States. In the years since the early 1980s, literally millions of Americans have been drawn into such projects: soup kitchens and food pantries on the front lines, and canned goods drives, food banks, and "food rescue" projects that supply them.

HUNGER HAS A "CURE"

What makes hunger in America unacceptable, to Boy Scouts and to the rest of us, is the extraordinary abundance produced by American agriculture. There is no shortage of food here, and everybody knows it. In fact, for much of this century, national agricultural policy has been preoccupied with surplus, and individual Americans have been preoccupied with avoiding, losing, or hiding the corporeal effects of overeating. Collectively, and for the most part individually, we have too much food, not too little. To make matters worse, we waste food in spectacular quantities. A study recently released by USDA estimates that between production and end use, more than a quarter of the food produced in the United States goes to waste, from fields planted but not harvested to the bread molding on top of my refrigerator or the lettuce wilting at the back of the vegetable bin. Farm waste, transport waste, processor waste, wholesaler waste, supermarket waste, institutional waste, household waste, plate waste; together in 1995 they totaled a startling 96 billion pounds, or 365 pounds—a pound a day—for every person in the nation.[2]

The connection between abundant production and food waste on the one hand, and hunger on the other, is not merely abstract and philosophical. Both public and private food assistance efforts in this country have been shaped by efforts to find acceptable outlets for food that would otherwise go to waste. These include the wheat surpluses stockpiled by Herbert Hoover's Federal Farm Board and belatedly given to the Red Cross for distribution to the unemployed, the martyred piglets of the New Deal agricultural adjustment (which led to the establishment of federal surplus commodity distribution), and the cheese that Ronald Reagan finally donated to the needy to quell the criticism of mounting storage costs. Accumulation of large supplies of food in public hands, especially in times of economic distress and privation, has repeatedly resulted in the creation of public programs to distribute the surplus to the hungry. And in the private sphere as well, a great deal of the food that supplies today's soup kitchens and food pantries is food that would otherwise end up as waste: corporate over-production or labeling errors donated to the food bank, farm and orchard extras gleaned by volunteers after the commercial harvest, and the vast quantities of leftovers generated by hospital, school, government and corporate cafeterias, and caterers and restaurants. All of this is food that is now rescued and recycled through the type of food recovery programs urged by Vice President Al Gore and Agriculture Secretary Dan Glickman at their 1997 National Summit on Food Recovery and Gleaning. "There is simply no excuse for hunger in the most agriculturally abundant country in the world," said Glickman, who urged a 33 percent increase in food recovery by the year 2000 that would enable social service agencies to feed an additional 450,000 Americans each day.[3] For Americans reared as members of the "clean plate club" and socialized to associate our own uneaten food with hunger in faraway places, such programs have enormous appeal. They provide a sort of moral relief from the discomfort that ensues when we are confronted with images of hunger in our midst, or when we are reminded of the excesses of consumption that characterize our culture. They offer what appear to be old-fashioned moral absolutes in a sea of shifting values and ethical uncertainties. Many of the volunteers I interviewed for my study told me that they felt that their work at the soup kitchen or food pantry was the one unequivocally good thing in their lives, the one point in the week in which they felt sure they were on the side of the angels. Furthermore, they perceive hunger as one problem that is solvable—precisely because of the abundant production—one problem about which they can do something concrete and meaningful. "Hunger has a cure," is the new slogan developed by the Ad Council for Second Harvest, the National Network of Foodbanks. It is not surprising, then, that hunger in America has demonstrated an enormous capacity to mobilize both public and private action. There are fourteen separate federal food assistance programs, numerous state and local programs, and thousands upon thousands of local, private charitable feeding projects which elicit millions of hours of volunteer time as well as enormous quantities of donated funds and food. In one random survey in the early 1990s, nearly four-fifths of respondents indicated that they, personally, had done something to alleviate hunger in their communities in the previous year.[4]

THE SEDUCTIONS OF HUNGER

Progressives have not been immune to the lure of hunger-as-the-problem. We have been drawn into the anti-hunger crusade for several reasons. First, hunger in America shows with great clarity the absurdity of our distribution system, of capitalism's approach to meeting basic human needs. Poor people routinely suffer for want of things that are produced in abundance in this country, things that gather dust in warehouses and inventories, but the bicycles and personal computers that people desire and could use are not perishable and hence are not rotting in front of their eyes in defiance of their bellies. The Great Depression of the 1930s, with its startling contrasts of agricultural surpluses and widespread hunger, made this terrible irony excruciatingly clear, and many people were able to perceive the underlying economic madness: "A breadline knee-deep in wheat," observed commentator James Crowther, "is surely the handiwork of foolish men."[5] Progressives are attracted to hunger as an issue because it reveals in so powerful a way the fundamental shortcomings of unbridled reliance on markets.

Second, progressives are drawn to hunger as a cause by its emotional salience, its capacity to arouse sympathy and mobilize action. Hunger is, as George McGovern once pointed out, "the cutting edge of poverty," the form of privation that is at once the easiest to imagine, the most immediately painful, and the most far-reaching in its damaging consequences.[6] McGovern was writing in the aftermath of the dramatic rediscovery of hunger in America that occurred in the late 1960s when a Senate subcommittee, holding hearings on anti-poverty programs in Mississippi, encountered the harsh realities of economic and political deprivation in the form of empty cupboards and malnourished children in the Mississippi Delta. Hunger was in the news, and journalist Nick Kotz reports that a coalition of civil rights and anti-poverty activists made a conscious decision to keep it there. They perceived in hunger "the one problem to which the public might respond. They reasoned that 'hunger' made a higher moral claim than any of the other problems of poverty."[7] The anti-hunger movement—or "hunger lobby" that they initiated—was successful in enlisting Congressional support for a major expansion of food assistance and the gradual creation of a food entitlement through food stamps, the closest thing to a guaranteed income that we have ever had in this country.

The broad appeal of the hunger issue and its ability to evoke action are also visible in the more recent proliferation of emergency food programs. "I think the reason . . . that you get the whole spectrum of people involved in this is because it's something that is real basic for people to relate to. You know, you're busy, you skip lunch, you feel hungry. On certain levels, everyone has experienced feeling hungry at some point in the day or the year," explained Ellen Teller, an attorney with the Food Research and Action Center whose work brings her into frequent contact with both emergency food providers and anti-hunger policy advocates. The food program staff and volunteers I interviewed recognized the difference between their own, essentially voluntary and temporary hunger and hunger that is externally imposed and of unpredictable duration, but the reservoir of common human experience is there. Hunger is not exotic and hard to imagine; it stems from the failure to meet a basic and incontrovertible need that we all share.

Furthermore, the failure to eliminate hunger has enormous consequences. As the research on the link between nutrition and cognition mounts, the social costs of failing to ensure adequate nutrition for pregnant women and young children become starkly obvious. And this, too, contributes to the broad spectrum that Ellen Teller mentioned. There is something for everyone here—a prudent investment in human capital for those concerned about the productivity of the labor force of tomorrow, a prevention of suffering for the tender hearted, a unifying concern for would-be organizers, a blatant injustice for critics of our social structure. Many anti-hunger organizations with relatively sophisticated critiques of the structural roots of hunger in America have engaged with the "feeding movement," the soup kitchens and the food pantries, in the belief that, as the Bread for the World Institute once put it, "Hunger can be the 'door' through which people enter an introduction to larger problems of poverty, powerlessness, and distorted public values."[8] For those progressives seeking common ground with a wider range of American opinion, hunger is an attractive issue precisely because of the breadth of the political spectrum of people who are moved by it.

Third, progressives have been drawn into the hunger lobby by the utility of hunger as a means of resisting, or at least documenting the effects of, government cuts in entitlements. In the early 1980s, especially, when Ronald Reagan began his presidential assault on the nation's meager safety net of entitlement programs for the poor, progressives of all sorts pointed to the lengthening soup kitchen lines as evidence that the cuts in income supports, housing subsidies, food assistance, and a host of other public programs were cuts that neither the poor nor the society could afford. While Reagan and his team claimed that they were simply stripping away waste and fat from bloated programs, critics on the left kept track of mounting use of emergency food programs as a means of documenting the suffering caused by the erosion of the welfare state. The scenario is being replayed, this time amid an expanding economy, as soup kitchens and food pantries register the effects of "the end of welfare as we know it."

Finally, of course, progressives are drawn to the hunger issue by a sense of solidarity with those in need. Most of us became progressives in the first place because we cared about people and wanted a fairer society that would produce less suffering. Few of us can stomach an argument that says that we should leave the hungry to suffer without aid while we work for a more just future. "People don't eat in the long run," Franklin Roosevelt's relief czar Harry Hopkins is reported to have said; "they eat every day."[9] Many of the more activist and progressive people I interviewed in the course of my emergency food study articulated similar sentiments. A woman who worked in the early eighties helping churches and community groups in southern California set up soup kitchens and food pantries to cope with the fallout from the budget cuts in Washington recalled the dilemma as she had experienced it. "As far as I was concerned, the people in Washington had blood on their hands . . . but I wasn't going to stand by and watch people suffer just to make a political point." As one long-time left activist in Santa Cruz put it when questioned about her work as a member of the local food bank board, "There are numbers of people who are very compatible with my radical philosophy who also feel that foodbanking is very important, because the reality is that there are ever increasing homeless and poor, including working poor, who need to be fed . . . the need for food has increased and the resources for providing it haven't. And if there weren't foodbanks, I think a lot of people would starve."

It is easy to see why progressive people have been drawn into anti-hunger activity in large numbers, and why they have been attracted to the soup kitchens, food pantries, and food banks, despite misgivings about these private charitable projects. I, personally, have counted myself an anti-hunger activist since the nation rediscovered hunger in the late 1960s. Nevertheless, after three decades in the "hunger lobby," and nearly a decade of observing and interviewing in soup kitchens, food pantries, food banks, and food recovery projects, I would like to offer a caution about defining hunger as the central issue.

THE CASE AGAINST HUNGER

The very emotional response that makes hunger a good organizing issue, and the felt absurdity of such want amid massive waste, makes our society vulnerable to token solutions—solutions that simply link together complementary symptoms without disturbing the underlying structural problems. The New Deal surplus commodity distribution program, which laid the political and administrative groundwork for most subsequent federal food programs, purchased surplus agricultural commodities from impoverished farmers in danger of going on relief and distributed them to the unemployed already receiving public help. It responded to what Walter Lippmann once called the "sensational and the intolerable paradox of want in the midst of abundance," by using a portion of the surplus to help some of the needy, without fundamentally changing the basis for access to food.[10] As Norman Thomas put it in 1936, "We have not had a reorganization of production and a redistribution of income to end near starvation in the midst of potential plenty. If we do not have such obvious 'breadlines knee deep in wheat' as under the Hoover administration, it is because we have done more to reduce the wheat and systematize the giving of crusts than to end hunger."[11]

For the general public, however, the surplus commodity programs were common sense, and they made well-fed people feel better. Few asked how much of the surplus was being transferred to the hungry, or how much of their hunger was thus relieved. As the *New York Times* predicted in an editorial welcoming the program: "It will relieve our minds of the distressing paradox."[12] And with the moral pressure relieved, with consciences eased, the opportunity for more fundamental action evaporated. Thus the token program served to preserve the underlying status quo.

Something very similar appears to be happening with the private food rescue, gleaning, and other surplus transfer programs that have expanded and proliferated to supply emergency food programs since the early 1980s. The constant fund-raising and food drives that characterize such programs keep them in the public eye, and few people ask whether the scale of the effort is proportional to the scale of the need. With the Boy Scouts collecting in the fall and the letter carriers in the spring, with the convenient barrel at the grocery store door and the opportunity to "check out hunger" at the checkout counter, with the Taste of the Nation and the enormous array of other hunger-related fundraisers, with the Vice President and the Secretary of Agriculture assuring us that we can simultaneously feed more people and reduce waste through food recovery, with all this highly visible activity, it is easy to assume that the problem is under control. The double whammy, the moral bargain of feeding the hungry and preventing waste, makes us feel better, thus reducing the discomfort that might motivate more fundamental action. The same emotional salience that makes hunger so popular a cause in the first place makes us quick to relieve our own discomfort by settling for token solutions.

In the contemporary situation, the danger of such tokenism is even more acute. There is more at stake than the radicalizing potential of the contradictions of waste amid want. The whole fragile commitment to public income supports and entitle-ments is in jeopardy. Food programs not only make the well fed feel better, they reassure us that no one will starve, even if the nation ends welfare and cuts gaping holes in the food stamp safety net. By creating an image of vast, decentralized, kind-hearted effort, an image that is fueled by every fund-raising letter or event, every canned goods drive, every hunger walk, run, bike, swim, or golf-a-thon, every concert or screening or play where a can of food reduces the price of admission, we allow the right wing to destroy the meager protections of the welfare state and undo the New Deal. Ironically, these public appeals have the effect of creating such comforting assurances even for those who do not contribute.

Promoting hunger as a public issue, of course, does not necessarily imply support for the private, voluntary approach. There are undoubtedly social democrats and other progressives who support expanded food entitlements without endorsing the emergency food phenomenon. Unfortunately, however, much of the public makes little distinction. If we raise the issue of hunger, we have no control over just how people will choose to respond. As the network of food banks, food rescue organizations, food pantries, and soup kitchens has grown, so have the chances that people confronted with evidence of hunger in their midst will turn to such programs in an effort to help.

Many private food charities make a point of asserting that they are not a substitute for public food assistance programs and entitlements. Nearly every food banker and food pantry director I interviewed made some such assertion, and the national organizations that coordinate such projects, Second Harvest, Food Chain, Catholic Charities, even the Salvation Army, are on record opposing cuts in public food assistance and specifying their own role as supplementary. When it is time to raise funds, however, such organizations, from the lowliest food pantry in the church basement to national organizations with high-powered fund raising consultants or departments, tend to compare themselves with public programs in ways that reinforce the ideology of privatization. You simply cannot stress the low overhead, efficiency, and cost effectiveness of using donated time to distribute donated food without feeding into the right-wing critique of public programs in general and entitlements in particular. The same fund-raising appeals that reassure the public that no one will starve, even if public assistance is destroyed, convince many that substitution of charitable food programs for public entitlements might be a good idea.

Furthermore, as the programs themselves have invested in infrastructure— in walk-in freezers and refrigerated trucks, in institutional stoves and office equipment, in pension plans and health insurance—their stake in the continuation of their efforts has grown as well, and with it, their need for continuous fund raising, and thus for the perpetuation of hunger as an issue. While many food bankers and food recovery staff argue that there would be a role for their organizations even if this society succeeded in eliminating hunger, that their products also go to improve the meal quality at senior citizen centers or lower the cost of daycare and rehabilitation programs, they clearly realize that they need hunger as an issue in order to raise their funds. Cost effectiveness and efficient service delivery, even the prevention of waste, simply do not have the same ability to elicit contributions. Hunger is, in effect, their bread and butter. The result is a degree of hoopla, of attention getting activity, that I sometimes think of as the commodification of hunger. As Laura DeLind pointed out in her insightful article "Celebrating Hunger in Michigan," the hunger industry has become extraordinarily useful to major corporate interests, but even without such public relations and other benefits to corporate food and financial donors, hunger has become a "product" that enables its purveyors to compete successfully for funds in a sort of social issues marketplace.[13] It does not require identification with despised groups—as does AIDS, for example. Its remedy is not far off, obscure, or difficult to imagine—like the cure for cancer. The emotional salience discussed above, and the broad spectrum of people who have been recruited to this cause in one way or another, make hunger—especially the soup kitchen, food pantry, food recycling version of hunger—a prime commodity in the fund-raising industry, and a handy, inoffensive outlet for the do-gooding efforts of high school community service programs and corporate public relations offices, of synagogues and churches, of the Boy Scouts and the Letter Carriers, of the Rotarians and the Junior League: the taming of hunger.

As we institutionalize and expand the response, of course, we also institutionalize and reinforce the problem definition that underlies it. Sociologists have long argued that the definitional stage is the crucial period in the career of a social problem. Competing definitions vie for attention, and the winners shape the solutions and garner the resources. It is important, therefore, to understand the competing definitions of the situation that "hunger" crowds out. What is lost from public view, from our operant consciousness, as we work to end hunger? In short, defining the problem as hunger contributes to the obfuscation of the underlying problems of poverty and inequality. Many poor people are indeed hungry, but hunger, like homelessness and a host of other problems, is a symptom, not a cause, of poverty. And poverty, in turn, in an affluent society like our own, is fundamentally a product of inequality.

Defining the problem as hunger ignores a whole host of other needs. Poor people need food, but they also need housing, transportation, clothing, medical care, meaningful work, opportunities for civic and political participation, and recreation. By focusing on hunger, we imply that the food portion of this complex web of human needs can be met independently of the rest, can be exempted or protected from the overall household budget deficit. As anyone who has ever tried to get by on a tight budget can tell you, however, life is not so compartmentalized. Poor people are generally engaged in a daily struggle to stretch inadequate resources over a range of competing demands. The "heat-or-eat" dilemma that arises in the winter months, or the situation reported by many elderly citizens of a constant necessity to choose between food and medications are common manifestations of this reality.

In this situation, if we make food assistance easier to obtain than other forms of aid—help with the rent, for example, or the heating bill—then people will devise a variety of strategies to use food assistance to meet other needs. It is not really difficult to convert food stamps to cash: pick up a few items at the store for a neighbor, pay with your stamps, collect from her in cash. Some landlords will accept them, at a discounted rate of course, then convert them through a friend or relative who owns a grocery store. Drug dealers will also accept them, again at lower than face value, and you can resell the drugs for cash. The list goes on and on. Converting soup kitchen meals is almost impossible, but there are items in many pantry bags that can be resold. In either case, eating at the soup kitchen or collecting a bag from the food pantry frees up cash for other needs, not only the rent, but also a birthday present for a child or a new pair of shoes. By offering help with food, but refusing help with other urgent needs, we are setting up a situation in which poor people are almost required to take steps to convert food assistance to cash.

Conservative critics of entitlements will then seize on these behaviors to argue that poor people are "not really hungry." If they were really hungry, the argument goes, they would not resell items from the pantry bag or convert their food stamps. Such behavioral evidence fits into a whole ideologically driven perception that programs for poor people are bloated, too generous, and full of fraud and abuse; it allows conservatives to cut programs while asserting that they are preserving a safety net for the "truly needy." Progressives meanwhile are forced into a defensive position in which we argue that people are indeed "really hungry," thereby giving tacit assent to the idea that the elimination of hunger is the appropriate goal. In a society as wealthy as ours, however, aiming simply to eliminate hunger is aiming too low. We not only want a society in which no one suffers acute hunger or fails to take full advantage of educational and work opportunities due to inadequate nutrition. We want a society in which no one is excluded, by virtue of poverty, from full participation, in which no one is too poor to provide a decent life for his or her children, no one is too poor to pursue happiness. By defining the problem as "hunger," we set too low a standard for ourselves.

WHERE TO?

The question of where we should direct our organizational efforts is inextricably tied up with the underlying issue of inequality. Above some absolute level of food and shelter, need is a thoroughly relative phenomenon. In an affluent society, the quality of life available at a given level of income has everything to do with how far from the mainstream that level is, with the extent to which any given income can provide a life that looks and feels "normal" to its occupants. In many warm parts of the world, children routinely go barefoot, and no mother would feel driven to convert food resources into cash to buy a pair of shoes, or to demean herself by seeking a charity handout to provide them. In the United States, where children are bombarded with hours of television advertising daily, and where apparel manufacturers trade on "coolness," a mother may well make the rounds of local food pantries, swallowing her pride and subsisting on handouts, to buy not just a pair of shoes, but a particular name brand that her child has been convinced is essential for social acceptance at the junior high school.

In this context, the issue is not whether people have enough to survive, but how far they are from the median and the mainstream, and that is a matter of how unequal our society has become. By every measure, inequality has increased in the United States, dramatically, since the early 1970s, with a small group at the top garnering an ever increasing share of net marketable worth, and the bottom doing less and less well. And it is this growing inequality which explains the crying need for soup kitchens and food banks today, even at a relatively high level of employment that reflects the current peak in the business cycle. Unfortunately, however, a concept like hunger is far easier to understand, despite its ambiguities of definition, than an abstraction like inequality. Furthermore, Americans have not generally been trained to understand the language of inequality nor the tools with which it is measured. Just what is net marketable worth, and do I have any? As the statistics roll off the press, eyes glaze over, and the kindhearted turn to doing something concrete, to addressing a problem they know they can do something about: hunger. Once they begin, and get caught up in the engrossing practical challenges of transferring food to the hungry and the substantial emotional gratifications of doing so, they lose sight of the larger issue of inequality. The gratifications inherent in "feeding the hungry" give people a stake in maintaining the definition of the problem as hunger; the problem definition comes to be driven by the available and visible response in a sort of double helix.

Meanwhile, with anti-hunger activists diverted by the demands of ever larger emergency food systems, the ascendant conservatives are freer than ever to dismantle the fragile income protections that remain and to adjust the tax system to concentrate ever greater resources at the top. The people who want more inequality are getting it, and well-meaning people are responding to the resulting deprivation by handing out more and more pantry bags, and dishing up more and more soup. It is time to find ways to shift the discourse from undernutrition to unfairness, from hunger to inequality.

NOTES

1. All quotations not otherwise attributed come from the transcripts of interviews I conducted in conjunction with my study of emergency food. For a more extensive treatment, see Janet Poppendieck, *Sweet Charity? Emergency Food and the End of Entitlement* (New York: Viking, 1998).
2. Foodchain, the National Food Rescue Network, *Feedback* (Fall, 1997), 2–3.
3. Ibid.
4. Vincent Breglio, *Hunger in America: The Voter's Perspective.* (Lanham, MD: Research/Strategy/Management Inc.,1992), 14–16.
5. For a discussion of the so called paradox of want amid plenty in the great depression, see Janet Poppendieck, *Breadlines Knee Deep in Wheat: Food Assistance in the Great Depression.* (New Brunswick, NJ: Rutgers University Press, 1986).
6. George McGovern, "Foreward," in Nick Kotz, *Let Them Eat Promises: The Politics of Hunger in America.* (Englewood Cliffs, NJ: Prentice-Hall, 1969) viii.
7. Nick Kotz, "The Politics of Hunger," *The New Republic* (April 30, 1984), 22.
8. Bread for the World Institute, *Hunger 1994: Transforming the Politics of Hunger.* Fourth Annual Report on the State of World Hunger (Silver Spring, MD, 1993), 19.
9. Quoted in Edward Robb Ellis, *A Nation in Torment: The Great American Depression, 1929–1939.* (New York: Capricorn Books, 1971), 506.
10. Walter Lippmann, "Poverty and Plenty," Proceedings of the National Conference of Social Work, 59th Session, 1932 (Chicago: University of Chicago Press, 1932), 234–35.
11. Norman Thomas, *After the New Deal, What?* (New York: Macmillan, 1936), 33.
12. "Plenty and Want," editorial, *New York Times,* September 23, 1933.

13. Laura B. DeLind, "Celebrating Hunger in Michigan: A Critique of an Emergency food Program and an Alternative for the Future," *Agriculture and Human Values* (Fall, 1994), 58–68.

Chapter Twelve

CUBA: A SUCCESSFUL CASE STUDY
OF SUSTAINABLE AGRICULTURE

PETER M. ROSSET

Our global food system is in the midst of a multifaceted crisis, with ecological, economic, and social dimensions. To overcome that crisis, political and social changes are needed to allow the widespread development of alternatives.

The current food system is productive—there should be no doubt about that—as per capita food produced in the world has increased by 15 percent over the past thirty-five years. But as that production is in ever fewer hands, and costs ever more in economic and ecological terms, it becomes harder and harder to address the basic problems of hunger and food access in the short term, let alone in a sustainable fashion. In the last twenty years the number of hungry people in the world—excluding China—has risen by 60 million (by contrast, in China the number of hungry people has fallen dramatically).

Ecologically, there are impacts of industrial-style farming on groundwater through pesticide and fertilizer runoff, on biodiversity through the spread of monoculture and a narrowing genetic base, and on the very capacity of agroecosystems to be productive into the future.

Economically, production costs rise as farmers are forced to use ever more expensive machines and farm chemicals, while crop prices continue a several-decade-long downward trend, causing a cost-price squeeze which has led to the loss of untold tens of millions of farmers worldwide to bankruptcies. Socially, we have the concentration of farmland in fewer and fewer hands as low crop prices make farming on a small scale unprofitable (despite higher per acre total productivity of small farms), and agribusiness corporations extend their control over more and more basic commodities.

Clearly the dominant corporate food system is not capable of adequately addressing the needs of people or of the environment. Yet there are substantial obstacles to the widespread adoption of alternatives. The greatest obstacles are presented by political-corporate power and vested interests, yet at times the psychological barrier to believing that the alternatives can work seems almost as difficult to overcome. The oft-repeated challenge is: "Could organic farming (or agroecology, local production, small farms, farming without pesticides) ever really feed the entire population of a country?" Recent Cuban history—the overcoming of a food crisis through self-reliance, small farms and agroecological technology—shows us that the alternatives can indeed feed a nation, and thus provides a crucial case study for the ongoing debate.

A BRIEF HISTORY

Economic development in Cuba was molded by two external forces between the 1959 revolution and the 1989-90 collapse of trading relations with the Soviet bloc. One was the U.S. trade embargo, part of an effort to isolate the island economically and politically. The other was Cuba's entry into the Soviet bloc's international trade alliance with relatively favorable terms of trade. The United States embargo essentially forced Cuba to turn to the Soviet bloc, while the terms of trade offered by the latter opened the possibility of more rapid development on the island than in the rest of Latin America and the Caribbean.

Thus Cuba was able to achieve a more complete and rapid modernization than most other developing countries. In the 1980s, it ranked number one in the region in the contribution of industry to its economy and it had a more mechanized agricultural sector than any other Latin American country. Nevertheless, some of the same contradictions that modernization produced in other Third World countries were apparent in Cuba, with Cuba's development model proving ultimately to be of the dependent type. Agriculture was defined by extensive monocrop production of export crops and a heavy dependence on imported agrichemicals, hybrid seeds, machinery, and petroleum. While industrialization was substantial by regional standards, Cuban industry depended on many imported inputs.

The Cuban economy as a whole was thus characterized by the contradiction between its relative modernity and its function in the Soviet bloc's division of labor as a supplier of raw agricultural commodities and minerals, and a net importer of both manufactured goods and foodstuffs. In contrast to the situation faced by most Third World countries, this international division of labor actually brought significant benefits to the Cuban people. Prior to the collapse of the socialist bloc, Cuba had achieved high marks for per capita GNP, nutrition, life expectancy, and women in higher education, and was ranked first in Latin America for the availability of doctors, low infant mortality, housing, secondary school enrollment, and attendance by the population at cultural events.

The Cuban achievements were made possible by a combination of the government's commitment to social equity and the fact that Cuba received far more favorable terms of trade for its exports than did the hemisphere's other developing nations. During the 1980s, Cuba received an average price for its sugar exports to the Soviet Union that was 5.4 times higher than the world price. Cuba also was able to obtain Soviet petroleum in return, part of which was re-exported to earn convertible currency. Because of the favorable terms of trade for sugar, its production far outweighed that of food crops. About three times as much land was devoted to sugar in 1989 as was used for food crops, contributing to a pattern of food dependency, with as much as 57 percent of the total calories in the Cuban diet coming from imports.

The revolutionary government had inherited an agricultural production system strongly focused on export crops grown on highly concentrated land. The first agrarian reform of 1959 converted most of the large cattle ranches and sugarcane plantations into state farms. Under the second agrarian reform in 1962, the state took control of 63 percent of all cultivated land.

Even before the revolution, individual peasant producers were a small part of the agricultural scene. The rural economy was dominated by export plantations, and the population as a whole was highly urbanized. That pattern intensified in subsequent years, and by the late 1980s fully 69 percent of the island's population lived in urban areas. As late as 1994, some 80 percent of the nation's agricultural land consisted of large state farms, which roughly correspond to the expropriated plantation holdings of the pre-revolutionary era. Only 20 percent of the agricultural land was in the hands of small farmers, split almost equally among individual holders and cooperatives, yet this 20 percent produced more than 40 percent of domestic food production. The state farm sector and a substantial portion of the cooperatives were highly modernized, with large areas of monocrops worked under heavy mechanization, fertilizer and pesticide use, and large-scale irrigation. This style of farming, originally copied from the advanced capitalist countries by the Soviet Union, was highly dependent on imports of machinery, petroleum, and chemicals. When trade collapsed with the socialist bloc, the degree to which Cuba relied on monocrop agriculture proved to be a major weakness of the revolution.

ONSET OF THE CRISIS

When trade relations with the Soviet bloc crumbled in late 1989 and 1990, the situation turned desperate. In 1991, the government declared the "Special Period in Peacetime," which basically put the country on a wartime economy style austerity program. There was an immediate 53 percent reduction in oil imports that not only affected fuel availability for the economy, but also reduced to zero the foreign exchange that Cuba had formerly obtained via the re-export of petroleum. Imports of wheat and other grains for human consumption dropped by more than 50 percent, while other foodstuffs declined even more. Cuban agriculture was faced with a drop of more than 80 percent in the availability of fertilizers and pesticides, and more than 50 percent in fuel and other energy sources produced by petroleum.

Suddenly, a country with an agricultural sector technologically similar to California's found itself almost without chemical inputs, with sharply reduced access to fuel and irrigation, and with a collapse in food imports. In the early 1990s average daily caloric and protein intake by the Cuban population may have been as much as 30 percent below levels in the 1980s. Fortunately, Cuba was not totally unprepared to face the critical situation that arose after 1989.

It had, over the years, emphasized the development of human resources, and therefore had a cadre of scientists and researchers who could come forward with innovative ideas to confront the crisis. While Cuba has only 2 percent of the population of Latin America, it has almost 11 percent of the scientists.

ALTERNATIVE TECHNOLOGIES

In response to the crisis, the Cuban government launched a national effort to convert the nation's agricultural sector from high input agriculture to low input, self-reliant farming practices on an unprecedented scale. Because of the drastically reduced availability of chemical inputs, the state hurried to replace them with locally produced, and in most cases biological, substitutes. This has meant biopesticides (microbial products) and natural enemies to combat insect pests, resistant plant varieties, crop rotations and microbial antagonists to combat plant pathogens, and better rotations, and cover cropping to suppress weeds. Synthetic fertilizers have been replaced by biofertilizers, earthworms, compost, other organic fertilizers, natural rock phosphate, animal and green manures, and the integration of grazing animals. In place of tractors, for which fuel, tires, and spare parts were largely unavailable, there has been a sweeping return to animal traction.

SMALL FARMERS RESPOND TO THE CRISIS

When the collapse of trade and subsequent scarcity of inputs occurred in 1989-90, yields fell drastically throughout the country. The first problem was that of producing without synthetic chemical inputs or tractors. Gradually the national ox herd was built up to provide animal traction as a substitute for tractors, and the production of biopesticides and biofertilizers was rapidly stepped up. Finally, a series of methods like vermicomposting (earthworm composting) of residues and green manuring became widespread. But the impact of these technological changes across subsectors of Cuban agriculture was highly variable. The drop-off of yields in the state sector industrial-style farms that average thousands of hectares has been resistant to recovery, with production seriously stagnating well below pre-crisis levels for export crops. Yet the small farm or peasant sector (20 percent of farmed land) responded rapidly by quickly boosting production above previous levels. How can we explain the difference between the state- and small-farm sectors?

It really was not all that difficult for the small farm sector to effectively produce with fewer inputs. After all, today's small farmers are the descendants of generations of small farmers, with long family and community traditions of low-input production. They basically did two things: remembered the old techniques—like intercropping and manuring—that their parents and grandparents had used before the advent of modern chemicals, and simultaneously incorporated new biopesticides and biofertilizers into their production practices.

STATE FARMS INCOMPATIBLE WITH THE ALTERNATIVE TECHNOLOGIES

The problems of the state sector, on the other hand, were a combination of low worker productivity, a problem predating the Special Period, and the complete inability of these immense and technified management units to adapt to low-input technology. With regard to the productivity problem, planners became aware several years ago that the organization of work on state farms was profoundly alienating in terms of the relationship between the agricultural worker and the land. Large farms of thousands of hectares had their work forces organized into teams that would prepare the soil in one area, move on to plant another, weed still another, and later harvest an altogether different area. Almost never would the same person both plant and harvest the same area. Thus no one ever had to confront the consequences of doing something badly or, conversely, enjoy the fruits of his or her own labor.

In an effort to create a more intimate relationship between farm workers and the land, and to tie financial incentives to productivity, the government began several years ago to experiment with a program called "linking people with the land." This system made small work teams directly responsible for all aspects of production in a given parcel of land, allowing remuneration to be directly linked to productivity. The new system was tried before the Special Period on a number of state farms, and rapidly led to enormous increases in production. Nevertheless it was not widely implemented at the time.

In terms of technology, scale effects are very different for conventional chemical management and for low external input alternatives. Under conventional systems, a single technician can manage several thousand hectares on a "recipe" basis by simply writing out instructions for a particular fertilizer formula or pesticide to be applied with machinery on the entire area. This is not so for agroecological farming. Whoever manages the farm must be intimately familiar with the ecological heterogeneity of each individual patch of soil. The farmer must know, for example, where organic matter needs to be added, and where pest and natural enemy refuges and entry points are. This partially explains the inability of the state sector to raise yields with alternative inputs. Like the productivity issue, it can only be effectively addressed through a re-linking of people with the land.

By mid-1993, the state was faced with a complex reality. Imported inputs were largely unavailable, but nevertheless the small farmer sector had effectively adapted to low input production (although a secondary problem was acute in this sector, namely diversion of produce to the black market). The state sector, on the other hand, was proving itself to be an ineffective "white elephant" in the new historical conjuncture, incapable of adjusting. The earlier success of the experimental "linking" program, however, and the success of the peasant sector, suggested a way out. In September 1993, Cuba began radically reorganizing its production in order to create the small-scale management units that are essential for effective organic-style farming. This reorganization has centered on the privatization and cooperativization of the unwieldy state sector.

The process of linking people with the land thus culminated in 1993, when the Cuban government issued a decree terminating the existence of state farms, turning them into Basic Units of Cooperative Production (UBPCs), a form of worker-owned enterprise or cooperative. The 80 percent of all farmland that was once held by the state, including sugarcane plantations, has now essentially been turned over to the workers.

The UBPCs allow collectives of workers to lease state farmlands rent free, in perpetuity. Members elect management teams that determine the division of jobs, what crops will be planted on which parcels, and how much credit will be taken out to pay for the purchase of inputs. Property rights remain in the hands of the state, and the UBPCs must still meet production quotas for their key crops, but the collectives are owners of what they produce. Perhaps most importantly, what they produce in excess of their quotas can now be freely sold on the newly reopened farmers markets. This last reform, made in 1994, offered a price incentive to farmers both to sell their produce through legal channels rather than the black market, and also to make effective use of the new technologies.

The pace of consolidation of the UBPCs has varied greatly in their first years of life. Today one can find a range from those where the only change is that the old manager is now an employee of the workers, to those that truly function as collectives, to some in which the workers are parceling the farms into small plots worked by groups of friends. In almost all cases, the effective size of the management unit has been drastically reduced. It is still too early to predict the final variety of structures that the UBPCs will evolve toward. But it is clear that the process of turning previously alienated farm workers into farmers will take some time—it simply cannot be accomplished over-night—and many UBPCs are struggling. Incentives are a nagging problem. Most UBPCs are stuck with state production contracts for export crops like sugar and citrus. These still have fixed, low prices paid by state marketing agencies, in contrast to the much higher prices that can be earned for food crops. Typical UBPCs, not surprisingly then, have low yields in their export crops, but also have lucrative side businesses selling food produced on spare land or between the rows of their citrus or sugarcane.

FOOD SHORTAGE OVERCOME

By mid-1995 the food shortage had been overcome, and the vast majority of the population no longer faced drastic reductions of their basic food supply. In the 1996-97 growing season, Cuba recorded its highest-ever production levels for ten of the thirteen basic food items in the Cuban diet. The production increases came primarily from small farms, and in the case of eggs and pork, from booming backyard production. The proliferation of urban farmers who produce fresh produce has also been extremely important to the Cuban food supply. The earlier food shortages and the rise in food prices suddenly turned urban agriculture into a very profitable activity for Cubans, and once the government threw its full support behind a nascent urban gardening movement, it exploded to near epic proportions. Formerly vacant lots and backyards in all Cuban cities now sport food crops and farm animals, and fresh produce is sold from private stands throughout urban areas at prices substantially below those prevailing in the farmers markets. There can be no doubt that urban farming, relying almost exclusively on organic techniques, has played a key role in assuring the food security of Cuban families over the past two to three years.

AN ALTERNATIVE PARADIGM?

To what extent can we see the outlines of an alternative food system paradigm in this Cuban experience? Or is Cuba just such a unique case in every way that we cannot generalize its experiences into lessons for other countries? The first thing to point out is that contemporary Cuba turned conventional wisdom completely on its head. We are told that small countries cannot feed themselves, that they need imports to cover the deficiency of their local agriculture. Yet Cuba has taken enormous strides toward self-reliance since it lost its key trade relations. We hear that a country can't feed its people without synthetic farm chemicals, yet Cuba is virtually doing so. We are told that we need the efficiency of large-scale corporate or state farms in order to produce enough food, yet we find small farmers and gardeners in the vanguard of Cuba's recovery from a food crisis. In fact, in the absence of subsidized machines and imported chemicals, small farms are more efficient than very large production units. We hear time and again that international food aid is the answer to food shortages—yet Cuba has found an alternative in local production.

Abstracting from that experience, the elements of an alternative paradigm might therefore be:

(1) *Agroecological technology instead of chemicals:* Cuba has used intercropping, locally produced biopesticides, compost, and other alternatives to synthetic pesticides and fertilizers.

(2) *Fair Prices for Farmers:* Cuban farmers stepped up production in response to higher crop prices. Farmers everywhere lack incentive to produce when prices are kept artificially low, as they often are. Yet when given an incentive, they produce, regardless of the conditions under which that production must take place.

(3) *Redistribution of Land:* Small farmers and gardeners have been the most productive of Cuban producers under low-input conditions. Indeed, smaller farms worldwide produce much more per unit area than do large farms. In Cuba redistribution was relatively easy to accomplish because the major part of the land reform had already occurred, in the sense that there were no landlords to resist further change.

(4) *Greater Emphasis on Local Production:* People should not have to depend on the vagaries of prices in the world economy, long distance transportation, and super power "goodwill" for their next meal. Locally and regionally produced food offers greater security, as well as synergistic linkages to promote local economic development. Furthermore such production is more ecologically sound, as the energy spent on international transport is wasteful and environmentally unsustainable. By promoting urban farming, cities and their surrounding areas can be made virtually self-sufficient in perishable foods, be beautified, and have greater employment opportunities. Cuba gives us a hint of the under-exploited potential of urban farming.

Cuba in its Special Period has clearly been in a unique situation with respect to not being able to use power machinery in the fields, forcing it to seek alternatives such as animal traction. It is unlikely that Cuba or any other country at its stage of development would choose to abandon machine agriculture to this extent unless compelled to do so. Yet there are important lessons here for countries struggling to develop. Relatively small-scale farming, even using animals for traction, can be very productive per unit of land, given technical support. And it is next to impossible to have ecologically sound farming at an extremely large scale. Although it is undeniable that for countries wishing to develop industry and at the same time grow most of their own food, some mechanization of agriculture will be needed, it is crucial to recognize—and the Cuban example can help us to understand this—that modest-sized family farms and cooperatives that use reasonably sized equipment can follow ecologically sound practices and have increased labor productivity.

The Cuban experience illustrates that we can feed a nation's population well with a small- or medium-sized farm model based on appropriate ecological technology, and in doing so we can become more self-reliant in food production. Farmers must receive higher returns for their produce, and when they do they will be encouraged to produce. Capital-intensive chemical inputs—most of which are unnecessary—can be largely dispensed with. The important lessons from Cuba that we can apply elsewhere, then, are agroecology, fair prices, land reform, and local production, including urban agriculture.

Chapter Thirteen

THE IMPORTANCE OF LAND REFORM IN THE RECONSTRUCTION OF CHINA

WILLIAM HINTON

From the early 1920s through 1949, when the Peoples Liberation Army liberated Beijing, the Chinese people, rising in revolution under the leadership of the Communist Party of China, targeted domestic feudalism, bureaucratic capitalism, and foreign imperialism as the three mountains on their backs that had to be thrown off. In the 1920s and early 1930s, the landlord-dominated feudal land system was the central issue, and land reform—equal distribution of the land to all who labored on it—formed the heart of the revolutionary program. After 1937, when the Japanese embarked on the military conquest of China, their imperialist invasion, threatening China's very existence as an independent country, preempted all other political issues. Chinese revolutionaries responded by forging a united front with all forces, including those bureaucratic capitalists holding state power and those landlords in the countryside, who were willing to join in resistance to Japan. For eight years, mobilization for land reform in the countryside gave way to rent-and-interest reduction schemes, a Communist Party policy to which all resisters gave lip service, but not all landlords and usurers put into practice.

LAND TO THE TILLER, THE CENTRAL ISSUE

After the Japanese surrendered in 1945, land reform again took the center of the political stage and dominated domestic politics in China throughout the period of the postwar civil war and even for several years thereafter. This dominance lasted more or less intact until all peasants everywhere—with minor exceptions such as a six-year delay in Tibet—took over the land they tilled. This stage of the revolution, the anti-imperialist, anti-feudal stage, was called by Mao Zedong the New Democratic Revolution. It was a massive armed uprising, primarily of peasants, that prepared the ground for socialism but did not place socialism as such on its agenda.

The New Democratic land reform in China was without doubt the most massive expropriation and distribution of property and repudiation of debt in world history. As I wrote in *Fanshen*, the Draft Agrarian Law of 1947

> was destined to play as important a role in China's Civil War of 1946-1950 as the Emancipation Proclamation played in the American Civil War of 1861-1865. Lincoln's Emancipation proclamation confiscated without compensation $3 billion worth of property in slaves, put an end to the possibility of compromise between the industrial North and the slave-holding South in the military contest then raging; made the slave system itself, rather than regional autonomy, the nub of the conflict; cleared the way for the recruitment of hundreds of thousands of emancipated black men into the Union Army; and spread the war into every corner of Confederate territory with devastating effect.

> Mao's Draft Agrarian Law confiscated without compensation $20 billion in land (no figures for the value of debts canceled are available); put an end to all possible compromise between the Communist Party and the Kuomintang; made country-wide overthrow of the landlords and compradores, rather than the defense of the Liberated Areas, the main aim of the war; facilitated the capitulation and recruitment of huge blocks of Chiang's soldiers into the People's Liberation Army; inspired peasant unrest in the far corners of China; and gave impetus to demonstrations of workers, students, merchants, and professional people in urban centers throughout the Kuomintang area.

The massive distribution of the property at the core of Chinese feudalism that followed promulgation of the Draft Law enabled almost every poor peasant and hired laborer in China to *fanshen*, to turn over, to stand up, to acquire land, often tools, a share in a draft animal, a section or two of house, even a few clothes—in other words the basic prerequisites for self support, and this egalitarian material base undergirding peasant society remains intact to this day.

LIBERATING PRODUCTIVE FORCES

More important in the long run than the equalization, however, the thorough and universal land reform liberated hitherto tightly constrained productive forces, primarily the surplus labor power of the Chinese peasants, and by providing returns from land of their own as incentive, led this huge force to increase production rapidly not only on land already tilled but on land newly reclaimed, not only on irrigated fields already in place or restored but on fields newly watered, and by new sideline and industrial projects never before undertaken that added greatly to individual incomes. All this steadily increased the days worked per year from below 150 to 200, 250, even 300. The latter figures became possible once cooperation pooled individual forms into collectives that could mobilize both labor and resources for ever larger projects and enterprises. As the utilization rate of labor power increased, output grew, as did incomes.

The liberation of productive forces through the transformation of productive relations—who owns what, who works for whom and under what arrangements—was the key. Historically, when any agricultural surplus piled up in the hands of landlords they either bought more land with it, loaned it out at usurious interest rates, spent it on high living, or buried it in the ground for safe keeping. None of this added one jot to production. Most of the loans were for festivals of consumption—weddings, first year survival parties for sons, funerals—or they were for emergencies like accidents and illness. They rarely added any input to agriculture, except perhaps for those loans advanced for seed. The result was economic stagnation.

When the agricultural surplus piled up in the hands of peasants individually or collectively, they reinvested much of it in expanded production. The lively market created by their inputs, together with their increasing demands as consumers, stimulated the whole economy. As Mao Zedong wrote in his "Ten Great Relationships," "if you want to develop heavy industry you must pay attention to developing agriculture and light industry."

The liberation of productive forces through land reform led to rapid development in China in all spheres—agriculture, light industry, heavy industry, and infrastructure. On the average, during the next thirty years the Chinese economy grew from 7 percent to 8 percent a year (even when factoring in the declines suffered during the hardship years 1959-1961). This was one of the fastest rates of growth in the world. This growth was firmly rooted in the land reform of 1946-1953 and could not have occurred without it.

Conventional wisdom has it that policy extremes imposed by Mao brought crop failures, hunger, and finally monstrous famine to China from 1959 to 1961. Actually, severe political combat between contending headquarters inside the leading bodies of the Communist Party were tearing the party apart from top to bottom, making it difficult to carry out coherent policies to combat three successive years of bad weather—the unprecedented floods and droughts that were the underlying cause of the crisis. Having obscured the cause, media and academicians alike then grossly exaggerated the effects. Twenty years later, by reverse extrapolations of some dubious population statistics, they turned a food crisis that had hitherto attracted very little attention outside China into the worst famine in history. Though some famine deaths did occur, such disasters were minimized by universal rationing, grain redistribution, reduced requisitions, the coarse milling of food grains, and expanded sown acreage. Far from being the cause of the trouble, collective strength helped overcome it.

POOLED PRIVATE HOLDINGS TRANSFORMED INTO USE-RIGHTS

Collectivization, by pooling holdings and distributing income in proportion to work performed, blocked polarization—the concentration of land and productive equipment in the hands of a few exploiters. A decision made during the Cultural Revolution, later transferred land ownership from local communities to the state, but reserved firm use-rights to rural land for the members of village-level collectives or brigades group-by-group, thus preserving the core function of land reform, assuring to every rural individual access to a fair share of land.

Now that the "reform" has broken up most agricultural cooperatives, the use-rights to land are apportioned not to collective groups, the teams that made up the rural brigades and kept their accounts together, but to families as accounting units, with land allocations to each based on the number of members. Thus every individual still enjoys use rights to a proportionate share of land. This method also preserves the core function of land reform— to every tiller a plot of land to till.

This underlying egalitarian arrangement makes China quite different, say, from India, Pakistan, or the Philippines where no thoroughgoing large-scale land reform has ever taken place. There, large masses of landless and destitute people form a huge reserve army of rural proletarians with no reliable sustenance, no place to go, and no place to return to that they can call their own.

Since the Deng "reforms" began in the early 1980s, many Chinese peasants with land use-rights at home have left their native places looking for something more lucrative to do than hand hoe the small strips allocated to them. In the off season as many as 100 million roam the country looking for work, especially in the boom-bust coastal provinces and the major cites. Some find work, many do not. But all of them, when down on their luck, have the option of returning home. Non-roaming family members—women, children, old folks, the ill, and the disabled—have usually raised some crops in their absence. Returning wanderers can still eat and find shelter under their own roof.

Nowadays as privatization and market relations gain dominance, contradictions and tensions in the countryside, brought on by social polarization, are escalating. As conflicts sharpen, the subsistence substructure provided by universal land use-rights adds greatly to the stability of a system and a situation that, if not backed up by these inalienable prerogatives inherited by hundreds of millions of rural people from land reform days, could easily become quite unstable, even explosive. Whether or not this outcome is positive can be debated. Unfolding as one of the great ironies of modern history, the vast liberating social equalization that accompanied the Communist victory in 1949 is now coming back into play by providing a huge and relatively compliant reserve army of labor for the development of capitalism—unfortunately not the brand of autonomous national capitalism familiar to the West as it developed, but a capitalism warped by strong compradore tendencies that can drag China back into the kind of neocolonial nightmare that brought on the upheaval in the first place.

REVANCHIST FORCES REPUDIATE LAND REFORM

Beginning in the early 1980s, strong revanchist tendencies began to surface in China which have strengthened year by year. Whereas the brunt of the "reformist" attacks used to concentrate on socialist collectivization, today repudiation even extends to the land reform of the New Democratic Revolution. Some localities are building People's Life Museums, thinly disguised celebrations of gentry life as it was led in the good old days, without any hint of the sources of gentry wealth or the class conflicts which these generated. Foreign academicians, meanwhile are writing books like Friedman, Pickowicz, and Selden's *Chinese Village, Socialist State* that bad-mouth the whole revolution, starting with a so-called "leveling and terror" land reform that had, they say, no objective basis in land concentration, land deprivation, or the class conflicts generated thereby. These attacks are off the wall, completely unjustified exercises in revanchism. By any objective standard—political, economic, social, or cultural—land reform in China must be judged an outstanding success. The goal of the movement was to break up, once and for all, the elitist, hierarchical, autocratic, wasteful, corrupt, and above all stagnant landlord-dominated feudal system and replace it with grassroots communities of equal, small holders laboring on their own land, responsible for their own livelihood and basically running their own affairs, led by Communist Party members recruited from among the best, most active, most dedicated men and women of the locality. If the dedication didn't always last after they tasted power, the potential for honest service to the community was still much greater than when hereditary gentry parceled out the posts.

On the whole, throughout the nation over a period of five or six years, peasant communities achieved their New Democratic revolutionary goals with results that exceeded expectations, whether it be the rapid expansion of crop production, the development of simple sidelines through mutual aid, the election of representative village councils, the empowerment of women, first steps toward universal primary education, widespread literacy campaigns, or an unfolding grassroots street theater. What better foundation could be laid for the establishment of an expanding economy generated by self-governing citizens than these villages, no longer shaped and constrained by members of a landed elite that knew how to exploit but not to build, yet still regarded themselves as the only worthy representatives of Chinese civilization.

SOCIAL EQUALITY UNDERGIRDS DEMOCRACY

As the American Civil War ended Thaddeus Stevens asked:

> How can republican institutions, free schools, free churches, free social intercourse, exist in a mingled economy of nabobs and serfs; of owners of 20,000 acre manors with lordly palaces and the occupants of narrow huts inhabited by "low white trash"? If the South is ever to be made a safe republic let her land be cultivated by the toil of the owners and the free labor of intelligent citizens . . . . This country will be well rid of the proud, bloated and defiant rebels . . . the foundations of their institutions must be broken up and relaid, or all our blood and treasure have been spent in vain.

America rejected Stevens' solution—forty acres and a mule for every freed slave and white tenant. The land went back to its erstwhile owners. Rural blacks went from slavery to peonage on the cotton plantations of the South, while the race question burgeoned into a lasting curse that has exacted an enormous price from all Americans ever since.

There were not many 20,000-acre manorial estates in China, and most landlords did not live in palaces. If anything, there was even a reverse correlation between the size of the holding and the venality of the landlord. Those with the sparsest holdings lived under the most pressure to collect the last modicum of rent lest they themselves be forced to swap their gown for a pair of work pants and a hoe. Many American academics had a hard time finding landlords in China because they could not believe that rentiers collected as little and lived as poorly as many undoubtedly did. But the class standards used by the peasant associations were well grounded, and people who lived off the land but did not work it lost their holdings, whatever their size, from the Amur to the South China sea. They got back, like everyone, a working peasant's share.

Thus China solved in a thoroughgoing manner what America failed to solve as slavery ended in the South, what India failed to tackle after winning independence, and what the Philippines aborted after MacArthur's return.

The difference this has made is profound, as any comparison of China with Mississippi, India, or the Philippines will demonstrate.

COOPERATION BETWEEN SMALLHOLDERS BOTH NATURAL AND NECESSARY

The more or less universal equality established by land reform made possible the next great step taken by the Chinese Revolution in the countryside—cooperative agriculture through land pooling village by village. Cooperation cannot arise between nabobs and serfs, nor even between petty landlords and their tenants. Their interests are too opposed. But cooperation between equal small holders is both natural and necessary.

Conventional wisdom has it that almost three decades of cooperative agriculture in China (1956-1983) led only to disaster. In preparing to break up the collectives, which they never favored in the first place, advocates of the individual family contract system vigorously promoted the theory that cooperation as a form of organization was generically unsuited to peasant agriculture. But in reality, after experiencing serious growing pains, the collective system as finally consolidated in the 1970s functioned successfully. A team of young specialists analyzing the situation on behalf of "reform" leaders in the early 1980s found that 30 percent of the rural collectives, those leading the way, were doing well, an additional 40 percent in the middle were viable but faced problems, while 30 percent at the bottom were in serious trouble and required drastic overhaul. With 240 million peasants prospering through cooperation, with another 480 million in village collective units basically successful, how could it be said that cooperation could never succeed in the agricultural sector?

The *China Daily* of April 10, 1996, reconfirmed the success of rural cooperation historically. Agricultural scientists at the Chinese Academy of Science found that the average annual increase in grain production from 1949 to 1984 (a period that includes the "three hard years" of 1959 to 1961 when output fell sharply) was 7.42 percent. This kept grain production well ahead of population growth, which averaged 2.4 percent. After 1984, as the Deng reforms took hold, however, the rate of increase in grain production slowed. In 1993 it fell to 1.34 percent, a level below that of population growth, which by that time had slowed to 1.5 percent. Since family contracts only became universal in 1982-1983, the bulk of this higher 7.4 percent growth rate was generated by an all but universally collectivized agriculture— a major achievement that contradicts what most commentators have been affirming.

DEMOCRATIC POTENTIAL NOT FULLY REALIZED

It goes without saying that before the "reform," the democratic potential embodied in so many communities of equal small holders cooperating to build a better life had not been fully realized in China. In not a few cases, core revolutionary civil rights norms had been badly betrayed by power holders who turned their home villages into a new type of feudal fief practicing favoritism based on kinship. Still the basic structure for autonomous, self-governing communities dedicated to prosperity and social service through collective action remained and could be activated by the vigorous application of party rectification, mass education, and a requirement that all cadres regularly join physical work. A rectification campaign, inspired by Chen Yonggui and Dazhai, the model village chosen by Mao, was gathering strength when both Mao and Chou Enlai, strong backers of the Dazhai road, died. Hua Guofeng, Mao's chosen successor, tried hard to maintain socialist momentum with two national Dazhai conferences and a national capital construction meeting that convened at several key spots where large-scale works for transforming nature were in progress. But the resurgent procapitalist opposition, now led by Deng, proved too strong. Deng outflanked Hua, who had no base in or strong ties to the military, and at the Third Plenary Session of the Eleventh Central Committee, Deng led the whole party to change course.

Stressing the fact that many villages were still stagnating, which was true, and reiterating the theory that cooperation and agriculture were by nature mismatched, which was not true (but served the interests of those who opposed the socialist transformation to begin with), the Deng "reformers" began dissolving collectives wholesale, beginning at places where communes, brigades, and teams were least successful. Using every means of pressure and persuasion, especially credit, farm supply, and tax policies that discriminated against collectives, they kept this drive going until they had almost entirely privatized agricultural production in China and dismantled a system that had taken almost thirty years to build. Many peasants welcomed the change, some simply went along with the tide. Others bowed under escalating pressure. Only a few highly successful collective units were able to resist and survive unchanged. As I said above, however, cooperation between equal small holders is not only natural but necessary.

WHAT MAKES COOPERATION NECESSARY?

In Chinese peasant communities, given the small size and scattered distribution of the land use-rights, any given family with rights to an acre or two may till ten strips in as many different places. This fragmentation ensures fairness in regard to good and bad, near and far, steep and level holdings, but it condemns peasants to endless ground breaking with hand-held hoes. It also makes mechanization virtually impossible and freezes labor productivity at medieval levels. Those who carried through the family contract "reform" counted on gradual consolidation through subcontracting that would transfer land use-rights into the hands of the more efficient producers, but this is happening very slowly, if at all. Few of any peasant's individual strips are adjacent to those of any of his or her neighbors. As a practical matter, scale can only be established through cooperation—that is to say through land pooling. Almost any village in the vast lowlands of China that wants to form a modern mechanized farm can put together 500 to 1,000 acres virtually overnight. This is a very good size for medium-scale mechanization. Widely applied it could make China competitive in labor productivity with any other part of the world.

Equally important, viable nonfarm enterprises requiring scale to succeed can also often be established only through cooperation. Communities can do what individuals can rarely do—accumulate investment funds in big enough amounts to finance such industrial projects as brick and tile kilns, coke and slaked lime ovens, cement mills, iron, bauxite, and coal mines, pig iron smelting, various types of iron foundries, machine and repair shops, sawmills, porcelain manufacture including the making of glazes, pharmaceuticals including antibiotics, dye and dye fixing chemicals, furfural (used for lacquers, dyes, and synthetic resins) made from corn cobs, wool and silk carpet weaving, garment making, food processing such as flour milling, bean noodle, tofu and corn starch making, processes that yield by-products for livestock raising and feed for dairy cattle, pigs, and poultry. Raising animals and birds is not considered farming in China. Neither are orchards, tree farms or medicinal herb gathering and processing, all of which yield good returns where appropriate. The list is long, very long.

The number of such nonfarm enterprises has reached as high as 20 million in rural China in recent years. Though many fail, many new ones start up. While some of these are private and some are organized along capitalist lines in the form of joint stock companies, the largest number are financed and managed by communities using collective accumulation funds. This whole massive development has its roots in the equal small holder communities created by land reform, in the land use-rights inherited by all, and in the accumulation practices of the collective period.

Agricultural mechanization, in the long run the only way out for peasants anywhere, depends on both the processes mentioned above: first, the creation of reasonable scale through land pooling to make mechanization possible; second, the provision of alternative employment through sideline and industrial enterprises to those released from the land by the machines. The surplus funds earned by the enterprises are as important as the jobs. These enable the community to buy the tractors and implements, the motors and the pumps that release the labor from the land.

All facets of this dialectical phenomena are mutually interdependent, each supports the other in providing conditions for the advance of the whole. When managed well the results can be surprising. In one North China village the support given by the industrial sector to the farming sector in terms of machinery supplied and by the newly mechanized farming sector in turn to the industrial sector in terms of labor power released raised per capita income in a few years from 1,623 yuan in 1987 to 8,502 yuan in 1993. What made this difference was a massive shift to high labor productivity both on the land and off it. Yet very few left the village—a living example of Mao's advice to peasants to "leave the land but not the village."

FAMILY CONTRACTS CAUSE ENVIRONMENTAL HAVOC

Without such a diversification process on a large scale, a process which the current family contract system neither favors nor promotes, rural China is running into increasingly severe problems. One example may serve to illustrate the adverse effects of the family contract system on the sustainability of agriculture.

All over China peasants on the noodle strip plots allocated by the Deng reform are depleting the organic matter in the soil. The depletion is due to lack of human, animal, and mechanical power to incorporate crop residues back into the land where they belong. Most families simply do not have enough able-bodied workers to process stalks and straw not to mention enough money to pay someone else to do it. Whether the interval between crops is long or short they burn most residues to get them out of the way. While burning may leave some useful minerals behind, it destroys key nutrients as well as the most important substance of all, the organic matter so plentiful in wheat straw, corn stover, soybean stalks and other plant residues—organic matter absolutely essential for soil structure, soil flora and fauna, earthworms, bacteria, fungi and microbial life of all kinds. It is essential also for increasing moisture absorption and retention, for releasing minerals to plant roots, and many other complex processes which contribute to healthy plant growth.

Traveling from Beijing to Northwestern Hubei at corn harvest time not so long ago, we found the whole countryside shrouded in smoke, especially in the late afternoon. As people prepared to leave the fields they set fire to the corn stalks they had stripped of ears that day. The blazes flared on into the night, myriad scattered points of light glowing near and far. It was as if whole constellations of stars had fallen from the sky and continued to sparkle across mountain and plain, north, east, south, and west.

The damage done by this destruction is incalculable, both in the present and in terms of future consequences. The monetary value of the crop residues burned over the whole country, residues more or less equal in weight to the grain harvested, comes to tens of billions of dollars, while the ecological damage done by its destruction must be counted as several times that. Such losses are not sustainable over the long haul. Yet, under the current family contract system there is no way to counter them. Thus for the 75 percent of the population that are still peasants, family contracts head down a dead-end road that can only lead in the long run to the liquidation, rather than the consolidation, of the equities held by small holders, and turn all but a few select tillers into propertyless proletarians with nothing to sell but their labor power.

This outcome looms in sharp contrast to Mao's open ended strategy; the advance of cooperation through stages, from mutual aid to lower-stage co-op, then to higher stage co-op, and on to communes where the cooperative economy may intersect with and eventually merge with that of the state. Mao's vision was dialectical, projecting a society in constant development, communities at different levels all moving forward toward higher levels of multifaceted cooperative production at speeds determined by their own potential and their own internal dynamism. Far from being one sided as Mao's critics proclaim, his vision was well-rounded, comprehensive, and far seeing. It pointed the direction for China's vast rural population.

COOPERATIVE BREAKUP LEADS TO MIXED RESULTS

The "reforms" of the 1980s brought the whole cooperative process to a halt while it was still at an early stage. They turned the clock back thirty years to the point where land reform left off in the early 1950s. Those few scattered village collectives that refused to dissolve worked together on pooled assets, made the most of their economies of scale, and prospered beyond all expectations. Of the village collectives that dissolved, actually the vast majority, only those in certain favored regions have been able to diversify into a wide variety of industrial activities linked to the urban centers of the regions where they reside. The rest of the communities, the overwhelming majority nationwide, in spite of vastly increased inputs of fertilizer, pesticides, and improved seeds, have stagnated. They are held in check by lack of capital (which communities, with production privatized, no longer accumulate), extreme fragmentation of all arable land (thus aborting mechanization), remote locations and poor communications, and unfavorable price ratios between needed agricultural inputs and the food and fiber they produce and sell. Most of all they are held in check by the anarchy that flows from "go it alone" ideology–not "public first, self second" that brings out the best in human nature, but "some must get rich first" that brings out the worst.

If these communities don't again get organized, if their members don't, in various ways, relearn how to work together, their problems can only get worse, polarization can only accelerate, and economic stagnation can only deepen. Going it alone on scattered noodle strips is a dead-end road.

NEW CLASSES BRING CHANGE
AND IRRECONCILABLE CONFLICT

The great land reform of the middle of the Century was a crucial turning point in China's history. Peasant rebellions had many times stormed "heaven" and ended dynasties, but never before had such an overthrow so thoroughly transformed social relations or set in motion such deep and lasting change. Such change was possible because a society and an economy shaped by Western imperialist penetration and intervention had brought into being new classes in China, a bourgeoisie and a working class, both victimized by feudalism and ready to fight for change. Together activists of these new classes mobilized the peasantry, the only force strong enough to take on a feudal establishment backed up from abroad, and led rural millions to rise in revolt. Their final victory was as remarkable as it was complete.

The first great sea change the new regime brought about, land reform, cleared the way for advance on all fronts. But as the dust settled not one, but two roads opened, one socialist, the other capitalist. The disparate class forces leading the revolution, most critically the leaders of the Communist Party itself, split into two factions representing the two classes contending for hegemony, workers on the one hand, bourgeoisie on the other, each with its own agenda and each with its own mass base. Thus began a struggle over China's future that continues to this day. From 1949 on no policy has gone uncontested, no initiative unopposed. As long as Mao lived, the socialist road predominated, most of the time. But after Mao's death his successor, Hua Guofeng, failed to consolidate his position. "Reformers," so called, took power. They cast doubt even on the need for land reform and dismissed three decades of socialist construction as thirty wasted years. Professing the use of capitalist methods to build socialism, they then set to work using socialism to build capitalism.

CAN THE REVERSAL BE REVERSED?

Still, it is not too late to reverse the reversal. The village structure that formed the basis for collective agriculture remains intact. Many thousands of communities, even mountain communities, have the opportunity to pool land and farm on a scale as efficient as any in the world. They also have the opportunity to support and supplement this modernization with village sidelines and industries that offer alternative employment to all, raise productivity on the land and off it, and raise standards of living. They could reactivate the principles of Mao's development ladder, break out of the current rural stagnation, and create a cooperative commonwealth of unprecedented strength and productivity. If this ever comes about (it is happening down below, in isolated spots where people are feeling their way toward something new), the land reform of the New Democratic Revolution would realize its full potential at last and show the way to all the peasant peoples in the world who are losing out in the rush to globalization.

APPENDIX

RESOURCE LIST

BIODEMOCRACY AND ORGANIC CONSUMERS ASSOCIATION

6114 Highway 61
Little Marais, MN 55614
T: 218.226.4164   F: 218.226.4157
<http://www.purefood.org>
Promotes food safety, organic farming, and sustainable agricultural practices through education, activist networking, grassroots lobbying, boycotts, protests, media and public relations, and litigation.

BLACK FARMERS AND AGRICULTURALISTS ASSOCIATION

P.O. Box 61
Tillery, NC 27887
T: 252.826.2800   F: 252.826.3244
<http://www.coax.net/people/lwf/bfaa.htm>
An education and advocacy organization working in conjunction with the National Land Loss Fund and other groups to respond to the staggering decline of African American farmers and landowners.

CENTER FOR AGROECOLOGY AND SUSTAINABLE FOOD SYSTEMS

University of California at Santa Cruz,
Farm & Garden
1156 High Street
Santa Cruz, CA 95064
T: 408.459.2799   F: 408.459.2799
Demonstrates a viable community supported agriculture model for small-scale farming and regional food systems.

CENTER FOR FOOD SAFETY

666 Pennsylvania Avenue, SE, Suite 302
Washington, DC 20003
T: 202.547.9359   F: 202.547.9429
<http://www.centerforfoodsafety.org>
Advocates testing, labeling and regulation of genetically engineered foods and strict national organic food standards; the prevention of potential animal and human health crises caused by food borne illness; and educating the public on the hazards of industrial agriculture.

CENTER FOR RURAL AFFAIRS

101 S. Tallman Street
P.O. Box 406
Walthill, NE 68067
T: 402.846.5428   F: 402.846.5420
<http://www.cfra.org>
Does advocacy and service work to demonstrate positive alternatives for rural areas in job creation, economic opportunity
for beginning farm families, agricultural
marketing and farm stewardship practices.

FEDERATION OF SOUTHERN COOPERATIVES

P.O. Box 95
Epes, AL 35460
T: 205.652.9676   F: 205.652.9678
<http://www.federationsoutherncoop.com>
Supports family farmers and African
American farmers in particular, in developing strategies for land retention. Assists
in the development of cooperatives and
credit unions as a collective strategy for
economic self-sufficiency.

FOOD WORKS

64 Main Street
Montpelier, VT 05602
T: 802.223.1515   F: 802.223.8980
Aims to bring an integrated, unified
approach to elementary education
through the development of local,
place-based curriculums centered
around community garden projects.

**GENESEE VALLEY ORGANIC COMMUNITY
SUPPORTED AGRICULTURE**

25 Nelson Street
Rochester, NY 14620
<http://www.gvocsa.org>
A cooperative of consumers and farmers.

GLOBAL EXCHANGE

2017 Mission Sreet, Suite 303
San Francisco, CA 94110
T: 415.255.7296   F: 415.255.7498
<http://www.globalexchange.org>
A human rights organization dedicated to
romoting environmental, political,
and social justice around the world.

HARTFORD FOOD SYSTEM

509 Wethersfield Avenue
Hartford, CT 06114
T: 860.296.9325
<http://www.hartfordfood.org>
Develops and manages food programs
for and with low income communities

INTERNATIONAL FORUM ON GLOBALIZATION

Building 1062, Fort Cronkhite
Sausalito, CA 94965
T: 415.229.9350   F: 415.229.9340
<http://www.ifg.org>
An alliance representing over 60 organizations in 25 countries formed to stimulate
new thinking, joint activity, and public
education in response to economic globalization and its impact on democracy,
human welfare, local economies, and the
natural world.

**INTERNATIONAL SOCIETY FOR ECOLOGY
AND CULTURE**

P.O. Box 9475
Berkeley, CA 94709
T: 510.548.4915   F: 510.548.4916
<http://www.isec.org.uk>
Works with institutions and communities
to promote ecological regeneration, community renewal, and economic localiza-
tion and challenges the view of a
universally beneficial global economy.

INSTITUTE FOR AGRICULTURE AND TRADE POLICY

2015 First Avenue, South
Minneapolis, MN 55404
T: 612.870.0453   F: 612.870.4846
<http://www.iatp.org>
Assists public interest organizations in coalition building and influencing policy that affects consumers, farmers, and rural areas through monitoring, analysis and research, education and outreach, and information systems management to create environmentally and economically sustainable rural communities.

INSTITUTE FOR FOOD AND DEVELOPMENT POLICY

(Food First)
398 60th Street
Oakland, CA 94618
T: 510.654.4400   F: 510.654.4551
<http://www.foodfirst.org>
Highlights root causes and value-based solutions to hunger and poverty around the world, with a commitment to establishing food as a fundamental human right. A progressive think tank and education-for-action organization.

LAND INSTITUTE

2440 E. Water Well Road
Salina, KS 67401
T: 785.823.5376   F: 785.823.8728
<http://www.landinstitute.org>
Seeks to develop a program of natural systems agriculture which will save soil from being lost or poisoned while maintaining the ecological stability of the prairie and providing a grain yield comparable to that from annual crops.

NATIONAL AGRICULTURAL LIBRARY

10301 Baltimore Avenue
Beltsville, MD 20705
T: 301.504.5755   F: 301.504.6856
<http://www.nalusda.gov>
Houses the largest collection of agricultural information for researchers, educators, policymakers, and the public. Serves as the key coordinating center for international agricultural data coordinating and resource information sharing.

NATIONAL CAMPAIGN FOR SUSTAINABLE AGRICULTURE

P.O. Box 396
Pine Bush, NY 12566
T: 914.744.8448   F: 914.744.8477
<http://sunsite.unc.edu/farming-connection/farmpoli/natcamsa/home.htm>
A network of diverse groups shaping policy to foster sustainable food and farming systems.

NATIONAL FARMERS UNION

11900 East Cornell Avenue
Aurora, CO 80014-3194
T: 303.337.5500   F: 303.368.1390
<http://www.nfu.org>
Mission is to protect and enhance the economic interests of farmers and rural communities by supporting the maintenance and growth of family farm and ranch agriculture.

NORTHEAST ORGANIC FARMING ASSOCIATION OF VERMONT

P.O. Box 697
Richmond, VT 05477
T: 802-434-4122
<http://www.nofavt.org>
A nonprofit association of consumers, gardeners and diversified farmers working to strengthen agriculture in Vermont.

NORTHEAST SUSTAINABLE AGRICULTURE WORKING GROUP

P.O. Box 608
Belchertown, MA 01007
T: 413.323.4531   F: 413.323.9594
<http://www.smallfarm.org>
A regional network of organizations and individuals working to create a sustainable regional food and farming system.

PESTICIDE ACTION NETWORK (NORTH AMERICA)

49 Powell Street, Suite 500
San Francisco, CA 94102
T: 415.981.1771   F: 415.981.1991
<http://www.panna.org>
Campaigns to have pesticides replaced with ecologically sound alternatives. Links health, consumer, labor, environment, progressive agriculture and public interest groups with supporters to promote safe and effective pest management through research, policy development, education, and advocacy.

RURAL DEVELOPMENT CENTER

P.O. Box 5415
Salinas, CA 93915
T: 408.758.1469
A community-based agricultural training and resource center.

U.S. DEPARTMENT OF AGRICULTURE

14th & Independence Ave., SW
Washington, DC 20250
T: 202.720.2791
<http://www.usda.gov>
Provides assistance to farmers, communities, and consumers through a wide range of services and programs.

CONTRIBUTORS

MIGUEL A. ALTERI is associate professor of agroecology at the University of California, Berkeley and a tireless promoter of grassroots approaches to sustainable agriculture in Latin America. He is the author of *Agroecology: The Science of Sustainable Agriculture* (Westview, 1995).

FARSHAD ARAGHI is associate professor of sociology and director of the sociology program at Florida Atlantic University. He has written on peasants in the world economy and is currently working on the politics of global restructuring and the local/global dialectics. He is coeditor of the *International Journal of the Sociology of Agriculture and Food*.

LAWRENCE BUSCH is a University Distinguished Professor in the department of sociology at Michigan State University.

FREDERICK H. BUTTEL is professor of rural sociology and environmental studies at the University of Wisconsin in Madison. He is author or editor of several books, including *Environment and Modernity* (London: Sage, 1999).

JOHN BELLAMY FOSTER is associate professor of sociology at the University of Oregon. He is coeditor of *Monthly Review* and *Organization and Environment* and author of *Marx's Ecology: Materialism and Nature* (2000) and *The Vulnerable Planet: A Short Economic History of the Environment* (1999, 2nd ed.), both published by Monthly Review Press.

WILLIAM D. HEFFERNAN is a professor of rural sociology at the University of Missouri in Columbia, Missouri.

ELIZABETH HENDERSON makes her living as an organic farmer and spends her spare time writing (for *The Natural Farmer* and other publications) and organizing for the Northeast Organic Farming Association of New York, the New York Sustainable Agriculture Working Group, and the Wayne County Agricultural and Farmland Protection Board.

WILLIAM HINTON, author of the classic study of the Chinese Revolution, *Fanshen* (University of California Press, 1997), first went to China in 1937 and has spent much of his time there since.

R.C. LEWONTIN holds the Alexander Agassiz chair in zoology at Harvard University. He is the author of *Biology as Ideology* and *The Genetic Basis of Evolutionary Change* and is the coauthor of *Not in Our Genes* and *The Dialectical Biologist.*

FRED MAGDOFF is professor of plant and soil science at the University of Vermont. He is the author of numerous scientific articles and of the book *Building Soils for Better Crops* (University of Nebraska Press, 1993).

LINDA C. MAJKA is an associate professor of sociology at the University of Dayton. She is coauthor with Theo Majka of *Farm Workers, Agribusiness, and the State* (Temple University Press, 1982).

THEO J. MAJKA is professor of sociology at the University of Dayton. He is coauthor with Patrick Mooney of *Farmers' and Farm Workers' Movements: Social Protest in American Agriculture* (Twayne, 1995).

PHILIP McMICHAEL is professor of rural and development sociology and the director of the International Political Economy Program at Cornell University.

GERAD MIDDENDORF is a doctoral candidate in the department of sociology at Michigan State University.

JANET POPPENDIECK, professor of sociology at Hunter College of CUNY, is director of the Center for the Study of Family Policy. She is the author of *Sweet Charity: Emergency Food and the End of Entitlement* (Viking Press, 1998).

ELIZABETH RANSOM is a doctoral candidate in the department of sociology at Michigan State University.

PETER M. ROSSET is the executive director of the Institute for Food and Development Policy/Food First, based in Oakland, CA. He has a Ph.D. in agricultural ecology and teaches at Stanford University

MIKE SKLADNY recently completed his doctorate at Michigan State University.

ELLEN MEIKSINS WOOD is the author of *The Origin of Capitalism* (Monthly Review Press, 1999), *The Retreat from Class* (Verso, 1998, 2nd ed.), and coauthor with Neal Wood of *A Trumpet of Sedition* (New York University Press, 1997). She is coeditor of the collections *Capitalism and the Information Age* (1998), *Rising from the Ashes? Labor in the Age of "Global" Capitalism* (1998), and *In Defense of History* (1997), all published by Monthly Review Press.

INDEX